MONTANA GHOS

MONTANA GHOST DANCE

Essays on Land and Life

John B. Wright

 UNIVERSITY OF TEXAS PRESS, AUSTIN

"Degrees of Gray in Philipsburg," copyright © 1973 by Richard Hugo, from *Making Certain It Goes On: The Collected Poems of Richard Hugo* by Richard Hugo. Reprinted by permission of W. W. Norton & Company, Inc.

First edition, 1998

Requests for permission to reproduce material from this work should be sent to Permissions, University of Texas Press, Box 7819, Austin, TX 78713-7819.

⊗ The paper used in this publication meets the minimum requirements of American National Standard for Information Sciences—Permanence of Paper for Printed Library Materials, ANSI Z39.48-1984.

LIBRARY OF CONGRESS CATALOGING-IN-PUBLICATION DATA

Wright, John B. (John Burghardt), 1950–
    Montana ghost dance : essays on land and life / by John B. Wright. — 1st ed.
      p.   cm.
    ISBN 0-292-79121-6 (alk. paper). — ISBN 0-292-79120-8 (pbk. : alk. paper)
     1. Montana — Description and travel.   2. Montana — Geography.   3. Montana — Environmental conditions.   4. Land use — Montana.   I. Title.
F735.W75   1998
917.86—dc21   97-33741

To James J. Parsons

GEOGRAPHER • TEACHER • FRIEND • BEAR

CONTENTS

MON

BRITISH COLUMBIA

ALBERTA

GLACIER N. P.

Rocky Mountain Front

Libby

Cut Bank

Kalispell

Flathead Lake

Polson

St. Ignatius

Choteau

Fort Benton

Missouri R.

Great Falls

Clark Fork

Blackfoot R.

River

Gates of the Mountains

CONTINENTAL

ROCKY

MTNS

Missoula

Stevensville

Helena

DIVIDE

Philipsburg

Hamilton

BITTERROOT VALLEY

Anaconda

Butte

Three Forks

Bozeman

Livingst

BIG HOLE VALLEY

Bannack

Dillon

Virginia City

PARADISE VALLEY

YELLOWSTONE NATIONAL PARK

TANA

SASKATCHEWAN

NORTH DAKOTA

SOUTH DAKOTA

Havre Chinook

Malta

Glasgow River

Missouri

Jordan

Glendive

Lewistown

River

Harlowton

Miles City

Yellowstone

Billings

LITTLE BIGHORN BATTLEFIELD N.M.

WYOMING

PREFACE

THIS IS THE book I swore I would never write.

For most of my twenty-five years in the state, all of Montana felt like prized troutwater. The most ethical thing to do was keep quiet about it. But now, the place has been found by the rest of the world. Montana is being filmed, claimed, mined, settled, and misunderstood like never before. The cat's out of the bag.

Many newcomers are burdened by myths and ill-prepared to live in the tangible Montana. Many long-termers are grimly holding on to cherished, fading legends about being here.

So I felt it was time to add a few thoughts about some of the actual trends that are rearranging the Big Sky. The specifics are about Montana, but the same issues are hitting all of the Rocky Mountain West.

This story has many sides. I make no claim of being all-inclusive. This is not a manual for saving Montana.

Following are heartfelt and hard-won words about a few of the dramas being played out. And some ideas about what we might do about them. I've worked on resource conservation issues for a quarter of a century in Montana. I've earned my living as a county planning director, housing rehabilitation specialist, land use consultant, conservation easement designer, and teacher. I'm on the board of the Five Valleys Land Trust in Missoula and help out a bit with land protection projects. These subjects have been on my mind awhile.

In places, I decided to get out of the way and let other voices be heard. When people know what they're talking about, the best we can do is listen, but any errors or missteps are solely mine.

This book is both anecdotal and fact-driven. My notion was to be deeply personal but fair. But judge for yourself. Montana has got a lot of acres to it. It's easy to get turned around. I know one thing for certain. These immense expanses contain the real lessons of land and life we so desperately need to learn.

Geography is how we search to find our way.

And boy do we need to figure out where we're going. The cataract thunders before us. We can already see the spray rising downriver. Time to choose our route wisely.

Jack Wright
Missoula
March 1997

ACKNOWLEDGMENTS

ROUND UP the usual suspects.
Gratitude to Bruce Bugbee for his bountiful knowledge and good heart.

Many thanks also to Land Lindbergh, Dave Odell, and Bob Kiesling for taking the time to talk.

The Montana Land Reliance, Five Valleys Land Trust, and all the other land trusts in the state provided real data and tangible optimism.

The names of those who have helped would fill phone books.

Here are just a few: Beth Pollack, Emma Bovary Zunz Goldman Peele, Jamie Kay of Missoula's "Fine Lines," Frank Waldbillig, Bill Long, Daryl Goebel, Chris Field, Paul Starrs, Dave Larson, Elmer Cyr, Pat Williams, Merrill Riddick, Vince Swann, Jim Carculis, and all the folks at that certain bar.

I owe you all a round. Even if I don't win at keno.

My friends in the Geography Department at New Mexico State University have been terrific and loyal. Thanks to Bob Czerniak and Mike DeMers. Muchas gracias to René Casillas for being supportive. And as always, to Mum and Cathy, the deepest kind of love.

J.W.

MONTANA GHOST DANCE

1

GHOST DANCE

IN ONE OF Charlie Russell's paintings, an elderly Indian man kneels in downcast prayer beside a bison skull. Telegraph wires vibrate overhead as a woman wearing Gay Nineties finery pedals by on a bicycle. In the sky are the spirits of fallen warriors on painted ponies. They seem to be calling to him.

Painful cultural shifts are a way of life in Montana. There has never been a steady version of land and life here. But with all the recent changes, it's hard to even know what to call the place anymore.

Joseph Kinsey Howard called the state *High, Wide and Handsome*. That's a great book, but a lot's happened since 1943. Many figure that Montana is *The Last Best Place*. Yet last stands have a poor record in Little Big Horn country. *A River Runs through It* has been taken over by the realtors. The listings use the expression to describe every twenty-acre tract with two feet of frontage on an irrigation ditch. We've been getting whiplash from slapping each other on the back about how great Montana is. Meanwhile it is getting less great right before our eyes.

Charlie Russell once said: "The West is dead! You may lose a sweetheart, but you won't forget her." In *For Whom the Bell Tolls*, Ernest Hemingway wrote: "Think about Montana, *I can't*. . . . it will just be nothing. That's all it will be. Just nothing." But this is no time to surrender to hopelessness.

Geography changes with our intentions. It is contingent upon our hearts. We get to choose—to find the proper medicine to heal our landscapes and ourselves. This will mean pulling back from catchphrases and putting our hands to the work before us. The places we come up with will be role models for our children. Do we want terrains of short-term greed and long-term upheaval? Or do we want communities where well-managed resources and ample beauty are the center of a sufficient prosperity?

All a rational person can do is choose conservation, the balanced use and stewardship of resources. But in Montana, rationality is losing traction to extremism—developmental extremism. People have to decide if that is what they truly believe in.

The growth promoters say things will be different this time. No more boom and bust in Montana. Endless growth all around. Jobs galore. Lower taxes. Room for more people, but everyone a Montanan.

You bet.

The mines will reopen—copper, silver, moly, and gold, pure ore healing over the old pits and failed prospects. We'll get back to the real deal—metallurgy and dynamite—extraction wherever and however we please. The missing forests will reappear for the taking, and over-take them we must. It's for their own good. Yet, even as the land is reduced to raw resources, the rivers will stay full of trout, the mountains will run thick with elk, and the ranches will still raise the world's best beef, wheat, and barley. We can cash in and nothing much will change. So what if subdivisions and houses cover places where we used to pick serviceberries, buck bales, and hunt deer. Even with all the growth, Montana will always be rural, unpopulated, and safe. And the traffic will never get bad.

To the boomers, the laws of physics and plain sense can be revoked by the damn-straight rightness of the dream. Their idea is that the future will be the past made perfect. She'll work out this time. Then all this newfangled doubt can simply be cast away.

Less mercantile souls have their own dream. One that arrives in lengthening stays in memory. It has been embellished by romance but still carries true weight. They remember Montana before the current explosion of growth and extraction. Before the housing frenzy turned a basic need into a luxury and gold fever threatened our precious good chance at a future rich with open land and clean water. They remember the state as a hidden kingdom.

Now it is getting hard to manifest a day without the longing, the rising empty ache from the waning of a world. See all those houses— that was the place where the Arabian horse ranch used to be. That bench covered with trailers was always a bunchgrass prairie, a blanket of clarkia, a piece of prime Hereford land. I was married in that meadow where a log mansion is now. A person used to be able to come to this canyon, river, lake, meadow—and be all alone. No more.

This is the way we mourn, speaking the changes, listing the losses, writing geographic obituaries from the driver's side.

To most Montanans, there is now a nagging pain about life that all the economic promises cannot cure. This pain comes from an idea: the past is the best that could ever be and there is no recapturing it. But in silent lonely measures we are haunted by a repeating wish—if only prayers could bring it all back. It isn't the first time this has happened.

Early in 1889, word swept across the Indian West that a messiah had come to return all the dead and make the land brown with 60 million buffalo again. It started with the Utes and the Bannocks then diffused to the Mohave, Pawnee, Shoshone, Cheyenne, and Sioux. Dozens of Indian languages repeated the message: "There is a new messiah, and he is an Indian. There is a sacred dance you must learn and songs you must sing. Soon the Indian dead will live again and the white men will be swallowed up. The messiah's name is Wovoka and he is an Indian like us."

Wovoka was a Paiute from Nevada. Some called him Jim Wilson. His dad was a mystic and Wovoka was raised on stories that always ended with the white man dying off and the West returning to paradise. Even Christian Indians called Wovoka "Our Father" once they learned Christ wasn't white.

His words were bold: "I am the man who made everything you see around you . . . I have been to heaven and have seen your dead friends." Wovoka was even said to have scars on his hands, fleshy evidence of crucifixion.

His message was impossibly perfect. The ruined earth would be remade from the sheer cleansing power of the dream. The old world would return and all the newcomers, the violent greedy outlanders, would flee or die from a lack of connection to the land. All Indians would be alive again and the bison herds would stampede back in endless numbers. The nightmare would end from strong medicine, in the elegance of a rhythmic new ceremony.

It was known as the ghost dance.

Indian people joined hands and slowly moved from right to left, swaying in rapture, their shifting feet raising soft currents of dust. No drums were heard, only a steady drone of singing. The dancing went on for days. Most took no food or water. People occasionally collapsed from fatigue or spirit and were revived shouting ecstatic visions of the dead walking back to rejoin the living. Rumors spread of the returning ones. Sightings were even reported of long-dead relatives driving vast herds of bison in from remote valleys. The dance was working!

A complete need for hope is what it was.

The ghost dance miracle movement spread across the West. White people grew uneasy and then panicky over the dancers. The insistent motion filled the whites' fearful hearts on the Pine Ridge Reservation, where the Lakota made "ghost shirts" in special designs that were said to make the wearer immune to bullets. On the Crow Reservation, a messiah named Sword-Bearer spoke the same message but was killed by gunshots anyway. This did little to shake the growing faith.

In the fall of 1890, Indian Agent D. F. Royer was in charge at Pine Ridge. The Sioux called him Lakota Kohipa-Koshkala ("Young Man Afraid of Indians"). Royer watched the ghost dancers for days, sensing the rising magic, abhorring it as violence. He urged President Benjamin Harrison to send in the Army. On November 17, they arrived. It was the Seventh Cavalry, defeated fourteen years before at Little Big Horn, losers of 221 men, including Custer himself. Revenge festered in the soldiers' hearts.

The Indians believed this signaled the coming of their messiah. The soldiers were the whites' last act of desperation before Eden returned. But just to be sure, 3,000 Sioux moved far off into the Standing Rock Reservation to resume dancing at Sitting Bull's camp.

An Army order was soon issued to arrest Sitting Bull and put an end to the "uprising." On December 15, 1890, 100 cavalry with light artillery and forty-three Indian Police officers (all Sioux) advanced on the camp. In the battle, six Indian Police and fourteen Sioux braves were killed, including the great Hunkpapa chief Sitting Bull.

Scores of braves, women, and children fled. The commander of the cavalry, E. V. Sumner, let them go. Since the Indians displayed no aggression, he also let them keep their guns. It seemed like the trouble was over. But in the pre-dawn darkness of December 23, Big Foot, along with 120 men and 230 women and children, sifted off toward the Badlands. They had heard that Lakota and other Sioux were endlessly ghost dancing off in the eroded hills, praying salvation closer with each footfall. Major S. M. Whitside saw this as a threat, and the Seventh was dispatched to head them off. The shivering people were captured without a fight. Big Foot was sick with pneumonia and agreed to go along without a parley—with no terms for surrender. Absent a struggle, the cavalry saw no reason to disarm the Lakota. The Indians and soldiers camped together along Wounded Knee Creek. The mood was strangely relaxed. Braves and troops talked and smoked cigarettes together, some even shared laughter.

Each group in its own way felt that all was well. The Lakota believed their ghost shirts would protect them from rifle bullets. This power might not even be needed: soon enough the soldiers would disappear forever. The Seventh Cavalry believed that their rifles and four Hotchkiss artillery pieces would prevent any conflict. They also had no idea what the ghost shirt drawings of buffalo and thunderbirds meant.

It would be a fatal misunderstanding.

Five hundred soldiers and 350 Lakota spent a bitterly cold night camped at Wounded Knee. The next morning, December 29, 1890, ice shone from every tent and tipi. Big Foot had become desperately ill and had no interest in war. Despite this and the presence of the entire Seventh Cavalry surrounding the Lakota, some of the officers still feared violence. An order was issued to disarm the Indians.

Yellow Bird, a powerful leader, began speaking. He told the people, "I have made medicine of the white man's ammunition. It is good medicine, and his bullets cannot harm you, they will not go through your ghost shirts, while your bullets will kill them."

There are many versions of what happened next. Some say the soldiers fired first, others the Lakota. No matter.

A thunder of gunshots filled the frozen air. Smoke and screams were everywhere. Half the Indians fell in the first seconds. More volleys came in a cross fire. People were firing blindly. Then Hotchkiss guns lobbed two-pound explosive shells into the screaming bloody piles of dying Sioux. The last steaming breaths of the slaughtered mixed with gunsmoke and artillery fumes. The madness subsided into scattered rounds fired at those trying to flee. Some women and children were chased two miles before being shot by mounted soldiers. There was raw premeditation in those murders. Several kids were coaxed out from under corpses with promises of rescue only to be hacked to death by cavalry swords. Then it was over.

One hundred and twenty-eight Indians were dead. Seventy more lay wounded. Thirty-one soldiers were killed. A bleeding woman was seen tearing off her magic shirt and stomping on it.

The ghost dance was over.

The wounded Lakota were taken to a nearby schoolhouse. They lay on the wooden floor stunned by grief, seized with pain and infection, demoralized by the failure of the dancing medicine.

Christmas decorations filled that awful room.

Three days later, troops were sent back to Wounded Knee to bury the Indian dead. The bodies were found frozen into contorted positions, fear and death spasms captured as flesh turned to ice. Big Foot's arms extended outward as if he were still trying to rise. Women were found sheltering their babies from a death they could not stop. A young girl covered her eyes against what she could not help but see.

A long trench was dug as a mass grave. The bodies of the Sioux were heaved into the pit, smashing violently against each other, frozen parts breaking on impact. Some corpses were stripped of clothing and sexually mutilated. Ghost shirts were taken by the troops as trophies, a people's final hope transformed into sarcastic souvenirs.

In 1891, Congress awarded Medals of Honor for "distinguished conduct" to eighteen of the soldiers involved.

This is a story that will always need retelling. It defies comprehension. Yet we must acknowledge it as recent and real and never try to minimize all that it represents about us. Soldiers and settlers were not only courageous, tough-hided adventurers in a grand American West; their souls and ours are tainted with racism, conquest, and genocide. Or at least silent, unthinking complicity with these things.

This is lesson enough. Yet the lessons keep unfolding the deeper you look. It seems that the ghost dance is back. But this time the whites are dancing.

During the 1990s, Montana has been discovered by out-of-staters seeking a beautiful place that still makes sense. Some 80,000 more people lived here in 1997 than at the start of the decade—a 10 percent increase. In-migration accounts for three-quarters of that rise. One of every three people moving in is from California. Montanans feel inundated, even oppressed, by these stereotypic "fornies" hefting cell phones and stock portfolios. I've even heard people mutter, "We've been Indianized." That demeans the memory of what transpired at places like Wounded Knee. But the mutterings say a lot.

Montanans are now sensing the faintest shadow of the losses the Indians experienced when their world changed forever. The barest bit of that unimaginable pain can now be physically comprehended.

Some might call it karma.

What comes is anger, confusion, and bitterness. Most Montanans feel an intense nostalgia for a less crowded past. Extreme environmentalists want to block all change, make all the land wilderness, deny that they use wood, fiber, food, metal, and gasoline. Even the resource extractionists are unhappy with the shifts taking place under their feet, with the rising opposition to the state's motto—"Gold and Silver"—still flying boldly on courthouse flags. No one seems particularly cheery about the cultural revolution. Confidence is getting hard to find. Entire ways of life seem to be drying up; even the landscape itself is fading, being transformed at an urgent pace into something we have no words for. The national magazines call it "The New West." Most reasonable people figured that, with a few changes, the old one would be just fine.

We don't really know what to do about all this. We don't even know if we're supposed to care so much. After all, isn't this just normal? Places grow, land is converted to realty or gold, communities become contraptions, and the tally is supposed to have us come out ahead, right? Isn't this just the real world? It surely must be childish to hurt so much. After all, you can't do anything about it: that would be wrong, wouldn't it? I believe in free enterprise, earning a living, and private property rights—so that settles it.

This is what we tell ourselves. But the sadness won't stay convinced. The Big World is coming and we know in our gut that everything is at risk.

It is easiest to blame the new people, so that's who takes the hit. "They're not like us; they don't understand the place and walk around telling us how to live; they're trying to turn Montana into Los Angeles or Seattle!" These things are said despite the inconvenient fact that

Montanans are the ones selling the houses, land, and businesses to the newcomers. Montanans are the ones who weakened state law to make things easier on mining corporations.

We're the ones who get to set the rules and mostly we've just taken the money.

It's like the joke making the rounds. A rancher shuffles into his local bar and orders a shot and a beer. He's royally upset. His buddy sidles over and says, "What's the trouble?" "Goddamn Californian took over my land," the rancher replies, taking a long pull of lager. "How the hell'd that happen?" says the buddy. "Sonuvabitch met my price," grunts the rancher.

Human nature insists that problems are caused by someone else. The Devil has out-of-state plates.

People like New York millionaire Robert M. Lee tend to reinforce the image. Lee bought 342-acre Cromwell Island in Flathead Lake and built a $25 million, 30,000-square-foot concrete mansion. Security forces in speedboats patrol the perimeter of the island.

But that's only part of the picture. People are rankled by more than just palatial new houses and rich, insensitive louts. What is troublesome is the entire load of changes—changes that touch the very nature of life that Montanans of all political views have so long taken for granted. What we once assumed eternal is now endangered and the nausea never seems to subside.

Groups of Montanans are now symbolically joining hands, forming secret circles, repeating their own songs of desperation for a return to the way things were. Developers, environmentalists, miners, legislators, militia cases, and patriotic ranchers—each group has its own version of the "Golden Age of Montana." And its own desperate ghost dance. Our barrooms and silences are now filled with shuffling feet. The song is that the past was better. It is a stubbornly seductive message partly because for each of us, at first glance, it seems pretty true.

Decades ago Montana had far fewer people and passed for a part of Canada to the average American. Mining proceeded and the jobs were at least there. Loggers were heroes; it was as simple as that. Wilderness was true, not legislated. Our towns were smaller, friendlier. You could afford to buy a house and not lock it even once.

But when we brush aside even the first wisps of nostalgia, some tough realities come thudding in. Montana has always been a place of newcomers and of animosity from those who arrived a few years or months before. It is a territory born of booms and glooms, of destructive exploitation of the environment, of perplexing toxic legacies from the complete freedom to mine, of onslaughts on wild places brought up short only by the limits of the marketplace, of logging made possible only by the largesse of the federal treasury. Mostly, Montana has been a place of recurrent cycles of population growth and rude conflict over what the ideal state should be. We've seldom agreed on much.

Sometimes people have tried to conjure up a permanent, more modest future. One that has an eye on limits and fairness. But usually we've stared back to the way things used to be and damn well should be again. Whether it was metal or solitude, it all seemed limitless back then.

The past reels away and defies recapture. And still we try. All this longing is understandable. But there's just a wee problem—we can't go back. Despite our fondest desire, it can't be done.

So it's time to stop ghost dancing. We're just burning daylight. It's time to figure out some fair, stout ways of conserving as much of the goodness as we can. There is no way for this to be easy. Some of our most cherished ideas are going to have to be reassessed. Not even one of us can get 100 percent of what we want. But maybe all of us can agree on enough to still make lives that take our breath away.

The frontier is done. Time to own up to it. Montana and the Rockies now have the fastest-growing population in the fastest-growing industrialized country in the world. The state has long been a resource colony. But today what's at stake is that final irreplaceable resource—Montana itself.

For me there is no subject more important than the future of the Big Sky. Partly this is provincial: I purely love this contrary, marvelously beautiful part of the world. But there are worse sins than caring for your province.

Mostly, though, in Montana we can see the whole nine yards—both senseless land degradation and honest attempts at caring for the ground. It's the cultural double helix in a single view. Both options lie before us as transparent as Beartooth water. In few other places are the traces of our decisions more visible and the price of choosing wrong so precious.

It settles clear as this—our lives will be a tough draw if we don't conserve Montana.

Despite the appearance of things, most Montanans know this in their chests and bones. The developmental and environmental extremists may rant until they run out of wind; it won't change the fact that most Montanans fall in the middle—as eventual conservationists. Sure, not all of them, many days it feels like far too few of them, but enough Montanans get around to it sooner or later to give us pride in the place. Twenty-five years of working on resource choices in the state has taught me at least that.

Historian Walter Prescott Webb wrote that "the West should not be looked at from the outside, but from the inside, from the center." That's what I've aspired to in the following nine essays—to tell stories from inside Montana, to make each one a different piece of the tale.

This is a book about Montana myths, old-timers, emigrants, elk, Freemen, ways of seeing the landscape, land conservation and land trusts, the fate of the Blackfoot, Bitterroot, Paradise, and other valleys, and ways of saving places we cannot bear to lose.

Mostly this is a geography book about where we are.

Every Montanan could write one. This is only mine. About all I do is stay close to the truth, or at least my truth of the matter. I hit the extreme developers much harder than the extreme enviros. The developers have the money, power, and influence to put their agenda into action; they are the driving force in landscape change. Most of the time those wanting every acre of Montana to be pristine and preserved lack the means to be more than marginal voices. Again, the real work—land stewardship—falls in the middle. But as a conservationist I can comprehend, feel, and many times support a good share of the environmental agenda. I confess that many of the resource extractors remain a mystery to me.

One last thing: since I won't be asking all the questions, I make no claim of having anything like all the answers. These are just my stories. Some things to think about.

But take it as it comes. I've tried to be fair but given all that's at stake, I trust I can be forgiven for letting my heart take the reins once in a while.

Add your own experiences where they fit. Get out a map and follow along. Reject what sounds wrongheaded. But at least give these words a go. All that's up for grabs is Montana.

That's all.

2

ST. PATRICK'S DAY IN BUTTE

BUTTE ON St. Patrick's Day is about as Montana as it gets. This rough-boned city of abandoned copper mines, grotesque runoff, and rusting gallows frames may be down a few hands but it still knows how to throw a party. There's a lot to celebrate and to forget.

No place in the state has seen things go more cattywampus.

Butte started as a small gold and silver shantytown. In 1880, Marcus Daly used the California capital of magnates like George Hearst to create the Anaconda Copper Mining Company. The first red metal was concocted by smelting ore out in the open. Stacks of rock and logs were set ablaze in town. The air turned to tear gas. The smelter town of Anaconda was then built miles away to better handle the job. Soon, 60 million pounds of copper a year was being mined from a warren of underground tunnels that chewed away at the foundation of the growing city. Daly, William Andrews Clark, and other "Copper Kings" quickly assembled fortunes. Clark was earning $17 million a month when workers averaged a couple of bucks a day toiling in deathly conditions. Copper is a metal the color of dried blood.

By 1920, Butte had a population of 60,000. The need for copper for wire, pipe, tanks, ships, and artillery shells kept the mines cranking for decades. Cities were built and wars were won with Butte's help. The profits just kept rolling in. The Anaconda Company—or just "The Company" to Montanans—used this wealth to control the state government. The Company employed thousands of miners, bribed hundreds of officials, and bought up dozens of newspapers in case someone might take offense and write it down.

In 1955, ore-digging shifted to the massive Berkeley Pit. To make room, buildings in the northeast section of the city had to be relocated. Butte was consuming itself. Now even low-grade ore (less than 1 percent copper) could be economically exploited.

The bust came anyway. In 1972, Anaconda's holdings in Chile were nationalized. A worldwide glut of copper caused prices to collapse. PVC pipes and fiber optic cables took an increasing toll on demand. In 1976, for some reason, ARCO bought The Company. Nobody has ever figured out why. Not even ARCO.

All operations in Butte and Anaconda were soon shut down. The Berkeley Pit was abandoned after producing 21 billion pounds of copper, 90 million pounds of molybdenum, 90 million ounces of silver, and 3 million ounces of gold. An 800-foot-deep lake of mine acids and groundwater now fills the 1½-square-mile crater. The noxious broth is rising at a rate of 2 feet per year. EPA's "Preferred Plan" for cleaning up the Superfund Site is this: let's wait until the year 2022, when the Pit is bank full with 56 billion gallons of venomous soup—then we'll figure a way to clean it up. In 1995, 342 migrating snow geese landed in the Pit and died from drinking the toxic water. A tall white statue, "Our Lady of the Rockies," stands poised atop the Continental Divide watching it all play out.

The landscape around Anaconda is equally famished. Decades of chloride and arsenic fumes have desertified grasslands and deforested mountainsides for miles. Black slag heaps line the highway leading to Wisdom. People use boards and scraps to sculpt their names in the spew. A Jack Nicklaus–designed golf course rolls over the Old Works site. Sod had to be imported. Not even knapweed would grow in the rank heavy-metal debris. The 585-foot-tall smelter stack looms above town like the chimney of a sinking ship.

The population of Butte is down to 33,000—about half what it was seventy-five years ago. Even with 300 mining jobs at the Southeast Berkeley Pit, Butte has the highest rate of lack-of-work of any major city in Montana. There's talk of turning much of it into a national historical park. But today, one of the main industries is cleaning up toxic waste. There's lots to do. In his novel *Red Harvest*, Dashiell Hammett called his fictionalized Butte "Poisonville." He was right on the money. ARCO has already spent over $250 million cleaning up the mess, but progress has been a mite slow. What's done tends to stay done.

But, on St. Patrick's Day at least, Butte is the best place to be in Montana.

The copper city is as anachronistic and defiant as leaded gas. The bars are legit, no ferns or wine coolers allowed. I suspect there's an ordinance. Just cold beer and hard liquor—in line with God's actual plan. Snooce chewing is about mandatory. Just spit the juice into your empties and try not to hand-blow your nose upwind of the ladies.

My favorite bars shall remain nameless. Just a simple courtesy. But there are plenty to go around. By my count Butte has 104 bars and 49 churches. Seems about right.

Uptown Butte is where St. Patty's Day kicks in. Blocks of historic stone and brick buildings line Broadway, Park, and other main streets. The styles are a mulligan stew of Greek Revival, Gothic, modified Queen Anne, and absolutely Vernacular. Yet it all hangs together with a rowdy authenticity that planned downtowns can't quite muster. Still, too many storefronts and upstairs offices stand empty. Even the "New Ames Hotel" hasn't had a customer since the days of JFK and full shifts in the Pit.

Yet espresso shops seem to be everywhere. This Seattle affectation has spread all over Montana—even to the streets of tough-luck Butte. People who need espresso to get through the day may be living the wrong lives.

There are two highlights of Butte's St. Patrick's Day celebration— the parade and the bar crawl. Both involve the consumption of heroic quantities of alcohol. This is the land of the thirteenth step—go back to drinking.

The streets are packed to the gunwales with Butte Irish and thousands of "Scandahouvians" borrowing the day. I normally avoid clusters like this but seem drawn to Butte as a reminder of lives being led in ways exactly opposite from my own.

Besides, it's a blast.

On this St. Patty's I was steering my way solo through waves of partyers. I always seemed to be going somewhere everyone else was coming from. People were dashing around, bumping happily into each other, climbing fire escapes, and howling with pleasure. It was like a monkey's wedding.

Around the next corner a group of beered-up crew cuts were forming flying wedges to cram themselves into a bar already in complete violation of all known fire codes. The defenses could not be breached. They bounced off the crush of people and spilled backward onto the sidewalk, stacking up like Cromwell's army after a failed run at the outer walls of Dunnottar Castle.

I managed to locate a beer and slunk partway into an alley to let the throngs slide past. The ground was strewn with plastic cups and flattened cans. Even the air tasted like beer. Bagpipe music seeped over from the next block and I cut through the back alleys to find the parade. A woman was sunning herself on a stoop watching an infant strapped into one of those curved plastic kid-holders. She was smoking a cigarette and had some sort of homemade tattoos on her hands. Prison art.

Through another alley and past an open window. Inside, a small old man was calmly watching television. He sat on a brown crushed velvet sofa, slippers on, hands folded, doilies covering the end tables. A black-and-white war movie flickered from the set—D-Day all over again.

I wasn't paying attention and almost tripped over a young guy reduced to all fours loudly retching green beer onto the cracked asphalt. His shiny leprechaun hat was badly askew. It had lost its top and slipped down over his face. The thing was a perfect megaphone for what he was engaged in. Erin Go Braugh is exactly the noise he made.

Finally Broadway, the parade route. A pipe-and-drum corps was marching by to great cheers. The sound always takes me back to England watching bagpipers move along a beach below the white cliffs of Dover. My English and Irish genes sent chills shivering all over. Then came floats full of queens and princesses teething real smiles on their big day. Veterans, politicians, fire engines, and brass bands followed, all as green as good intentions could provide.

I watched the crowd closely. Here were the faces of Butte, a swirl of

Irish, Welsh, Polish, Finn, Czech, German, and more. So many old men, ears mangled or hips torqued, hands missing parts or eyes failing behind opaque headlamp lenses. These were the guys. Union guys. The miners who found the metal for shells and tanks, who implemented two world wars. The ones who made all that money for The Company. The very lives that were made possible by the work but were so limited by the pay. And now they stood as tall as ache would allow, having a beer, fierce pride still present, despite all the reasons against it, despite all the chances to decide it wasn't so.

Yes, on St. Patrick's Day at least, Butte is the best place to be in Montana.

After the parade, the revelers figured it was time to bear down and get legitimate about drinking. I decided to head home before the DUI's started hitting the roads and then each other. On the downgrade to my truck, I stopped across from the old Metals Bank building and raised my little pocket camera to take a shot. It was now a Mexican restaurant. Less need for vaults these days. The mining money has long since left the state on wire transfers. Even the wire left the local ground.

Suddenly I heard a blast of laughter, belch, and argument roar out from behind me. An old gentleman shaped like a sack of grain wobbled out of Fat Jack's Bar. He scanned me for defect and found plenty.

"Git out!" sackman yelled in my direction. His eyes were somehow going six places at once.

"Git out! Let Montana be Montana!"

Our man had something on his mind. I hung in there waiting for it as he gathered himself for another salvo.

"Let Montana be Montana!" he yelled again.

I was beginning to detect a theme. A couple of passersby glanced over, but mostly people just ignored it all. In Butte, a fracas in the street is hardly cause to alert CNN.

I walked over to the guy. "I'm just taking a picture of the old bank."

"You just git out!" he bellowed. I did a mental countdown for the refrain. He didn't disappoint.

"Let Montana be Montana!" he barked, eyes still arguing amongst themselves. "Damned out-of-staters comin' in takin' our jobs!"

Ah, I'd been branded a tourist or newcomer, either one a capital crime at best.

"Wait a minute, I'm from Missoula," I said, trying for friendly. "And I used to live just up the road."

St. Patrick's Day in Butte

This threw him back on his worn-down heels. You could actually watch the data tunneling through synapses blocked by an overburden of whiskey ditches and Pabst Blue Ribbon beer. The news finally arrived.

"Oh."

That's all. Fine. He started moving off in a penguin's shuffle and I returned to my camera, lining up the right angle.

But sackman wasn't done. Apparently the news wore off.

"Git out! Let Montana be Montana!" he yelled at me, like he'd come up with it fresh.

Now I was pissed. I strode over to him ready to get to the bottom of this thing.

"What the hell is your problem? I'm just taking a damn picture!"

"You out-of-staters wreckin' things," he slurred. Apparently I was personally responsible for the coup in Chile, the invention of PVC, and The Company's decision to sell out—for every exact thing that made copper fall from grace.

"I've lived in Montana for years, wasn't born here but I've worked all over the state," I said. That was my first mistake.

"So you just git out then!" he raged righteously, waving me away with a swoop of his arm.

But I knew something he hadn't banked on. Nearly all of the miners that worked in Butte in the old days came from outside the state. Many were foreigners. A real minority were native Montanans.

"Wait a minute," I said. "Where were you born?"

He grunted, sending a slow-motion message to his feet to go find another whiskey ditch. The delay in transmission gave me an opening.

"Well, come on, where the hell were you born anyway?"

His face started to swell up, purple veins mapping the contours of his bulging, drink-ravaged nose. He was about to burst. Three, two, one . . .

"I'M FROM CHICAGO BUT THAT DON'T MEAN SHIT!!!" he roared. And he actually believed it.

Then with a disgusted shake of his head, sackman inched away using his best version of quick. A moment later the ancient miner was folded back into the crowd of green-wrapped Butteans and gone.

It turns out that irony will track you down anywhere. An Illinoian anointing himself something sacred—a native.

But what is a real Montanan anyway? Does it come from an accident of birth? Just the luck of the romantic draw? If Montana is a born-to clan, it kind of lessens the sheen a bit. With no way to lose the status, with no act unethical enough to bring on banishment, where's the honor in it?

And what about "letting Montana be Montana?" What in the name of sweet reason does that mean?

Is the real Montana made of fertile ranchland, lots of elk, and clean cool water? Or is it a place where mining corporations ransack the land, export the earnings, and leave unemployed communities in the toxic lurch? Each of these is equally typical of the state.

Is the real Montana safe and tolerant, or is it a haven for militias and Freemen full of paranoia and festering racial hate? Again, it seems to be both.

Is it a state where all the new growth is welcomed or detested? Both.

It seems we've got to do something big, rangy, and tough. We've got to figure out what letting Montana be Montana really means. More than that: we've got to secure a Montana in line with geographic reason and our true needs. That sounds like democracy.

For most of the state's history, things have been either handed to us or shoved down our collective throats. The wild land and beauty were just here; we didn't have to earn them. The desecration and damage were just done; we sanctioned them. But since the state was so big, there seemed space enough for everything.

Those days are gone. Montana is still 147,138 square miles but its remoteness is being corroded by fax modems, gold fever, and ravenous real estate promotion. There is no numerical speed limit, so the miles won't protect us anymore.

Now it's up to us. Many have already devoted long lives to protecting their place. Montana is rich in conservationists of every stripe. The state has been on the innovative edge of land conservation partnerships for decades.

But die-hard enthusiasts of endless development have always hefted a lot of power in Montana. Power that has often been maintained by the relentless hawking of ideas that are not on cordial terms with the truth.

Likewise, most of the newcomers, Californians and otherwise, tend to see Montana more as a myth than a true place. They've come for the idea of Montana, the one they saw in the movies, the one that's unspoiled, the one that somehow stays perfect while the rest of America fails.

There's enough astonishment here to feed a world of misunder-

St. Patrick's Day in Butte

standings. One Fourth of July, the young daughter of some friends stood watching her first fireworks display. Explosions of red, purple, green, and blue filled the tremendous night.

"Does the sky just *do* that?" she gushed.

In the heavens of Montana, with Perseid meteor showers, dry lightning storms, glowing Milky Way sashes, and curving curtains of Northern Lights, it was a fair question.

Montana has its share of grand ascensions. And more than its portion of hooey. To find the marrow of this place we've got to be able to tell which is which.

3

MYTHS

"MYTHS ARE things that never were, but always are."
A philosopher whose name I can't remember figured that
one out.

But the word "myth" has two meanings. One is an untruth—sheer
boneheaded bullshit. No shortage has ever been reported. The other
definition is more compelling. A myth is a story that helps explain a
sacred history and the origin of a way of life. It is a narrative about the
land, a fable about the nature of things where we live.

Montana's myths tend toward stories of a tightly held but false geography. Montana writer Bill Kittredge calls it "reliving the old fictions." All of us, both locals and newcomers, have been susceptible.
And new layers get added on every day.

The antidote is to become disillusioned: to let the chaff blow away even if this challenges our proudly held notions of land and life. Then we can begin to craft the new myths we so dearly need—the lasting stories of land stewardship and lives deep in belonging.

Here are some facts behind ten of Montana's more persistent myths.

MYTH #1: THE PRISTINE LANDSCAPE

The most powerful myth about the Americas since 1492 and of the West since the settlement era is that the landscape is pristine. This notion still runs deep and beyond reason. It resists intrusions of reality so steadfastly for the simple reason that we desperately want it to be so.

The human need for Eden is widely known.

Trouble is, Europeans invaded a "New World" that was already pretty worked over. The Ice Age megafauna—the woolly mammoths, mastodons, ground sloths, and saber-toothed tigers—had already been rendered extinct by human hands. Archaeologists studying Folsom and Clovis points and paleontologists counting the bones call it the "Overkill."

Paleo-Indians and more recent tribes used fire extensively to clear and modify forests across the Americas, even in the "untouched" Amazon Basin. Grasslands were widely expanded and manipulated by flames to assist in hunting.

Agricultural fields covered immense areas. Sacred mounds, agricultural terraces, raised fields, and other remakings of the earth were common. Over 200,000 farming mounds have been found in the United States. In Wisconsin alone, thousands of Indian fields have been located, many more than 300 acres in size.

Indigenous cultures created extensive irrigation systems: the Aztec chinampas or "Floating Gardens," the Inca ditches in the Lake Titicaca region, the Hohokam canals near present-day Phoenix, and hundreds more.

The Incas built 24,000 miles of roads paved with fitted stones. The Mayas constructed 800 miles of causeways. In 1541, Gaspar de Carvajal traveled up the Amazon River and wrote of an "extensive system of highways leading deep into the forests from a string of riverbank cities." The Anasazi built cities, roads, and trade centers in Chaco Canyon and throughout the Southwest.

Clear evidence of serious soil erosion has been found everywhere ancient agriculture took place in the New World. Eroding soils from corn fields, perhaps as much as long-term drought, led to the "disappearance" of the Anasazi into the modern Hopi, Zuni, Laguna, Acoma, and other Pueblo nations.

Large cities were built all over the Americas, not just in the Maya, Inca, and Aztec empires, but in what is now the United States. Cahokia in Illinois had a population estimated at over 25,000 prior to the arrival of Columbus.

So the recent movie *1492—The Conquest of Paradise* was, well, a movie. The New World was a working landscape, not Shangri-La.

Montana historian K. Ross Toole once said, "Montana is not pristine, but these things are relative." Very relative when you consider what came after European settlement.

At first, Montana's isolation formed a moat against exploitation. The many Indian nations that jostled for position here were not farmers, built no roads except what horses' hooves and travois would carve, burned the land for hunting but replicated lightning-caused fire, and did not render bison or elk extinct. Their imprint on the land, limited by technology and temperament, was relatively soft. But most were relative newcomers to the ecosystems they inhabited.

With the settlement of North America by the Spanish, English, French, and Russians, a chain reaction of tribal dislocations echoed out across the landscape. When Lewis and Clark passed through Montana in 1805, none of the Indians they encountered claimed to have lived in the region 150 years before. The Blackfeet were from Canada, the Plains tribes from the Great Lakes; several nations had been pushed east into Montana from the Pacific Northwest.

The Lewis and Clark Expedition provided the first written physical geography of the Louisiana Purchase. The extraction of resources and rapid transformation of the landscape could now begin. And the transformers meant business—they still do. This unbroken tradition reaches us essentially intact. It is one of Montana's most ardently defended customs, almost part of the gene pool.

The narrative of impacts on Montana is long: the slaughter of wildlife, over-mining, over-logging, over-grazing. Best to just recite a few examples.

John Jacob Astor's American Fur Company and scores of other outfits trapped out beaver and other furbearers from Montana's rivers. These animals never returned to some watersheds.

Excessive hunting was the rule early on. In 1854, Sir George Gore, a wealthy Irish bachelor, traveled across Montana and the Rockies on a three-year binge of carnage. The party of "Sir Bloodsport" included thirty men, twenty-five wagons, 112 horses, three milk cows, and lots of ammo. Gore ended up shooting 2,000 bison, 1,600 deer and elk, 100 bears, and thousands of birds of every feather.

The wildlife of the West seemed endless. It wasn't.

The estimated 60 million bison that grazed across North America were hunted to near extinction for their hides and bones. This overkill was much more than commerce—it was an act of war designed to destroy the food supply of the Plains Indian nations. By the 1880s, only a few hundred bison survived in Montana. The species has now recovered somewhat but is mostly raised as livestock.

By 1910, elk were wiped out in Utah, Nevada, New Mexico, and most of the West. Montana's herds were about gone. Yellowstone National Park was their last sizable refuge. The herds roaming the West today are mostly descendants of animals transplanted from the park.

Montana's legendary "wild trout" fisheries have a secret—they're dominated by non-native species. Rainbow, brown, and brook trout are introduced exotics. Only fish like the cutthroats, Arctic grayling, and bull trout are locals. Despite the relatively high quality of fishing in the state, the news isn't all good. Two-thirds of the state's Westslope and Yellowstone cutthroat trout populations may soon disappear due to the introduction of non-native trout, habitat destruction, and over-fishing. Exotic lake trout have invaded Yellowstone Lake and are rapidly devouring cutthroats. Even conservative Governor Marc Racicot acknowledges that "our state fish has virtually run out of room." The fluvial Arctic grayling was once found in all of Montana's cold-water streams. Today, this graceful iridescent fish swims only in the upper reaches of the Big Hole River. Bull trout have been eliminated from many watersheds by sedimentation from logging operations. A federal court has ordered the U.S. Fish and Wildlife Service to reconsider listing the bull as an endangered species.

The news is even worse for exotic trout. "Whirling disease," a perplexing tail-blackening parasitic ailment, is sweeping through Montana's river systems. It damages the cartilage of infected fish who whirl in circles until a predator finds them. Others just starve to death. Over 90 percent of the rainbow trout in the world-famous Madison River have already succumbed. Rainbow populations have plummeted from 3,000 to 300 fish per river mile and catch rates have collapsed by 75 percent. Biologist Dick Vincent, head of Montana's whirling disease task force, believes that in "some rivers, we're looking at a real threat to the entire species." This spore-borne disease accidentally entered the United States in 1958 in a shipment of trout fillets from Denmark. All of Colorado's streams quickly became infected by this aquatic "Andromeda Strain." Soon all of Montana's may be as well. Vincent believes that "brown trout are holding the whole system up." But now even brown trout are beginning to die.

Montana's forest lands have also endured much. In 1902, the Anaconda Company built its first smelter. Over 300,000 cords of fuelwood alone began to be cut from the region's mountainsides each year. The forests of the Big Hole and Blackfoot basins were carted off at a full canter. Poisonous fumes of ash, fluoride, and arsenic killed trees as far north as Philipsburg.

Prior to the creation of the National Forests in 1906, timber poachers stripped millions of board feet from public lands. Following World War II, the annual legal harvest from the National Forests increased dramatically. In the 1960s, clearcutting—the act of sawing down all standing trees—replaced true forestry. In the Bitterroot National Forest, conservationists were stunned to see terraces being bulldozed into mountainsides after the timber was clearcut. Sedimentation rates soared and streams became entombed in mud. On some slopes you can stand knee-deep in the absence of soil.

Today, the mining of timber continues in stands farther and farther out in the backcountry. The cost of road building and harvest now exceeds what the logs bring at the sawmill. Since 1979, the U.S. Forest Service has lost over $4 billion on its timber programs. One hundred of 120 national forests are losing money. So-called "deficit sales" are now the norm in Montana with the federal treasury used to subsidize logging operations. Despite the argument that these cuts ensure "community stability," timber towns are now in awful financial straits from decades of over-harvest and export of raw logs. Because of dwindling supply, the cut from federal land has dropped by two-thirds in the 1990s. The loggers took too much too quickly. Jack Ward Thomas, former Chief of the U.S. Forest Service, set the agenda for change when he took the job in 1993. He informed agency staffers that the new rules were simple: "Tell the truth, obey the law, and listen to biologists." The fact that these words needed to be said revealed the severity of the agency's problems. Thomas recently resigned without substantial change having taken place. However, the new Chief, Mike Dombeck, repeated the same message to Congress: "the health of the land must be our first priority . . . failing this, nothing else we do really matters." Dombeck concluded that just as "it took decades for today's unhealthy forest conditions to develop, it will take an equally long time to reverse them."

The stakes are high.

A drive through the Kootenai, Lolo, and other national forests reveals mile after mile of cutover public lands. Parts of the Yaak River watershed look like the Tunguska blowdown in Siberia. Nature needed a meteorite to deforest 1,200 square miles. We've skinned off far more than that using chainsaws and D-9 Cats. While many areas of the state are regrowing reasonably well and responsible logging is more common than extreme environmentalists would admit, much of the time it has been just cruise, cut, and haul. So—newcomers get ready—national forests are not butterfly preserves. They're commercial timberlands. America's public forests are laced with 360,000 miles of logging roads—that's more than fourteen times the circumference of the world at the equator. Water quality, recreation, and wildlife have often paid the price. Unfortunately, the overall record of private timber companies like Plum Creek and Stimson may be no better. There has been a 150 percent increase in timber harvest on Montana's corporate lands since 1985.

The mining industry has generally treated the land like dirt. Users of trifles like clean water take note—Montana is sometimes not what it seems.

A 1996 report prepared for the Western Governors Association gives the scale of the disturbance. Montana has 19,751 mine sites covering 148,000 acres. Some 2,200 of these are active mines currently operating under state permits. Montana has 1,118 miles of mine-polluted rivers and creeks. Mine spoils cover 14,038 acres; 20,862 acres have been excavated. Another 1,845 acres are now prone to cave-ins. Montana has 1,174 hazardous mining structures. Statewide reclamation costs have been estimated at $912 million. That figure is mighty low. A quarter of a billion dollars has already been spent in Butte and Anaconda alone.

The Butte region is a desolation row from the era of go-for-broke copper mining. They made it. The Anaconda Company is no more, and its industrial watershed—the Clark Fork River—is broken. This drainage contains the country's largest EPA Superfund cleanup problem. It includes four sites: the Silver Bow Creek project, encompassing the Berkeley Pit mining complex and 140 miles of the Clark Fork River from Butte to Missoula; the Milltown Dam at the confluence of the Blackfoot and Clark Fork rivers; the Anaconda smelter area; and the pentachlorophenol-choked Montana Pole Treatment site in the Butte Valley.

Smelter complexes in need of cleanup also exist at Great Falls (aluminum), East Helena (lead), and Columbia Falls (aluminum). Montana is pockmarked with eight Superfund sites.

Gold mining is also a clear and present danger.

The Zortman-Landusky operation in the Little Rocky Mountains is the state's largest gold mine. A heap-leach system is used in which cyanide is drizzled onto piles of ore taken from open pits. Cyanide is the same stuff used in gas chambers. Pollution plumes have leaked into the Missouri and Milk rivers. In 1996, two lawsuits settled with the Pegasus Gold Corporation required a $32 million upgrade of waste-treatment facilities and the payment of $3 million in fines.

The Seven-Up Pete Joint Venture—an immense open-pit gold mine—is gearing up in the upper Blackfoot River watershed. More on that irony later. Also on the drawing board is ASARCO's Rock Creek Project, a copper and silver scheme that would take ore from beneath the Cabinet Mountains Wilderness.

Montana's extractionist myth is that God is a miner and He disapproves of all forms of demonic regulation.

There are some notable exceptions to this poor record. Cases that give us proof that a mine can be a good neighbor.

Montana's eighteen coal mines produce about 35 million tons annually from strip mines in eastern Montana. Back in the 1970s, the Montana Power Company (through its subsidiary Western Energy) proposed to build four coal-fired electrical power plants and a new town at Colstrip. Citizen groups like the Northern Plains Resource Council fought the proposal, citing massive potential environmental and social impacts. Extensive air pollution, groundwater contamination, and landscape destruction were feared.

To date, most of those impacts have not materialized. Western Energy has strip-mined about 11,000 acres and reclaimed half of it. If you don't believe that, walk through the replanted grasslands and see for yourself. While a few localized cases of acid runoff have been reported, Colstrip works. Would it have come out this way if environmentalists hadn't duked it out with the companies to require sensible operating standards? Absolutely not. But the point is, it works.

Most of the other changes in Montana's landscape show up in our daily papers.

In the spring of 1996, sixty tons of chlorine and potassium cresylate spilled into the Clark Fork River near Alberton when a Montana Rail Link train derailed. Fish and forests died immediately. More than 500 people were forced to evacuate the area for weeks. Those exposed to the gas cloud still complain of health problems like joint and muscle pain, body aches, burning skin, numb lips, blurred vision, and extreme fatigue. Lawsuits are pending.

Twenty-six people were hospitalized in Ronan recently when a truckload of Diazonon, Rovral, Amine 4, and other pesticides spilled during a wreck on Highway 93.

The Confederated Salish and Kootenai Tribes are forcing the Yellowstone Pipeline Company to remove its gasoline pipeline from the Flathead Reservation because of a long history of leaks and spills. Now the company is proposing to rebuild the line through the remote Ninemile Valley, a place renowned for its pack of endangered gray wolves.

The myth of a pristine Montana dissipates the closer you look.

Leafy spurge, spotted knapweed, flannel mullein, cheatgrass, and other exotic weeds infest millions of acres across the state.

The *Giardia* intestinal parasite is now found in almost all of Montana's water. Twenty years ago you could drink from any high-country stream. No longer. After three painful rounds of giardiasis, I now filter everything I drink on camping trips.

Wintertime air quality in Missoula and Billings violates federal Clean Air Act standards so often that oxygenated fuels must be used. Missoula's air quality is poorer than Pittsburgh's or San Francisco's. Woodstove regulations have been enacted to reduce the winter's brown pall of smoke.

And on and on it goes.

But if it's so awful, why do people love Montana? Because right next to the ruins are portions of wild country that have arrived in a nearly direct line from the Big Bang. Each day we drive by ranchlands full of wildlife and real evidence that stewardship survives—that we belong. Belief is carried in our bones.

Throughout Montana's hell-bent history, that has been the tension. The conflicting urges to exploit and conserve define this place. The primal issue of life here can be simply put: "What happens to the land?" We may violently disagree about the answer but few would debate that, to paraphrase Shakespeare, the land's the thing.

Yet landscape change has come from both sudden maraudings and subtle increments of loss. It's hard to know what's "natural" anymore. The danger is that we may forget. Newcomers often remark how pretty the yellow fields of leafy spurge are. Locals can only grimace. Actress Meg Ryan, fresh into the Paradise Valley, calls Montana "not even remotely spoiled yet." Old-timers can only shake their heads remembering what was. In *The Big Sky*, Boone Caudil spoke of nineteenth-century Montana: "It's all sp'iled, I reckon . . . the whole caboodle." Each person lives with a personal sense of the state. It's mostly what we talk about. As historian Joseph Kinsey Howard wrote: "the development of Montana must be primarily the responsibility of Montanans, and to do that they must first learn its cultural and economic history."

Kinsey's right. If we emerge memoryless into our daily lives, if we pull back from a clear-eyed look at what has already happened in Montana, there seems little possibility we can fix the problems lying out there beyond our windshields. To do this, both newcomers and natives are going to have to cast aside the myth of a pristine Montana that can endure all we ask.

The real Montana is a calloused cultural landscape, hand-riven by generations of claimers. We've often spent the place with a lavish and improvident hand. Too often we've acted like it would never wear out.

It's often said "You can't eat the scenery." Montana shows that some people try.

MYTH #2: THE CLIMATE ITSELF

The cold is obvious. Montana holds the U.S. record for the coldest temperature ever recorded—minus 70 degrees F on January 20, 1954, at Rogers Pass in the upper Blackfoot drainage.

But then there's heat. Montana routinely exceeds 100 degrees in July and August, except when it's snowing on our barbecues. On July 5, 1937, it reached 117 degrees at Medicine Lake.

Montana has the largest range of recorded temperatures of any state—187 degrees. North Dakota comes in second with a mere 181 degrees. Alaska is third with 180.

In any given year Montana will be colder than Moscow and hotter than Cairo. A benign stretch of seasons will only toss 30 below and 105 above at us.

Droughts and floods come so often that figures for average precipitation are meaningless. The valley bottoms might get fourteen inches one year, six the next, twenty-two the next. Winter snowpacks can reach twenty feet or barely take hold.

Montanans, like most Westerners, have often confused weather with climate. We'd kind of prefer that Montana were milder and wetter than it is. This has set us up for generous portions of hell-to-pay.

In 1880, the Montana Territory had only about 275,000 cattle. With a string of mild winters and the bison killed off, cartels began overstocking the rangelands of eastern Montana. Three years later, over 600,000 head grazed out in the big open. Then the winter of 1886–1887 arrived. Temperatures fell to 40 below and kept dropping. Blizzards buried what remained of the depleted grasslands. It hit 63 below at Miles City. Starving, snow-blind cows pressed together in coulees desperately trying to survive. Most did not. When spring finally arrived, over 60 percent of the cattle in the territory were dead — 362,000 animals. Losses in some areas were over 95 percent.

After a succession of moist years, people sometimes decide that the damned aridity has been healed. In their book, rain follows the plow. Following passage of the Enlarged Homestead Act in 1909, some 85,000 homesteaders arrived on Montana's northern plains — the High Line. From 1910 to 1916 it was unusually wet, sixteen inches of rain, double the long-term figures. Yields of wheat exploded and wartime demand kept prices high. Then the war ended and prices collapsed. Drought returned in 1919 and crops failed. By 1920, 65,000 High Line settlers went bust and left the state.

The lesson is that extreme is about as normal as Montana gets.

Chinook winds will do as a reminder. During winter, cold air builds west of the Continental Divide and spills over the mountains into central and eastern Montana. As the air descends, it compresses and heat is created. Basic physics, Boyle's Law. The sudden warm-ups along Montana's chinook belt, in places like Browning, Choteau, Havre, and of course, Chinook, can be epic.

The most remarkable temperature change ever recorded in the United States occurred at Great Falls on January 11, 1980. In seven minutes it went from 32 degrees below zero to 15 degrees above. At Havre, a rise of 43 degrees in fifteen minutes has been recorded. Weather observer Grayson Cordell witnessed a gain of 26 degrees in forty-five seconds, again at Havre. An 80-degree climb in four hours occurred at Kipp where thirty inches of snow disappeared before people's eyes. No wonder the word "chinook" means "snow-eater" in several Indian languages.

Just for symmetry, Montana also holds the national record for the most rapid decrease in temperature. On January 23, 1916, Browning was luxuriating in a chinook. The air was a balmy 44 degrees and people were out in their shirtsleeves. Twelve hours later it had plummeted to 56 degrees below zero.

So what is the truth of Montana's climate? Montana is so big it has nine official climate zones. Conditions in the wet, mountainous northwest bear little resemblance to what the atmosphere cooks up for folks living out on the plains of the southeast. There's no "typical" Montana climate.

Then there's altitude. Montana ranges from 1,820 feet where the Kootenai River enters Idaho to 12,799 feet at the summit of Granite Peak in the Beartooths. Biogeographers call the vertical pattern of intervening environments "life zones."

The floodplain zone is the lowest, a place of cottonwoods, ponderosa pines, and abundant, sometimes trailer-drowning amounts of water. Semiarid steppes or subhumid prairies cover the benches and rolling plains. These are Montana's sunniest, driest, hottest, and sometimes coldest environments. In the winter, cold air drains into the valleys and forms lakes of frigid air. During these "inversions" temperatures can be as much as 15 degrees warmer 500 feet above the valley bottoms.

A lower treeline caused by dryness forms the boundary between grasslands and forests. The humid montane and subalpine forests ascend upslope until cold and freezing winds create an upper treeline. The alpine zone with its brief, flower-filled summer caps the peaks. Year-round snowfields and scores of small glaciers remind us that rumors of the demise of the Ice Age may have been greatly exaggerated.

Slope aspect is just as critical. At the same elevation, forests grow on the shady, cool, north-facing slopes and grasslands or conifer parklands mantle the sunny, warm, south-facing aspects. Building a home in the shade can add two months to winter. Montana is a place where you need to learn the lay of both the land and the sky.

Promoters of the state have always done their best to confuse the matter. In 1909, the state published an almanac and distributed it all over the country. Among the pages of absolute bunk about boundless harvests, endless land, and bullet-proof prosperity was this bit of climate data: "The winters are warm, sunlit and inviting. Cold periods are infrequent and of short duration, as the prevailing winds of winter bring the balmy atmosphere of summer."

With money at stake, liberties are taken.

Among the state's current promotions is the "Invite a Friend to Montana" program. Not even one photograph shows anyone cold. Cold would be bad for business. Even the ski areas bill themselves as both snowy and warm. Winters like that can happen—in Colorado.

Myths about climate and the weather are held by newcomers and oldcomers alike. "Red sky at night, sailors delight." "A wet March makes a sad harvest." "Expect stormy weather when ants travel in lines." "When the cows lie down, rain is coming." "When the stars begin to huddle, the earth will soon be a puddle." I confess to not getting that last one.

Native Montanans are partial to the rule of extremes. In the past, they argue, things were always wetter, drier, colder, or hotter than today. In their memories, the most extreme events were habitual. It adds luster to conversations.

The newcomers drive into town with a head full of summer expectation and winter dread. Most end up being stunned it isn't snowier in the valleys, how sunny it can be, but how cold and long winters are. They learn that some years have only two seasons—winter and rodeo week. Other years fetch up a 50-degree Christmas and a Fourth of July blizzard. The phone lines light up back to Los Angeles and La Jolla with half-meant excitement over all this. But most newcomers hold on to a secret folklore—with their arrival, the winters will back off into mildness. If rain follows the plow, maybe warmth follows the Mercedes.

The first stretch of weeks that crackle below zero generally cinches in this sort of thinking. So do events like the Montana's Pleistocene winter of 1996–1997. Missoula, Kalispell, and the Bitterroot Valley— the "Banana Belt"—received between nine and twelve feet of snow.

When it comes to Montana's climate, it's an ill wind that blows no minds.

MYTH #3: A LACK OF NATURAL HAZARDS

Many people moving to Montana are fleeing landscapes roiled up by earthquakes, fires, floods, and other natural hazards. They fancy that the biggest threats here are icy roads and cholesterol.

Well, fancy this.

Much of central Montana lies within one of the country's most active earthquake regions—the Intermountain Seismic Belt. This curving swath extends from Yellowstone National Park through Helena and north along the Rocky Mountain Front. The entire belt is in Seismic Zone 3—areas having North America's highest risk of damaging earthquakes. Seismologists consider Yellowstone, the Paradise Valley, Livingston, Bozeman, and Helena to have significant potential for destructive temblors. California's San Andreas Fault is also included in Seismic Zone 3.

Montana has been severely shaken by large earthquakes. In 1925, structures were leveled in Three Forks from a Richter magnitude 6.8 event. In October 1935, Helena experienced two destructive quakes in two weeks. These 6.3 and 6.0 shakes cracked houses, wrecked chimneys, broke glass, and caused several million dollars in damage. Over 1,200 quakes hit Helena in the next three months. Hundreds of minor quakes have been detected ever since. In the Flathead Lake region, swarms of magnitude 3 to 4 earthquakes are recorded each year.

The Yellowstone region is very seismically active. Most of what is now the park catastrophically exploded 600,000 years ago. The "hot spot," a plume of magma, is still in operation. Another explosion is assured at some future date—maybe in another 600,000 years, maybe next Wednesday.

In 1959, a major earthquake hit Hebgen Lake near Yellowstone. This 7.1 magnitude shudder caused an entire mountainside to crash down into the Madison River Valley. Twenty-eight people were killed when a campground and main highway were buried. Their bodies have never been recovered from the massive pile of debris. Earthquake Lake formed in back of the landslide. Houses and roads were flooded out and abandoned. Damage was reported in every town within 100 miles of the epicenter. Today, the mountainside is still raw and fifteen-foot-high active fault scarps slice across the region. In 1975, a magnitude 6 earthquake again hit the Hebgen Lake region.

A swarm of earthquakes was recorded in Yellowstone Park during 1996 with magnitudes reaching up to 4.5. These events scared thousands of people but caused no damage. Seismicity has noticeably increased over the last ten years. When will the Yellowstone region produce another deadly quake? "That's the $64,000 question," says University of Utah geophysicist Robert Smith.

Montana's rivers can also cause tremendous damage. Severe flooding has occurred in Montana in 1908, 1927, 1938, 1948, 1953, 1964, 1975, 1981, 1996, and 1997. Despite hundreds of dams and reservoirs built to control runoff, nature still finds a way to remind us of the true order of things: floodplains get flooded.

The most damaging floods come when above-average snowpacks are melted by rainstorms and suddenly high springtime temperatures.

In June 1908, it rained for thirty-three days in a row in western Montana. The Clark Fork River charged out of its banks and washed away most of the Milwaukee Road Railroad line between Butte and Missoula. Scores of houses were damaged or destroyed. Missoula's Higgins Street Bridge was swept downstream toward Lake Pend Oreille.

In June 1964, torrents poured over and around the Gibson Dam along the Rocky Mountain Front. Pieces of buildings were washed fifty miles downstream.

In May 1996, snowpacks in many Montana drainages stood at 180 percent of normal. Temperatures reached the nineties and many rivers quickly rose to flood stage and beyond. The Yellowstone began to threaten Livingston. I was doing fieldwork nearby and watched it happen. In the morning the sandbags seemed to be working. By afternoon, the river was passing through the front doors of houses and politely exiting through the back. Decks became wharfs. Over 150 people were forced to evacuate. The same thing happened the following spring.

In 1996, the Bitterroot River also reached 100-year flows. Thousands of acres were inundated and the Victor Bridge was destroyed. A more sobering fact: the high water of 1996 claimed the lives of six people in the Missoula/Bitterroot area alone.

When it isn't too wet in Montana, it's often too dry.

Forest fires are the most serious natural hazard here. For decades we have fought them bravely if not wisely. The forests and grasslands of the state have evolved with fire, yet until recently we have viewed flames as a satanic destroyer—as something to be cast out of paradise. The cost of this ignorance has been high.

On August 9, 1949, a lightning-caused fire broke out in remote mountain country beside the Missouri River downstream of Helena. Fifteen experienced smokejumpers parachuted into Mann Gulch to put it out. The heat was ghastly, over 100 degrees, and the grasslands were tinder dry. Then the wind came up. A drowsy little char was instantly transformed into a firestorm. The men ran upslope trying to escape. All but two died. Today the landscape is healthy, rejuvenated by the released fertility. Those thirteen dead smokejumpers are memorialized by crosses erected where they fell.

In 1988, Yellowstone Park caught fire. Both lightning and human carelessness were responsible. The nation demanded that the government "save" Yellowstone, the world's first national park. Waves of firefighters and the National Guard moved in to do battle. Fall rains and snows eventually put the fires out.

Today, we accept that burns were a natural part of the functioning of the park and an inevitable force in shaping the plant communities of the West. Yet suburban houses continue to be built in Montana forests and grasslands that are as fire-prone and fire-dependent as Mann Gulch and Yellowstone. A century of fire suppression has created a landscape crowded with far more fuel than nature would normally allow. Fires in the "urban-wildlands interface" (where cities spread into the boonies) have consumed thousands of houses across the rapidly populating West. But such losses are nothing new in the Big Sky.

In 1910, 3 million acres of west-central Montana were torched in a single fire, twice the acreage burned in Yellowstone in 1988. The 1910 fire is now called the "Great Burn." Eighty-five people were killed and the towns of DeBorgia, Taft, and Haugan were destroyed. Only the DeBorgia Schoolhouse survived. In 1980, I succeeded in having the building listed on the National Register of Historic Places. It was all that was left of the old days.

Fire is an element of life in Montana. The tree rings and fire scars of ponderosa pines and Douglas firs reveal fire frequencies ranging from seven to twenty years. Yet people continue to build log homes roofed with cedar shakes in forests that can be counted on to torch. Then they expect the fire department to protect them. Many also rebel against the use of controlled burns to lessen the risk. They like all the trees.

Fire ecologist Stephen Pyne puts it simply: "Carbon cannot be sequestered like bullion. Living systems demand a fire tithe. Refuse . . . and feral fire will return."

My house is in a ponderosa pine parkland. Photos from the thirties show a prairie with scattered large trees. Pine saplings are now packed in everywhere. Botanist Jim Habeck tells me that fire used to run through every seven years or so. My land hasn't burned in a century. I went prudent. My house has concrete siding and fiberglass-cored roofing shingles which are as fire resistant as metal. A moat of gravel and rock surrounds the place. I've spent days thinking like a fire, thinning out the fuel and carting it off. A recurring dream arrives every fire season. Flames charge up the hillside, yet my home is unscathed. I even imagine the paper's front page headline—"Why Did Jack Wright's House Survive?" But it's probably only a dream.

Montana doesn't have California's smorgasbord of hazards or Florida's volleys of hurricanes. But it isn't Walton's Mountain either.

MYTH #4: POPULATION

Journalist Joel Garreau includes Montana in a region he calls "The Empty Quarter." Geographers Frank and Deborah Popper call much of eastern Montana "The Big Open" or "The Buffalo Commons." It's as if no one lived here. That's part of Montana's mystique in a way. We've wanted it to be not only pristine but uncrowded—an edenic refuge, the fresh start. This sort of thinking has been around awhile.

Europeans imagined the "New World" as certain wilderness. Problem was, at the time of contact the Americas were home to about 54 million indigenous people. Berkeley historical demographer Woodrow Borah believes it may have been twice that many. Whatever the exact number, the New World was already pretty much spoken for.

Between 1492 and 1650, 90 percent of those voices were silenced by disease and the sword. That's 48 million Indian deaths. More would come. This holocaust may help explain the persistent myth that the American West was "unoccupied territory."

In 1492, about 4 million Indians lived in what is now the United States. Their numbers catastrophically collapsed and for a while the land really did seem either empty or unclaimed to white eyes. That's what all the wars were about.

Today, over 50,000 Indian people of many nations live in Montana—about 6 percent of the total population. Their reservations cover 13,055 square miles, a bit less than 9 percent of the state. The new wars are, in part, about how many people get to live on the rest.

Paul Meadows, a University of Montana researcher, sized it up this way: "Montanans are beginning to think—if we may use the editorial pages as evidence—that they have all the people they can handle. There is a fear that the state is reaching, if it has not already reached, its saturation point." Meadows wrote this in 1945. He went on to call for a state "population policy" recognizing that equilibrium or even loss "does not mean a declining economy or culture—a balance of land and people must be found." We still haven't found it. That's because bar rumors have too often passed for facts. A glance at the following myths about Montana's population might help clear the air.

Montana's Low Population Density

Montana is far bigger than all the New England states, New York, and New Jersey combined. At 147,138 square miles it's quite a spread—the fourth-largest state.

In 1997, Montana's estimated population stood at 879,000, a rank of forty-fifth in the Union. So the Big Sky has about 5.9 people per square mile, making it forty-eighth in crowdedness. Sounds like Montana is spacious beyond imagining.

Problem is, that density figure is useless. We need some new calculations with a bit of applied geography involved.

First, about 40 percent of Montana is controlled by the federal and state governments. People generally don't live on public lands. Subtract those areas and the state shrinks to 88,283 square miles.

Now, deduct the 13,055 square miles of Indian reservations. Montana is down to 75,228 square miles.

Since it isn't sensible to cover productive agricultural land with houses—Montana's 24,000 ranches and farms are a $2 billion industry—we'd best exclude some acreage here. It would also be wise to keep houses off a reasonable share of the state's big game winter-range habitats, historic sites, productive private forest lands, and scenic open spaces. Otherwise there'd be no point to living here. Still more land is simply undevelopable—too steep, rocky, or remote. And of course river and creek floodplains would be out as well.

So what's left?

If we take the conservative position that one-half of Montana's privately owned land either has a low physical capability for development or is entirely unsuitable for growth, the population density of the state shifts even more. Montana's revised area is now 37,614 square miles, and the state's density becomes twenty-three people per square mile. That's a fourfold increase. Hardly Hong Kong, but let's keep going.

Nearly all of the state's population growth in the 1990s is taking place in a few counties. Newcomers as well as in-state migrants are not

heading to the plains of Scobey, Brussett, and Ekalaka. They are settling near the mountains.

So what is the revised population density in the places where Montana is growing? Here are four examples using the same formula.

Missoula County (Missoula): 135 people per square mile.

Ravalli County (Hamilton): 105 people per square mile.

Flathead County (Kalispell): 98 people per square mile.

Gallatin County (Bozeman): 82 people per square mile.

These counties have densities more like Missouri, Mississippi, and
Hawaii than the rest of Montana. Regardless of how these calculations
are done, Montana is far more crowded than expected.

The 1990s—Montana's Biggest Population Boom

Not even close.

A look at the population trends in Table 1 deflates the "biggest
boom ever" theory. During the 1990s, Montana will probably grow by
about 100,000 people. This will be only the fourth-largest numerical

TABLE 1. MONTANA POPULATION GROWTH, 1870–1997

Year	Total Population	Number Change	% Change
1870	20,595		
1880	39,159	+18,564	+90
1890	142,924	+103,765	+265
1900	243,329	+100,405	+70
1910	376,053	+132,765	+55
1920	548,889	+172,836	+46
1930	537,606	−11,283	−2
1940	559,456	+21,850	+4
1950	591,024	+31,568	+5
1960	674,767	+83,743	+14
1970	694,409	+19,642	+3
1980	786,690	+92,281	+13
1990	799,065	+12,375	+1.5
1997	880,000 (est)	+80,935	+10

Source: U.S. Bureau of Census.

increase for any decade in Montana history. During the teens, mining expansion and a homesteading boom brought 172,836 newcomers into the state. This was back when Montana had half a million fewer people to start with.

During the 1990s, Montana's population will probably expand by about 13 percent. Again, the decade will only come in fourth overall. The 1880s saw a 265 percent rise. The 1980s brought a welcomed flat line—only a 1.5 percent expansion. In fact, only the 1920s, when Montana lost 2 percent of its population, showed less growth. The stall in the eighties may help explain why growth in the nineties seems so garish in contrast. We kind of got used to the quiet.

Montana also ranks substantially behind other western states in net in-migration between 1990 and 1995: 50,000 people, or a 6.3 percent gain in total population. Nevada has grown by 20 percent during that period from migration gains alone. Other states exceeding Montana's "newcomers" surge include Idaho (9.8 percent), Arizona (8 percent), and Colorado (7.5 percent).

Montana's net migration gain between 1990 and 1995 matched the state's net loss from 1985 to 1990. During that economically awful period, 137,000 Montanans moved out of state and 87,000 people moved in.

This is the Montana way. For the last fifty years, the number of births and deaths in the state can be graphed as a nearly even squiggle. But the line charting migration in and out of the state looks like the teeth of a ripper saw—sharp, erratic, and dangerously unpredictable.

The biggest-boom theory has little merit even in the "fast growth counties" of western Montana. Missoula County has averaged between a 20 and 33 percent increase in population every decade except the eighties since 1930. The 1990s boom is coming in at about 25 percent. Ravalli County (Hamilton) will grow by about 25–30 percent in the 1990s. It grew by 40 percent in the 1970s.

But other Montana counties are actually declining in population. Granite County (Philipsburg) had 4,328 residents in 1900. Then the mines closed. The current population is 2,548. Wheatland County (Harlowton) had 5,619 people in 1920. It may have peaked as high as 8,000 a few years earlier during the bonanza wheat boom. Today the county has 2,246 souls.

Montana is a demographically divided state.

The mundane conclusion here is that Montana's overall growth rates of the 1990s are not that unusual. The pace of the current boom has been reached or exceeded in seven of the last thirteen decades. That fact may be even more shocking than a record boom. Unrelenting growth has become nearly normal.

During the 1990s, Montana's population has grown about 1.5 percent per year. That sounds puny. But at that rate, the population will double in a bit over fifty years. China is growing at only 1.3 percent per year.

More sobering than any decade-long shift is Montana's long-term trend. Since 1950, factoring in all the ups and downs, the state has averaged a 1 percent increase in residents per year. That means a doubling time of seventy years.

Lewis and Clark came through in 1805—193 years ago. Driving around the state, we almost feel like we can reach out and touch those times. If Montana continues to grow at just 1 percent annually for the next 193 years here's what will happen:

Year 2068—1.8 million residents, the current population of Utah.

Year 2138—3.6 million residents, Colorado's present population.

Year 2201—7 million residents, more than the existing populations of Washington and Oregon combined.

In less than three average lifetimes, Montana's valleys will be transformed into a metropolitan sprawl. If that is not what Montanans want, we need to start talking about how to prevent it.

Californians

This myth has some truth.

About one-quarter of Montana's population growth in the 1990s comes from California in-migrants alone. There is even something called the Greener Pastures Institute in Los Angeles. People wishing to move to Montana just have to dial 1-800-OUT OF LA. License plate data from the California DMV support what Montanans already know: the Californians are arriving in record numbers, as many as 2,500 per year.

But we cannot forget the thousands of people who moved out of Montana during the 1980s. The majority went to California, Washington, and Oregon. A huge outflow to the West Coast also occurred during the 1920s, 1930s, 1940s, and 1960s.

That's the reality check: for much of Montana's history we have sent far more native sons and daughters to California and other states than we took in. We have used these places as an employment lifeline during hard times. So gulp hard—more often than not Montanans have been the damned out-of-staters.

But who are the newcomers?

The prevailing wisdom says they're rich. Dr. Christianne Von
Reichert, of the University of Montana Geography Department, has data that indicate otherwise. Her work with Bureau of Census surveys and IRS records describes the typical newcomer as between twenty and thirty years old, slightly more educated than resident Montanans, with an income under $20,000. Only about 4 percent of the recent in-migrants were earning more than $100,000 a year back where they came from.

But aren't they all building huge, garish houses? Many certainly are. A $500,000 home is not that uncommon anymore. In the late 1980s, it was almost unheard-of. Someone's building them and it sure doesn't seem to be Montanans. Just ask a carpenter. Evidence derived from driving around the valleys may be anecdotal, but the number of recently built palatial homes out there is staggering.

Despite this visual evidence, Dr. Von Reichert's data show that while 75 percent of Montana residents own a home, 60 percent of the recent in-migrants are renting. So Von Reichert's preliminary study says that most newcomers are not rich and can't afford to build.

Perhaps. But as my father used to say, data and facts are not the same thing.

Then there are the disenchanted out-migrants. People who find themselves marooned in a land where they don't fit. These are Californians and others who move here, build a place, try to find a job and can't, try to start a business and fail, wish to be part of a community and aren't welcomed, exhaust their savings, burn out on the cold weather, and then leave. The average length of stay by Californians is about two years.

"Sounds Good to Us" is what the front page headline gleefully announced in the October 16, 1996, edition of *The Missoulian*. In the story, a policy analyst in California talked of 350,000 new jobs being created and the beginnings of a substantial return flow of people to the once economically moribund Golden State. The October 10, 1996, issue of the *Wall Street Journal* had a similar front-page story about California entitled "Moving In: Influx of Immigrants Adds

New Vitality to the Housing Market." The sidebar read, "California's economy is off and running."

Montana's sawblade may be sharpening down to an eventual exodus. But history shows that this will only be followed by another round of returning.

MYTH #5: NATIVE MONTANANS

The bumper stickers are starting here now. The ones with an outline of Montana with "NATIVE" written boldly across it. I first saw this sort of thing traveling through Colorado back in the 1970s, and look how that's turned out. Colorado is losing 900,000 acres a year to development. In 1900, Colorado had Montana's 1990 population. Now it's closing in on 4 million. Those bumper stickers are a bad sign.

But what is a "Native Montanan?" Is it a Blackfeet, Sioux, Kootenai, Salish, Assiniboine, Bannock, Cheyenne, Chippewa, Crow, Gros Ventre, Kalispel, Piegan, Pikuni? These nations and others could claim an exclusive right to the name. But go back far enough and even they are immigrants. The anthropological truth is that Indians came from Asia. The indigenous people of the Americas came over the Bering land bridge at the end of the Ice Age. Due to repeated movements, most tribes have been in Montana just a few centuries. But if anybody can be called "Native Montanans," the Indian nations win hands down.

A more common myth goes like this. Montana was always place where "natives" (white people born here) were an overwhelming majority, and now all the newcomers are messing that up. This is often said with heartfelt emotion and extreme conviction. It's understandable given all the changes. Problem is it's mostly untrue.

In 1870, few whites living in Montana were native-born and Chinese people made up 10 percent of the population. About 39 percent of all residents were *foreign-born*.

During the homesteading era, every settler who came to Montana was a greenhorn newcomer equipped mostly with guts and determination. Settlers were lured in by advertisements for free or cheap land. The Milwaukee Road rail line put up posters all over the country showing a Montana farmer working a two-horse team. As the land was plowed open, gold coins poured out. The message was clear: come to Montana and release the obvious, pent-up prosperity; come claim the ungathered wealth. Most claimers failed and left in a huff. The settlers who stuck it out on hardscrabble homesteads are now revered as the real Montanans. Time will do that.

When statehood came in 1889, just 15 percent of the population had been born here. This means that 85 percent of all pioneer Montanans were out-of-staters.

In 1920, 165,000 of Montana's 548,889 citizens were foreign-born— 30 percent of the state's population. The mines and homesteads drew people in from around the world. Only about one-third of all Montanans had been born here. By 1940, those born overseas still made up 26 percent of the state's total. Just 46 percent of all Montanans had been born here.

So here's the payoff: the highest percentage of native-born population in Montana history was reached between 1970 and 1990—just 59 percent. In-migration during the 1990s has dropped this to about 54 percent. Despite that shift, Montana is more "native" today than during all but about twenty years of its existence.

But this varies depending on where you live.

Eastern Montana agricultural counties retain a very high percentage of Montana-born people: Daniels (77 percent), Philips (76 percent), Hill (73 percent), Golden Valley (72 percent). The die-hard folks of Butte also tend to stick close to home. Over 74 percent of Silver Bow County's residents are native Montanans. Californians tend to avoid the place. A porkie sandwich and jo jo potatoes are no substitute for sushi.

The state's rapidly growing counties are dominated by non-natives. Ravalli County has the lowest percentage of Montana-born residents —38 percent. Gallatin (46 percent), Park (Livingston) (48 percent), and Flathead (49 percent) are following suit. Missoula County is 52 percent native and dropping.

However, Montana's 54 percent overall figure is still quite high for the Western states. Only Mormon Utah has a greater total—70 percent. In contrast, just 15 percent of Nevadans were born there. The other Western states form a scatter: Alaska (36 percent), Arizona (37 percent), Colorado (42 percent), Idaho (52 percent), New Mexico (52 percent), Oregon (49 percent), Washington (50 percent), and Wyoming (43 percent). While Montana may not be as true-born as we expect, it remains far more native than most parts of the West.

A bizarre fact: 61 percent of California's seemingly transient population is native-born. The same figure holds true for the heart of the beast—Los Angeles County. Despite our preconceptions, California has a much higher percentage of natives than Montana.

But what is a real Montanan? It takes just an hour to change your license plates; a feeling of belonging takes much longer. That's why being born in the state is a source of understandable pride. But taken too far, it becomes a kind of cultural apartheid. Should people describe themselves by percentage of native blood? Should we call ourselves quadroons—one-quarter Montanan? How about octoroons—one-eighth? Character matters, not just nativity.

Years ago a friend of mine named Frank Waldbillig cut to the core of all this. He ranches near Philipsburg. His family's been around for a fistful of generations. He's the conservative chairman of the Granite County Commissioners. And still he said this: "It's not where you're from, it's what you bring."

That'll do.

But we've been a bit flexible on this matter of Montana-ness. When it suits us we've embraced an array of characters as our own. Most of them have been out-of-staters.

Here's a partial list of where these "Montanans" were born:

Lewis and Clark	"back East"
Charlie Russell	Missouri
Marcus Daly	Ireland
Norman Maclean	Iowa
Andrew Garcia	Texas
Dorothy Johnson	Iowa
A. B. Guthrie	Indiana
Granville Stuart	Virginia
Joseph Kinsey Howard	Iowa
Chief Joseph	Idaho
James Crumley	Texas
Bill Kittredge	Oregon
Richard Hugo	Washington
Rick Bass	Texas
Rick DeMarinis	New York
David Quammen	Ohio
Richard Ford	Mississippi

William Pitt Root	Florida
Tom McGuane	Michigan
Liver Eatin' Johnson	New York
Senator Conrad Burns	Missouri

In *The Last Best Place*, a compilation of writings about Montana, there were few native Montanans represented—Jim Welch, Ivan Doig, K. Ross Toole, Wally McRae, Frank Beer, and a few others. But this is nothing new. For good or ill, the history of the American West has mostly been made by non-Westerners. Here's a sketch gallery of the "outsiders":

Kit Carson	Kentucky
Jesse James	Missouri
Stephen F. Austin	Missouri
Judge Roy Bean	Kentucky
Lillie Langtry	England
Charles Goodnight	Illinois
The Virginian	Virginia
Zane Grey	Ohio
Frederic Remington	New York
Billy the Kid	New York
Calamity Jane	Indiana
Wild Bill Hickok	Illinois
Bat Masterson	Illinois
John Chisum	Tennessee
Jim Bridger	Virginia
Wyatt Earp	California

Montana and the West still manage to stay unique. Yet the people who defined the region and continue to do so are from everywhere.

Ranching itself is barely local. The breeds of cattle, sheep, and horses are mostly from Europe. The wheat, barley, and oats are from Eurasia. The tack is from Mexico. Even the words lariat, chaps, and buckaroo are derived from Spanish. Ranching originated when Anglo grazers started using Saxon feedlots. The Montana ranch evolved from English practices blended with North African pastoralism, Caribbean mercantile agriculture, the Spanish colonial rancho system of Mexico, and the steadying influence of the Midwestern Corn Belt.

Country and "Western" music came from Scotch-Irish and Mexican roots. Tumbleweed came from the steppes of Eurasia. Stetson hats originated in Philadelphia.

Even our names on the land are not the first. In Montana's cherished Glacier National Park, the whites and Blackfeet have given different names to the same places:

Lake McDonald	Sacred Dancing Lake
Mount Wilbur	Heavy Shield Mountain
Trick Falls	Running Eagle Falls

So on this business of "native Montanans," a cursory look at the stats reveals some reminders.

Every place in Montana has at least two names.

All Montanans originally came from somewhere else.

It is what you bring, what you choose to stand for, that makes a Montanan.

MYTH #6: MONTANA HAS A MINING AND TIMBER BASED ECONOMY

Used to. Not anymore.

Montana was once ruled by mining outfits like the Anaconda Company and major timber entities like U.S. Plywood, Diamond Match, and the Champion International Corporation. In his excellent book *Crossing the Next Meridian*, Charles Wilkinson calls such power brokers "the Lords of Yesterday."

In Montana, the days of the economic dominance of extractive industries are over. But mining and logging remain key job generators in a few counties and the "Lords" still wield stunning political clout statewide.

Yet here are the economic realities: The mining industry provides about 4,000 jobs—less than 1 percent of all Montana jobs and 3 percent of the Gross State Product. The wood products industry directly employs about 11,000 people—that's just 2 percent of all jobs in the state.

Despite this, the continuing folk wisdom is that mining and timber are still major economic sectors. Everything has changed about the Montana economy except our understanding of it.

MYTH #7: IT'S CHEAP TO LIVE HERE

Hollow laughter echoes across Montana. Just a few figures will suffice to put this one to rest.

PER CAPITA INCOME (1996):

Montana	$19,214
United States	$24,426

On average Montanans earn 21 percent less than the national average. Montana ranks forty-third in per capita income among the states.

COST OF LIVING INDEX FOR SELECTED RAPIDLY GROWING MONTANA CITIES (1996):

Missoula	102 percent of national average
Bozeman	101 percent of national average
Kalispell	101 percent of national average

AVERAGE SELLING PRICE OF HOMES IN 1996:

Missoula	$113,863
Bozeman	$134,241
Kalispell	$127,360

There was a time when Montana was a bargain. It still is in many rural areas, but try finding work there. The cost of living and housing may make the cities seem affordable. But try buying a house on the wages being paid. Living in Montana is very expensive.

MYTH #8: MONTANA IS A CRIME-FREE SAFE HAVEN

Crime is declining in the United States but rising in Montana. This is a complex fact.

In 1996, New York City had its lowest overall crime rate in thirty years. The homicide rate in this metropolis has actually declined 50 percent since 1990. Four precincts of the city—Greenwich Village, Midtown, Wall Street, and Central Park—had no murders at all in 1996. Zero. During that same period Missoula County had five killings.

Despite "reality" shows like COPS—you know the song, "Bad Boys, Bad Boys, What You Gonna Do?"—despite all the Kodacolor gore we see in the media, much of America is not as dangerous as it was a few years ago. Some places remain pretty awful. Los Angeles County has 2,000 homicides a year. Yet even that is a decrease from the 1980s. Homicide rates are also falling in Boston, Philadelphia, Dallas, Phoenix, and other major cities.

But it can still get pretty frightening out there.

Our perception is that Montana is a refuge from all this criminality—a paragon among places, the mountains and high plains rising ethically above barbaric national cycles of thievery and gunplay. Problem is—Montana's crime rate has jumped 22 percent since 1990 and is creeping up on the national average. But gross statistics should always be mistrusted. The Montana Board of Crime Control issues an annual report that breaks down the details by category of hurt. Here are the numbers.

In 1995, there were thirty-five homicides in Montana. Factoring in our population, this is half the national average. You are nearly six times as likely to be murdered in Los Angeles as in Montana. Eleven of those thirty-five deaths happened in rapidly growing Flathead County (Kalispell). Yellowstone County (Billings) had six homicides, Missoula County five, and Lewis and Clark (Helena) and Cascade (Great Falls) three each. Sudden death tends to be a side effect of larger populations.

We tend to blame the killings on outsiders, and sometimes we're right. A recently arrived teenager shot a Missoula store owner to death over a carton of cigarettes. Drifters murdered Montana native Patrick Duffy's parents in Boulder. The actor lost his mom and dad in one randomly evil instant. An itinerant California ranch hand killed Wayne Stevenson, a beloved rancher in the Hobson area. It was the first murder in Judith Basin County in fifty years.

But most of the shootings, knifings, and blunt-object beatings were inflicted by Montanans—usually as a result of a debt argument gone lethal, a drinking jag whirled into black out, or a love triangle turned to a flat line.

Sometimes it's simple depravity. Two local teenagers were arrested for allegedly killing popular Seeley Lake teacher Cliff Nelson. They were accused of entering the man's home and shotgunning him to death. The cops' working motive is this: he expected the boys to work too hard in school.

We tend to reprieve the murderous wretches of the past to the quaintness of the Wild West. Montana psychotics like "Rattlesnake Jake" Fallon, the Henry Plummer Gang, Charles "Longhair" Owen, and "California Jack" are now enlisted by chambers of commerce to sell fudge and T-shirts. You wonder how long until our current crop of homicidal maniacs are rehabilitated as marketing shills.

It's already starting. A Virginia City, Montana, museum recently acquired a .222 caliber rifle owned by Don and Dan Nichols, self-described "mountain men" who once lived in the woods near Bozeman. In 1984, these high-smelling specimens kidnapped a biathlete named Kari Swenson while she was cross-country skiing. Dan Nichols figured he needed a wife. The rifle was used to kill Alan Goldstein when he attempted to rescue Swenson. Kari was also shot and lives in constant pain. The men are now behind bars and Virginia City proudly displays the gun for tourists. Murder sure is colorful.

In the 1990s, the number of reported rapes and cases of domestic abuse in Montana have risen 45 percent and 102 percent respectively. The greater willingness of women to come forward may be responsible for these increases. Still, only 18 percent of all rapes are "cleared by arrest" according to police parlance.

Robberies are up 65 percent since 1990—but Montana's rate is still 86 percent below the national average.

Aggravated assaults are up 20 percent—yet Montana is still 70 percent below the national penchant for whip-ass.

Stolen vehicle cases are up 32 percent—Montana has now reached half the U.S. rate of grand theft auto.

Burglaries declined 4 percent in the decade—the state still has just two-thirds the national break-in rate.

Larceny—a catch-all of offenses ranging from shoplifting to theft from cars to stealing from unlocked buildings—has jumped 31 percent. Montanans' larcenous hearts now beat one-third faster than the American norm.

Drug offenses have skyrocketed 157 percent in Montana since 1990. Much of this increase is a result of the federal "War on Drugs." Missoula author Dan Baum's 1996 book *Smoke and Mirrors: The War on*

Drugs and the Politics of Failure helps explain the state's "drug problem." Baum painstakingly chronicles the nation's failure to face the
abject futility of this "war." Some of the statistics are stunning:

Number of Americans who died in 1969 from all legal and illegal
drugs: 1,601

Number of Americans who died in 1969 from falling down stairs:
1,824

The country's alleged "drug epidemic" during the sixties formed
the flawed rationale for what has transpired ever since:

Amount spent per year on the "War on Drugs": $13 billion

Number of illegal drug users in America: 11 million

Number of those who use marijuana: 9 million (82 percent)

Number of heroin addicts: 500,000 and holding steady

Number of cocaine users: 350,000 and declining

In 1996, Drug Czar General Barry McCaffrey said that cocaine use
had dropped 80 percent since 1981. Drug Enforcement Administra-
tion policies are not responsible—supplies are as high today as ever.
People are deciding the drug is dangerous and stopping.

But police departments in Montana are still given millions of dollars
to continue to wage this war. The state's relatively safe conditions
leave cops with time on their hands. Many occupy themselves with
waging this war on drugs and filling the state and federal prison system
with nonviolent offenders. Stockbrokers, city council members, baseball coaches, and other heinous sorts are regularly arrested for pot,
their houses confiscated, and their lives wrecked by long jail terms.

Offenses that in other places would be resolved by a suspended sentence or community service often result in hard time in Montana. In
part because of these policies, Montana's penal system is now vastly
overcrowded. In 1996, 251 inmates from the Deerlodge State Prison
were flown to a Texas facility to ease overcrowding. Deerlodge was
built to house 850 inmates; it now holds 1,300. Since 1980, Montana's
total prison population has risen sharply from 1,200 to 1,700 inmates.
With Deerlodge maxed out, convicts are being housed in county jails
all over the state. Governor Marc Racicot has asked the state legislature for $100 million to build more jail space.

It might appear Montana is having a dangerous crime wave. The truth is that about one-third of those incarcerated are nonviolent offenders doing time for such things as using drugs and stealing. Excessive mandatory sentencing for nonviolent crime is also a big part of the problem. If we found alternatives to warehousing pot smokers and other feral menaces to society, there would be no prison crowding in Montana. In-home incarceration, drug treatment, halfway houses, job training, and counseling come to mind and would probably be cheaper than building more cells. But governors and legislators like building more cells. It is politically expedient to look tough on crime.

We all want violent offenders put away. Most will never be rehabilitated. They ought to stay behind bars for what they have done. But building prison space mostly for nonviolent criminals doesn't quite add up. Jail construction has become a strange and expensive national craze. The United States of America now has a higher percentage of its population in jail than any other country on earth.

But in Montana, at least for now, life is still relatively safe. Even with a marked increase in the overall crime rate, only 2.9 percent of all major offenses are violent. Over 97 percent are property crimes—people taking stuff. In fact, "War on Drugs" arrests are not even reflected in official government statistics for "major crime." That's a telling admission.

Where is Montana the safest? Mostly where populations are low. McCone County (Circle) has 2,175 residents. Its 1995 total of reported crimes was four petty thefts and two stolen cars—that's it. Treasure County (Hysham) has 889 residents. In 1995, its crime stats totaled one burglary, two shopliftings, and a bar fight.

There are exceptions to the rule. Ravalli County (Hamilton) has the lowest percentage of native Montanans and vies with Flathead County for the title of fastest-growing jurisdiction in the state. Yet it ranks fortieth of fifty-six counties in the rate of major crime. Sometimes a booming population and an increase in out-of-staters does not make a place more dangerous.

However, overall there is a relentless formula at work. Our freedom from being killed, raped, and assaulted is declining as Montana grows. It isn't pot but increased population that is the biggest threat. Yet the numbers still reflect the Montana we love. There's no need to change the Area Code to 911. But at current rates of population growth, you wonder how long before that precious resource known as safety will be depleted.

Of course they don't, but Montana is sure getting a mean streak. And becoming a national laughingstock.

In 1996, *Esquire* magazine named Montana "the most dubious state in the union." The publication singled us out for the Freemen stand-off, the Unabomber, the militias, the Neo-Nazi upsurge, and the guy in Billings who refused to hand over fifteen rats to animal control officers. He fired thirty-five bullets at the police before being captured.

There have always been crackpots, back shooters, vigilantes, and puppy drowners hiding out there in the woods and coulees. Only now they are better armed, more aggressive, and tightly linked with legions of fellow travelers. It's all part of the post–Cold War psychosis of hate. The Commies have faded as an exterior threat. Those who define themselves by what they detest have found the U.S. government, women, nonwhite races, and non-Christian religions to be worthy replacements. And the number of haters is growing.

Montana is 94 percent white people, so racists of various pathologies seek refuge and support here. Sometimes they find it.

The Church of Jesus Christ Christian, the Neo-Nazi Aryan Nation, is headquartered in northern Idaho but is spreading into Montana. In 1994, flyers for the Aryan Youth Action meeting in Hayden Lake were disseminated across the state. Below a photo of Adolf Hitler were promises of family fun: "An Aryan Olympics, Skinhead Bands, Book and Flag Burning, a Swastika Lighting."

The Church of the Creator is of this same ilk. The Missoula chapter publishes a rag called *Racial Loyalty*. Inside are largely incoherent rants against the "Jewish press and peddlers of race mixing." T-shirts can be bought bearing the white supremacist slogan "RAHOWA"—RAcial HOly WAr. Recently, stickers with swastikas and the words "Deport Niggers" were placed on the windows of the Jeannette Rankin Peace Research Center in Missoula.

In 1996, the "Reverend" Slim Deardorff entertained thirty-five white supremacists at his lair outside of Superior. I encountered Slim when I worked in Mineral County back in the seventies. He used to fondle his twin side arms while regaling me with stories of the international Jewish banking conspiracy and the Trilateral Commission. He always paid for everything with silver dollars. To Slim, the use of paper money would speed the downfall of white, Christian civilization.

Superior's Mayor Hendrick makes the feelings of the town clear: "We don't agree with what he [Slim] is doing, and that's why he has to bring in outside people . . . nobody here will listen to him." I lived in Superior for nearly five years. The mayor's right.

Many such groups are tied to the national "Christian Identity" movement. These are not Nobel Laureates. Their scale of nature goes like this: Whites are the "true Israelites." Fact is, no whites come from that part of the world. Blacks are "subhuman." Problem is, all humans evolved in Africa. Jews are "the children of Satan." But I seem to recall a gentleman named Jehovah.

Other than that, it's a seamless case.

Joe Balyeat, the vice-president of the Christian Coalition in Montana, is an unapologetic advocate of something called "Christian Reconstructionism." Joe calls himself "an instrument of dominion" to enact God's plan. He's the kind of guy who squats with his spurs on. Among the more gracious elements of Balyeat's vision are capital punishment for homosexuality, blasphemy, heresy, and apostasy (thinking wrong thoughts). A lack of Christianity is even put forward as sufficient grounds for denying citizenship. Yet Balyeat has served as the campaign chairman for archconservative Rob Natelson—a Jew.

It gets curiouser and curiouser.

In 1991, several residents of Helena organized a visit by Archbishop Desmond Tutu. This esteemed African advocate of human rights spoke to large crowds. Following his visit, the organizers received this cheery little greeting card.

You help raise thousands of HEATHEN indians and LOWLIFE niggers, while your white brothers and sisters are home-less and hungry . . . May God Almighty have mercy on your souls . . . The body politic (FREE WHITE) of the state of MONTANA find your efforts and actions supporting COMMUNISM highly treasonous . . . BEWARE . . . this is your *only* warning . . . Beware for your families also—P.C.

P.C. stands for the Posse Comitatus, a right-wing vigilante group opposed to just about everybody but themselves.

In Billings, the Ku Klux Klan targeted the Montana Human Rights Network as part of a "Pro-Faggot Triad." Also accused were the local police chief and the Montana Association of Churches. The Klan papered the city with flyers targeting Jews and gays by name. Dawn Fast Horse, a Native American, awoke to find a swastika spray-painted on her house. She had to try and explain what that meant to her terrified three-year-old daughter.

In Ronan, Aryan Nation recruiting forms have been slipped into newspapers delivered all over town. In Great Falls, an African American leader has been repeatedly harassed by threatening racist phone calls. In Noxon, people with ties to the Aryan Nation sued the Sanders County Attorney seeking a "white, Christian judge." In Bozeman, swastikas, "faggot," and "child molester" were spray-painted over sidewalk art created for an AIDS awareness program. A foul warren of white supremacists now extends statewide. The movement is alleged to have ties with separatist Bo Gritz (rhymes with "fights"), who is creating a new community near Kamiah, Idaho.

The Montana Human Rights Network documents the incidents, tracks the groups, and works with local people to oppose racism, homophobia, religious intolerance, and violent intimidation. Organizing is already under way in Butte, Billings, Missoula, Bozeman, Fairfield, and many other communities.

Free speech is protected by the Constitution. But as Stacy Haugland of the Gallatin Human Rights Task Forces says, "A lot of people can't distinguish between free speech and hate speech." The "Reverend" Dan Hasset of the white supremacist Church of the Creator in Missoula has said he is willing to use "murder, treachery, lying, deceit, mass killing, whatever it takes to win."

Many fear this will also prove true of the Militia of Montana, widely known as "MOM." Organized by a white-bearded zealot named John Trochman, MOM is now one of the country's largest and best-organized militias. During 1994, MOM members toured the state giving presentations and drew crowds ranging from 200 to 800 people. But no one knows the actual number of members.

Fueled by paranoia over what they see as a looming New World Order, the country's militias, including MOM, consist mostly of disaffected white men. The disastrous outcome at the Branch Davidian compound in Texas and the unwarranted shooting deaths of white separatist Randy Weaver's wife and son at Ruby Ridge, Idaho, are cited endlessly by militia members as evidence of a federal war against "average Americans." They see the Brady Bill and the ban on assault weapons as the first steps toward disarming the public before the

United Nations completes a coup d'état. Some militia members are said to believe that a U.N. force from Belgium has been in the forests of Montana since 1952 awaiting orders. One video produced by a militia group shows a menacing-looking sign reading "Transfer Station." This, we're told, will be one of the places they bring us before sending us to prison camps. Of course, a "Transfer Station" is just a set of dumpsters, part of a rural solid-waste pickup system. That's how paranoid these people can be. No exotic explanation is needed for the way they think—they're dumb as a box of hair. And they're angry and armed to the overalls.

The growing fear is that these militia groups will not just talk the talk but will begin to walk the walk. Maybe the Oklahoma City bombing was that beginning. National militia leaders dismiss the movement's alleged involvement. Most say the government blew up the federal building to generate support for President Clinton's flagging antiterrorism and gun control bills.

Then there's the Freemen standoff near Jordan. This bizarre scene held the country's attention for eighty-one days. Facing federal charges of issuing millions of dollars in bogus checks, LeRoy Schweitzer, Rodney Skurdal, and about twenty others retreated to a 960-acre ranch and renamed it "Justus Township." The Freemen were accused of forgery and vast fraud, were in default on bank loans, and had a history of issuing threatening warrants against the Garfield County Commissioners, Sheriff, deputies, and judges. The Freemen chose to see routine law enforcement as evidence of an American police state. Signs were erected outside Justus Township warning people not to trespass. A "shoot to kill" order applied to anyone who disagreed.

These men and women from Arkansas, Utah, North Carolina, Texas, Canada, and Montana had convinced themselves they were free to disobey any U.S. law they disagreed with. Using an arcane and miasmic theory dating back to the Magna Carta, the Freemen gave seminars to large audiences on how to place phony liens on an enemy's property. Such liens were then allegedly used as collateral for generating huge money orders. The government claims that the money was intended to be used to finance right-wing violence.

The Freemen had been declaring their "common law" beliefs, intimidating local people, and professing race hate for years. It took the FBI and ATF almost two years to show up in Jordan. You can't help but figure their response time would have been a tad quicker if a bunch of heavily armed black guys had been cutting bad checks and threatening public officials with guns. Yet some folks in Garfield County actually felt sympathy for the Freemen's situation. There is a lot of difficult debt in Montana's ranch country these days, especially for newcomers not born on the land. Ironically, there is also no shortage of anti-government rage in the same people who would have yelled "Love it or Leave it" in the face of an antiwar protester back in the sixties. Curiouser indeed. Today, fourteen of the Freemen are facing an array of federal charges. It will be a long haul. Freeman Rodney Skurdal has bombarded the Montana Supreme Court with handwritten "filings." The court described these writings as "liberally peppered with Latin words and phrases, biblical admonitions, and references to various laws ranging from the Magna Carta to the Uniform Commercial Code."

Meanwhile, the accused Unabomber, a Chicago-born Montana resident, sits in a federal jail awaiting trial for his alleged campaign of death and explosive terror.

Montana really does have a mean streak these days. The Bureau of Alcohol, Tobacco and Firearms (ATF) reported that in 1995 Montana had 127 cases requiring its attention, one for every 6,850 people. The Montana federal district ranked number one in the nation in ATF actions. In that same year, Los Angeles had only 113 cases, one for every 141,593 people.

In 1996, the Gallatin County Commissioners felt compelled to ban the bringing of firearms into county buildings. Also included were Molotov cocktails, hand grenades, rocket launchers, and slingshots.

Is all this trouble being imported by non-natives? Does organized hate crime represent the real Montana? The answer to both has to be yes and no.

A 1996 Montana Bureau of Economic Research poll revealed that the highest level of support for the "Militia of Montana and similar groups" was among new arrivals—25 percent. But 21 percent of local Montanans expressed support. This isn't necessarily support for vicious forms of prejudice. The truth is known only in their hearts. Mine tells me that Montanans are still among the fairest and most dependably decent people in the country.

But looking through hate-crime reports is getting to be a depressing business. Deval Patrick, the former head of the U.S. Justice Department's Civil Rights Division, recently said that "tolerance seems to be in jeopardy." That national failure of character is now affecting Montana to an unprecedented degree. About all that hasn't happened here is a church burning.

Yup, it sure would be nice to blame it all on the outsiders.

But the banality of evil is this: the face of white supremacy, racial bigotry, and antigovernment violence is sometimes our neighbors. Sometimes it is us.

MYTH #10: THERE IS NO SPEED LIMIT

"Whoa Dude!" That's what the billboards advise.

Contrary to the spreading folklore, Montana *does* have a daytime speed limit. It's known as the "Basic Rule." Signs posted along the interstates read as follows:

DAY	Reasonable and Prudent
NIGHT	65 MPH

Basically we're being told not to drive stupid. Some visitors have preferred to do just that.

In July 1996, dozens of motorists cell-phoned the Highway Patrol to report that a panzer division of Mercedes-Benz prototypes was scorching along I-90 doing about 105 MPH. The fifteen test drivers blasted along in bumper-to-bumper formation all the way from Billings to Livingston before officers pulled them over for a little chat. Each received a $70 ticket.

So it's not the Montanabahn after all.

Locals know it. The average speed of in-state drivers went from 72 mph to 73 mph after the law changed. The old 65 mph speed limit had generally been ignored, but not by much. Those unlucky enough to get caught in those days were given a $5 "environmental ticket" for wasting fossil fuels. We were high on life and low on gas. You just handed over a fiver and went on your way. None of this ever appeared on your driving record.

Montanans have never much believed in speed limits. We dutifully hated the original 55 mph rule imposed by the federal government in 1974. We had to go along or lose millions in federal highway funds. Prior to that revolting development, Montana had always used the "reasonable and prudent" standard. And we trundled along just fine.

In the first six months since returning to the "Basic Rule," deaths on the interstates actually declined by 7 percent. The number of accidents increased 15 percent, but a tough winter may explain that as much as lead-footing. But the number of speeding tickets handed out has doubled.

Montana receives 8 million visitors each year, nearly ten times its population. According to Colonel Craig Reap, Commander of the Montana State Highway Patrol, "the highest speed vehicles are out-of-staters, and what I see when I'm out driving in my personal car indicates the same thing."

The French, as usual, have come up with the most baffling case of stupid. Montana Highway Patrol Officer Mitch Tuttle got a call from a Paris tire manufacturer wanting to test some new tread designs at 140 mph. Tuttle responded wryly, "I told him that's not what we consider reasonable and prudent."

But in December 1996, a jury decided that auto mechanic Don Williams was being perfectly prudent at 101 mph. Montanans do love their speed.

Happy motoring.

CONCLUSION

I once asked Bill Kittredge what the purpose of writing was. He responded "to tell the truth clearly." Mythology can both help and hobble our tries at getting truthful.

Myths can be stories that explain landscapes, cultural symbols, and God. They can remind us how to live right where we are. Sometimes they're gentle fun—beer-fueled campfire tales of clumsy mishaps or basic geographic matters requiring prideful embellishment. Many others are simply misunderstandings. But myths can also be vengeful, ignorant nonsense—vicious weapons unsheathed to exploit land and people.

Montana's future depends on us discerning the difference.

4

THE PURITAN EPIC, PROHIBITION AND MAGNETO-HYDRODYNAMICS PARTY

PEOPLE CALL the place Pburg and go on the best they can. I moved to Philipsburg in 1975. It is one of the complete ironies of my life that I went to conservative and contrary Granite County to be a land-use planner. This is like being a vegan at a testicle festival. For those unacquainted with the drill, Montanans like to deep-fat fry mountains of bull huevos, call them Rocky Mountain oysters, drink excessively, and gorge. I've always found the texture a dite stringy. The steers probably aren't too thrilled with the procedure either.

But Philipsburg it was. I drove up Broadway into the "downtown" and stopped at the county's only traffic light. It seemed to have one color—pink. A rancher in the 4 × 4 in back of me laid on his horn. Hell, everyone knows pink means go.

I made a hard left up a terrace slope and parked next to a grand, silver-domed building—the Granite County Courthouse. The Planning Office was in the basement. They're always in the basement.

Sylvan Lutey sort of greeted me. He was a skinny guy from Butte, and Butte's not the best place to grow up slight. It showed in his defense—firm and habitual. He carried a pinch of snooce in one cheek, combed his hair with Brillcream or some other aggressive lubricant, and figured me for exactly what I was, a greenhorn kid from Back Damn East somewhere. Things got much easier, but that first day I was ready to bolt.

There was no shortage of houses to rent in Pburg. One response to an ad in the *Mail* did the job. An impossibly nice older couple fed me cookies and cider, talked about Harry James music, then rented me a complete house for $40 a month. It was green with one bedroom and Paleozoic linoleum. There was even a yard full of basin wild rye. Sure it sat next to Broadway's "U-Turn" sign, but I got used to the headlights after a while. Pburg was famous for its dogs—packs of muttish, barking curs loudly settling a full slate of urgent matters. In time, I got used to the barking too.

My courthouse job turned instructive. I was raised in a town of 1,000 people, but that was in Maine. Over the next year, Pburg's 1,000 souls and the 2,000 others out there in Rock Creek, Maxville, Hall, Drummond, and Upper Willow gave me something more like an education than anything I'd ever known. I learned to shut up and listen. This was the beginning of my learning the actual Montana.

My days were spent reviewing housing developments at Georgetown Lake and wherever else good fishing brought construction. The developers had the upper hand in those days, as they do now, and about all we did was make sure the septic tanks worked and the roads were built to county specs. That was an eye-opener to a twenty-four-year-old who expected planners to actually plan a few things. But I did what I was told, hoping it would come to something later.

After the first month, I settled into a routine. Walk up to the courthouse, do what Lutey didn't have time for, walk down to the Gallery Cafe for lunch, up to work, then back downhill. At night I played a lot of guitar or bowled over at the three-laner upstairs of the Antlers Bar. I'd bowled several times on the *Rex Trailer's Junior Bowling* television show back in New England when I was young. Once I even got to meet Celtic great Bob Cousy when he was the guest host. But in Pburg, teenagers still manually re-set the pins. I was stunned that still went on.

Part of my daily pattern was an elaborate midmorning custom known as "coffee." This was nothing so ordinary as a ten-minute cup of Joe. No, this involved Lutey, County Appraiser Daryl Goebel, and folks from Assessing, Welfare, and such carpooling the whole 100 yards down to the Soil Conservation Service Office for an hour or more of hemming, yeehawing, and ardent prevarication. I loved it.

The taxpayers are right, sometimes government types do waste a lot of time. Goebel labored much harder than most. His thankless job was to assign dollar values to houses, barns, and businesses for the entire county. These appraisals formed the basis for property taxes. It was not a popular line of work. So to cheer himself up, Daryl played endless practical jokes on everyone in sight.

His weapon of choice was the telephone. One day I was left home alone in the office. The phone rang and I reluctantly answered. It was my most profound fear at that time—a crazed land developer.

"Ya, hi, this is Milt Merkin down here in Drummond, you the planner?" His voice sounded like the failing tranny of a Dodge.

"Yes, one of them," I answered, but I was bragging. I didn't know a thing.

"Ya, I'm going to put in a couple hunnerd trailer houses down by the river—they say it's floodplain so I figure two septics oughta do her."

I felt like my spleen had been crushed. After I'd babbled out some sort of "not sure, wait until Lutey gets back" gibberish, we hung up.

I walked next door to Daryl's office. He was calmly working on an appraisal card, neatly scaling out the dimensions of a laundromat.

"You won't believe the yahoo I just talked to!" I was looking for help wherever I could find it. "The guy's an idiot!" I was ranting now, giving him the full blow-by-blow.

Suddenly Daryl burst out laughing. The kid had been had. We laughed together for a long time, me from relief, maybe him too. Over the coming months he did this kind of thing so often I could hardly tell who was real anymore. One day I took a call and damn near blurted highly obscene and imaginative words at U.S. Senator Lee Metcalf.

Another time I was by myself trying to look busy when a wiry ranchwoman in her fifties walked into the office.

"Excuse me, I was told you were the planner," she said tentatively. "Are you Jack MeOff?"

Instantly her face detonated to crimson, embarrassment spreading to all known muscle groups.

"OH THAT DARYL!" she fumed and stormed out.

There we were: Pburg, 1975. As politically correct as passed wind. I was home.

Philipsburg was born in 1864 during a gold strike. It grew up in the 1880s when a silver mine took off at Granite, a boomtown high up on the shoulders of the Flint Creek Mountains. Pburg was the regional trade center complete with a train station, fancy Victorian storefronts, and a sprawling Chinatown. It spread east-west along a creek bottom with rows of houses and businesses rising up the terrace scarps and basin-fill benchlands.

But Granite was the essential story. Miners blasted ore from the deepening basement of the Combination Mine in shifts that never stopped. The earth yielded fortunes in native silver, silver sulfide, pink and black manganese, galena, and gold. The ore was sent 1,300 feet downhill along a gravity-fed Bleichert aerial tramway to the massive Bi-Metallic stamp mill where it was crushed and amalgamated.

By 1892, Granite had a swarming population of 3,000 living in a smurge of log cabins, clapboard shacks, and canvas tents. The mine managers lived in fancy homes along "Silk Stocking Row." Granite claimed seventeen saloons, many cafes, a weekly newspaper called *The Granite Mountain Star*, a brewery, hotels, a bank, Chinese laundries, two skating rinks (one roller, one ice), and four churches. A red-light district with a dozen brothels filled a swale below the handsome brick and stone Miners Union Hall. The companies, Granite Mountain and Bi-Metallic, paid fair wages and provided a hospital, hot pools, and a library for the workers. In ten years, $28 million in silver bullion was taken from the ground.

On August 1, 1893, all this seemed to come to an end. The federal government repealed the Sherman Act and abandoned silver-gold bi-metallism to back U.S. currency. The gold standard was on. The Treasury Department immediately stopped buying the 4.5 million ounces of silver a month the old law had required. Prices crashed. A massive silver panic spread across the West. Miners stampeded out of places like Granite and headed for the better prospects of the region's gold camps.

A. L. Stone, later a Dean of the School of Journalism at the University of Montana, watched the strange exodus sweep down the winding road from Granite into Pburg:

> It was the most complete desertion I have ever seen . . . The queerest, most incongruous procession ever . . . No one had stopped to pack. Everything was

thrown in helter skelter. Wheelbarrows, go-carts and burros had their place in the procession . . . Everyone was in a hurry and pushed and jostled to reach the bottom first . . . [some walked] carrying their hand luggage, frying pans or teakettles. Wagons that hadn't been used for ten years, creaked, and screeched down the incline. Bandboxes, babies, and bull dogs brought up the rear, and so it kept up all day and all night . . . a continual stream of almost panic-stricken people, leaving forever their homes on the mountain.

But somehow Granite didn't die. In 1898, the two mining outfits merged and geared the whole thing back up again. Over $1 million was extracted from the Flint Creeks each year. The mill pans ran red from ruby silver.

A photo of the 1903 Miners Union Day celebration in Granite shows a scene of obvious prosperity. The men sported suits, ties, and bowlers. Some held brass band instruments. The few women present wore white frilly dresses and Bella Abzug hats. American flags were draped over telephone and electric lines. The streets had brass drinking fountains.

But then the ore began to run out. Same as it ever was.

By 1905, the mine went down and water began flooding the deepest shafts. A World War I manganese boom brought back the good times. During the 1920s, Granite produced 90 percent of America's manganese dioxide. But then the Depression hit and the town was abandoned for good.

Through all this turbulence, Pburg survived. Ranching, logging, and retail trade provided steady, unspectacular work. But with the mines shut down, the town's population dropped from a peak of 3,000 in 1917 to 1,000 in 1930. When I drove into town that June morning in 1975 it still had just 1,000 claimers. Even after forty-five years with no mining, most hadn't given up on metal.

People call the place Pburg and go on the best they can.

On quiet nights after work, I began writing a geographic country song. It came a little bit at a time as things showed themselves. I just called it "Pburg."

Pburg ain't for pirates,
stealers on the silver sea,
'cause it seems like this earth is more
than ancient history.
All the moonlit copper crappers,

Puritan Epic, Prohibition and Magnetohydrodynamics Party

passing it all in style,
we'll make the most of the PreCambrian coast
'til our dust fills up the manganese mine.

I eased my way at first and eventually got to know a few of the retired miners and other old men plying the sidewalks between the
White Front and Club House bars. Heinie Winninghoff had run the
Ford dealership in Pburg since Henry Ford first got a bright idea.
Nineteen twenty-nine was a good year—ninety-nine cars sold. Nineteen thirty-two wasn't—just two. Living had showed him the full
menu. I never met anyone fairer. "Cowboy" Joe Johnson was rather
fond of cattle and horseflesh. But people called him that because of the
way he dressed—ransacked Levi's all over, a salt-etched felt hat, and
boots so worn he listed to starboard when he walked. Leroy "Shorty"
Rickard liked to gab about whatever version of his life felt best that
day. Specially if there was a shot of tequila at stake.

At first glance, some of the people I met seemed about as smart as
bait. But I was completely wrong. More often than not there was
ample intelligence hiding in there callused over by heartache. You just
had to wait out the B.S. to get let in.

So I continued to write "Pburg" in the key of G:

The moon and the stars of the local bars
making faces just like Monroe.
They answer the question
that the planet is destined
to swallow all them lonely souls.
Through all these scenes of disguise
and them long-told lies
I've been waiting for some kind of sign.
So let's drink another toast
to the PreCambrian coast
and climb on down this mine.

One day a toothless gnome in a tobacco-brown Stetson was creaking along out in front of the Club House Bar. It was Henry Hull. His
body looked like a cantilevered muppet gone too long without repair.
Henry paused and hawked up an impressive ball of mucus and spat it
on the street. He'd contracted silicosis, a chronic inflammation of the
lungs, from twenty-two years underground in the Butte copper mines.

MONTANA GHOST DANCE

Henry Hull really, really liked to mine. He wasn't particular about where or what—copper in Butte and South America, opals in Australia, gold "wherever God put the damn stuff." Not even one cell in him cared for "all them goddamned envioment people." His life was driven by a single immutable urge, to dig in the ground.

The old souls talk of travel,
breakin' rock with metal in mind.
They wander the streets
with wisdom and feats
That stepped across the vapors to time.

I sometimes visited Henry at his small house that loafed on one of Pburg's dirt side streets. Even with milk cartons scattered around to catch phlegm from his rotting lungs, the man still felt that mining was the proper nature of things. He was born in 1895 over on Rock Creek "back when you could ride a horse from the crick all the way to Pburg without having to cross one fence." He saw no conflict in wanting to mine the entire world while mourning the unturned landscape.

One time in his kitchen, Henry showed me a rock covered in what might have been gold spray paint. He assured me he'd "cooked the gold out" onto the surface. He claimed to have mastered the little known art of simultaneously baking gold bullion and roasting elk in a 1954 Hot Point range. When I didn't quite buy in, his eyes flashed a glint of lurking smarts and gleamed with ambiguity.

Henry had two violins. One was an ancient Amati that he played with some skill and more pleasure. His favorites were country fiddle tunes like "The Wabash Cannonball," "Soldier's Joy," and "The Wildwood Flower." But he wasn't above a stab at a polka or one of Johann Sebastian Bach's "little numbers." The other violin carried the inscription "Stradivarius 1762." I suspected this was like the spray-painted rock but held silent. Let him have this one.

I didn't agree with one thing Henry Hull said to me over that year. He was a nineteenth-century man ill acquainted with the twentieth. But the rule of shutting up still applied. I was here to listen—and write another verse:

Miner Henry he's a digger,
of delusion and delight.
He likes to tell jokes about niggers,

Puritan Epic, Prohibition and Magnetohydrodynamics Party

'cause he thinks that it breaks the ice.
He truly plays Verdi on a fiddle,
and he sways oceans with his light.
He's been busted in two by the wire,
that split the land and changed his life.

During that cherished, strange summer I must have passed the small ramshackle building across from Winninghoff Ford hundreds of times. Its hand-painted sign was nailed crookedly over the false front: "Merrill K. Riddick for President—Puritan Epic Party." It all seemed a shard peculiar so I always kept going. No telling what caliber of zealot was loaded in there.

Then one day I was eating a bowl of chili at the Gallery Cafe and Merrill Riddick walked in. He was already eighty years old by then and his gait showed it. Each footfall expended just that quantum of energy required to ensure forward locomotion. But he managed a persistent plod. The man looked like a dog's breakfast but he wore a black suit, white shirt, and uncertain necktie with the thin part hanging down a good foot or so below the wide. His glasses looked like a bughouse optician's final lab project—thick, bulbous circles of congealed silica smeared with bacon grease and typewriter carbon all squared off by black girders and rebar frames. The entire apparatus appeared to weigh more than a house cat. He was lumpy-round with a sparse crop of hair raked straight back, eyebrow dandruff, and a good measure of his right ear gone from what looked like a vicious badger mauling. And he was heading straight for me.

He torsioned himself up onto a stool and we exchanged nods. On his lapel was a pin the size of some college scoreboards: "Merrill K. Riddick for President—Puritan Epic Party."

"You're new," he decided after squinting up at me. How could he tell? The man was viewing life through 500-kilovolt powerline insulators.

"Yup, I work for the county," I answered, not wanting to own up to being a planner unless I had to.

"Oh, good—now, here's what I've been thinking." And he was off and running.

Over a beef pastie with fries I quickly concluded that Merrill K. Riddick really, really liked to talk. And what he lacked in precision he made up for in mass. I learned that the travels of Lewis and Clark, the role of Bessemer Converter in steel production, and the invention of the navigational gyroscope were all "linked together." To Merrill, everything linked up. Each day added data that whirled into the matrix of his own version of the Grand Unification Theory that had eluded Einstein until the end. To Merrill the payoff was this: something called magnetohydrodynamics (MHD) would solve all our energy problems. As near as I could figure he hadn't made it up and it had something to do with magnets. But Merrill's Big Idea went beyond physics into law, aeronautics, petrology, and the writings of Emma Goldman, Charles Lyell, and Michel Crèvecoeur.

And that was just our first conversation.

By late 1975, I was sharing soup with Merrill several times a week. Toward the end of the month I would pay and at the beginning of the next he would pony up when his government check came in. He was never one to ask for charity. This was a man whose actual life exceeded a novelist's dearest dream.

My first sense of the authenticity of the man came early. The windows of Merrill's "campaign headquarters" were taped over with news clippings and "white papers" he'd written on the prevailing issues of the day. This was the time of the Middle East oil crisis and skyrocketing gas prices. There, among his calls for digging up sections of Alberta to get at the hydrocarbon-rich "tar sands," was a photo of Merrill standing next to Charles Lindbergh.

"What's this?" I asked.

"Oh, I used to do a little flying," he grunted.

Indeed he did. And a lot more. Over the next few months I managed to strap together some of the details. They came slowly. He preferred to talk about the future.

Merrill was born on a farm in Wisconsin in 1895. His father, Carl, moved the family to a wheat and flax homestead near Lewistown, Montana, when the boy was eleven. He hated farm life as only a farmer's son can and quit school when he turned sixteen. With money he raised from selling his textbooks and trapping a mink, the odd youngster took a printing job in Great Falls. Then he worked harvesting ice from the Missouri River. Then it was door-to-door pan soldering. He finally made it to Seattle and snuck aboard an ore-hauling ship bound for China. Once at sea, Merrill got discovered. He was hired on as a cabin boy—a position he described as a "gofer." At a loading stop in San Francisco, Merrill grew terrified of the prostitutes and shanghai gangs working the streets of the Barbary Coast. He fled by boat—no Bay Bridge in those days—and found himself on the campus of the University of California at Berkeley. The kid dove into courses on structural geology, mineralogy, and engineering. Having "gotten most of it," he soon dropped out and took a job clearing fields for East Bay dairy farmers.

Then one day in 1916 the twenty-one-year-old stumbled onto famed stunt flyer Lincoln Beachey repairing his plane. It was the first aircraft Merrill had ever seen up close. They talked all afternoon and everything shifted. Merrill immediately joined the Army to become a pilot. A year later, silver flyer's wings were pinned to his itchy wool uniform. In 1917, he was sent to England, where his superb skills made him too valuable to lose in a dogfight. He trained hundreds of pilots during World War I and was decorated several times.

By the war's end, his dad, Carl Riddick, had been elected to the U.S. House of Representatives from Montana's Eastern District. Merrill flew into D.C. to visit but couldn't find the airport. Never big on ceremony, he decided to land his plane directly on Pennsylvania Avenue. "It was smooth and there weren't many drivers in those days," he explained. After a brief arrest, the congressman's son roamed around the sleepy Southern town talking to politicians, ambassadors, and bureaucrats to "see how the whole thing worked." Merrill decided it didn't work up to par but decided to keep flying. He could always run for something later.

Merrill joined the Harry Perkins Air Circus in 1919 and worked with a slender kid named Charles Lindbergh. Merrill was the older of the two and had soloed six years before Lindy. Riddick was billed as a "Wing-Walking Flyer" and gave the crowds their money's worth with stunts he characterized to me as "pretty insane nonsense." He soon left show biz to work as one of the country's first Air Mail pilots, once again right beside Lindbergh. But even this wore out after a while and Merrill sought a friskier way of life. So he began barnstorming all over the Midwest.

One night in Pburg in Merrill's cramped little quarters, he told me what came next. The only light in the room was a red-orange glow from all four burners of his electric stove turned up high. This was often Merrill's preferred means of heat and light production.

"I was barnstorming in Kentucky," he said. "My plane was a Jenny in those days, and I caught sight of a big group of folks having a picnic down in this field, so I decided to land and drum up some business." He smiled and hefted his glasses back in place. "I made a lot of money that day giving rides so I bought some new clothes and got a room at a first-rate hotel for a change." An even bigger smile. "The next morning this really pretty girl came by and asked to pay for a ride. Of course I gave it to her free. Well, we found out we had a lot in common, which was amazing since her father was a Baptist preacher, so we got married that same day."

"The same day?!" I blurted.

"You bet, but she eventually ended up dying." He allowed himself a few seconds to remember, then rebounded by talking about bornite ore and copper concentrates. But I saw the loss. His wife of thirty years, his Helen, died of cancer in 1949. Merrill had been living alone ever since, for an entire twenty-six years.

The rest of the man's story came in pieces scattered all out of order.

Merrill taught Franklin Delano Roosevelt how to fly before the polio hit. During World War II, FDR personally wrote asking him to teach a new crop of recruits aerial tactics and Merrill again served in England.

One of his students soloed after fifty-five minutes of instruction—a documented world record.

Merrill attempted to fly to Bombay in the late 1920s. The government stopped him in California, figuring that his certain death would be bad for international relations.

He wrote a book on cybernetics—in 1946.

During the Depression, Pulitzer Prize–winning author Upton Sinclair met several times with Merrill trying to get him to join the Socialist Party. While Merrill backed the idea of Social Security, he "was never a Socialist, just a Progressive." One of his planes was torched by an angry mob who disagreed.

Merrill wrote about jet aircraft, moon landings, and human ecology —in 1920.

Each time I had doubts about one of his stories, he'd pull a yellowed newspaper clipping, official government document or Spammed-over photograph from a pile to back it up. I finally asked him about the name—the Puritan Epic, Prohibition and Magnetohydrodynamics Party.

"Well, over the years I just kept adding bits to that deal. The Puritan Epic kind of speaks for itself." He put his hand to his chin for a bit and decided, "I should really add Ethic to it but it's already pretty long."

"Why the Prohibition?" I asked. "You drink sometimes."

"I'm not talking about liquor there, I'm talking about prohibiting illegal campaign contributions, violations of the Bill of Rights, all that

Nixon Watergate business." Merrill made a face like he'd eaten some spoiled lutefisk.

"And the Magnetohydrodynamics?"

"Well, MHD's just to let people know what's coming, there'll be an end to all the oil some day," he concluded.

He asked me to be his campaign manager for the 1976 presidential race. Of course I said yes. This mostly involved buying him stamps and bowls of soup at the Gallery Cafe.

Merrill was out of town a lot as the election heated up. He would buy one of those Greyhound Bus passes that allowed you unlimited travel for a month—always with the senior discount factored in. He'd sleep on the bus, eat out of grocery stores, and talk to anyone who'd listen. Senator Mike Mansfield was always gracious to the man. Whenever Merrill shuffled into the Capitol Building, Mike would always make time to have a cup of coffee and chat. Eventually, a federally funded MHD research facility was built in Butte. Turns out the damn thing works.

But I'm afraid that in 1976 much of his "press coverage" focused more on the "wacky old man" angle. Too bad. They missed hearing the real substance of that presidential season.

Another verse arrived:

> The flights of fancy
> and the spiritual chances
> of the aviation pioneer.
> He still crosses the nation,
> bus station to station
> until the driver says he's made it back here.

Merrill Riddick was the only man I ever met without two brain hemispheres, just one hot-wired cerebral contraption dancing in contradiction to most of what we assume to be true.

When my job was up in Pburg, I stopped over at Merrill's to say goodbye. By now he'd taken to parking an old hearse out back and using the coffin space as a bedroom. I dearly wanted something grand to happen that day—a capstone insight, a letter from Churchill, anything—but Merrill was too busy reading about molybdenum and "linking things up" to waste air on more stories. We chatted for a few minutes and soon I was back in the Opel heading for Missoula.

Out past Waldbillig's ranch I figured out the chorus:

The whirlpool winds away.
Spinning those fibers of fable
until all the people are able
to glide clean away.
So in my time off
I'll do my best to get off.
Cause I just might not find enough reasons
for me to go.

But songs are songs and life requires a living, so I left.

I saw Merrill less and less over the years—a drop-by on my way to fieldwork, a special trip for soup and dissertation at the Gallery Cafe, a Christmas visit—that was about it. Life sweeps us away.

One morning in 1988 the newspaper said he'd died. It was back in the Midwest somewhere. His senior citizen children were with him. Merrill had finally worn out. It had taken ninety-three years.

I sat on the ground and cried.

One of Montana's gifts is deep time. In a way, everything sticks around.

We see the imprint of generations of choices etched into the landscape. We touch eternity in the basement rocks. Somehow we know that we are separated from deer, marmots, and vireos by a few distant spins of the genetic wheel. Push things back farther and nature itself is new.

The Montana landscape is our way of remembering all that.

It reminds us to know our biology. To learn bird songs and pay attention to the wind. To know the history of what happened in each place and the people who made it. Mostly, this rangy landscape is a map of the lessons we need to gain.

One of Montana's gifts is deep time—and a tank full of High Line gas to enjoy it.

On Veterans Day, 1996, I awoke to find Missoula wrapped in a shroud of brown goo. Lolo Peak rose above the inversion layer like "Popo" above Mexico City. The paper said the air quality was officially "Poor." Thanks for the data.

I decided to leave town.

But where to go? The Bitterroot would be smegmatic, Mineral County squatted down-drainage from the scudding clouds of crud, and the Flathead required a kamikaze run over Evaro Hill.

Puritan Epic, Prohibition and Magnetohydrodynamics Party

I chose Pburg.

The route ran along three embattled drainages: the Clark Fork River, Rock Creek, and Flint Creek. It was bordered by hard-time mountain ranges with names still worth saying—Garnet, Sapphire, Flint Creek, John Long, Pintler. This was the grand traverse, and the memories were everywhere.

I drove past a small creek valley where long ago thirty of us buried a friend on the sly. No permits, no undertakers. Just the peace of his favorite spot.

Then came a crumbling brick electric house and an absence of rails. The Milwaukee Road had long since been melted into bridge spans and refrigerator bodies.

Then past the abandoned river meander remade as a farm pond. Past endless forest clearcuts checkerboarding the slopes where I first keyed out snowberry, ninebark, and ocean spray. To the collapsed log cabin. Evan Denney said he'd lie down in front of bulldozers to save it. Onward to D.J.'s warm spring and the pools for soaking away back-packing aches and serious residues. Memories came of making love to the hum of semis.

The land was growing fast with recollections: the gandy-dancer water-break spot, the aspen grove split by the interstate—fall colors still brilliant but now out of sync—the medicine caves and folded limestones, the cliff where paleo-Indian kids jumped into the frigid milky water of Glacial Lake Missoula on searing summer days at the waning of the Ice Age—I'm just sure of it—past boot-ripping volcan-ics to the sign west of Drummond—"World Famous Bullshippers"—to the huge hillside "D" whitewashed above the snake rocks where I first levitated from rattle noise, in that same broken country where Odie Omega Royal Brown nearly lost her life in 1931, long before Normandy, long before her real losses would come.

I downshifted. Then a turn south over the Clark Fork, more of a creek than the river here. It was still Butte-hammered, choked with algae and thirsty for the freshening flows of Rock Creek and the Blackfoot.

Then came the LDS Ward House right across from well-mowed fields and Mormon hay derricks. All is well. All is well.

New Chicago off to the left, just a squat of dry-rot buildings. The girl who used to live there liked Mexican beer, soil science, and Tom Petty music.

Through the bends where the dead skunks always are, to a brush-painted sign, and a family worth that acclamation:

Henderson Ranch
Est. 1869
Reg. Angus Since 1919
Archie, Margaret, Jim, Merri

Round bales, square bales, irrigation ditches cut on the contour— water applied with an even and optimum hand.

Past the same billboard: "The Wages of Sin is Death." The Arabian horses prefer to stare up at the snowpack filling the eastern peaks.

Into Hall (population: occasional). The old grocery still has good jerky. The new cafe has three signs saying "Open," its owners trying hard to ignore the inherent problem. Past the house where you can buy ranch-made honey in clear plastic bears. To the marshland where Christa Lee used to pick cattails for cat toys. Later, we'd laugh, watching Rabbit and Jumper turn the house allergic with rising columns of aquatic fluff.

A few miles on to the Douglas Creek rail crossing. One winter night I nearly T-boned a lumber train here. After eighteen years of ripped-out rails, I still slow and scan for trouble. Then the Wight Ranch. Several people at the Pburg Senior Citizen Center remain convinced that this is my home place. About all they can do with "he's not from around here" is assign me to a spread twelve miles north in the distant land of Hall.

As usual, I stopped at the maroonish-red roadcut where I first laid my hands on Granite County argillite. Crumbling touchstones lay all around.

Rolling again past Hokon Grotbo's place, the brick-and-clad house framed by Lombardy poplars where scotch and canasta used to keep the chill backed off. Hoke's gone now. Cigarettes. So many of them gone.

A few rolls farther. Marie Morrison's ranch. The blue house and its slender pole fences have been replaced by a double-wide trailer perching efficient and square on the sidehill. To the dinosaur-bone bedrock dike and the rounded-rock field. About 50,000 years ago the Boulder Creek glacier entered the valley and backed up a local lake. One spring day the ice dam burst, sending thousands of granite bowling balls careening out in a massive, lobate mudflow. The water sieved away. The rocks settled down. Junipers and Douglas firs are now getting thick in the cattle-beaten interstices. I stop to retrieve one of the cobbles. It will go with the others encircling my lilacs. In May, lavender and gray help cool off the yellow-flowered heat of the arrowleaf balsamroots in the prairies beside my house.

Through Maxville, a woodsy hideout still fuming about the 1,200-kilovolt powerline schlepping overhead along triple-decker towers right out of the *War of the Worlds*. I used to stop out here beside Flint Creek to breathe and seek constellations. For fifteen years, the warning strobe has been the only star.

Then the wooden bridge over Flint Creek, the place for dogs to swim and dally. The firs growing upslope are getting thick from an absence of needed fire.

I drove on until the Pintlers arrived. Here, where one of America's true mountain views reveals more of itself with each revolution, where a working-class Ford buys you perfection, someone decided to erect a new regional powerline corridor and exterminate beauty. Fifty-foot wooden poles were being penetrated in a linear picket. Each was strung with eight strands of serious wire cutting an electrified slash across the peaks. If they had simply been put on the other side of the road, we would barely notice.

Why do it this way? Beyond all the right-of-way technicalities and cost-benefit ratios was politics. The new line was a statement. They were fencing in the Pintlers. The message of the wire was a warning: "Listen, the land out here's got more work to do than be pretty. We can't eat pretty."

It was Montana in one gander. The lovely and the foul sitting side by side.

I was back in Pburg.

The town was still the same size, 1,000 people. But Granite County had lost 800 folks since I lived here and was sinking below 2,500. Same as always, no work.

The town was betting its future on tourism and the gussying up was everywhere. The old Burg Motel had been taken over and rechristened "The Inn at Philipsburg." Beware the dreaded "at." "At" is mercantile code for pretentious and expensive. About all they did was repaint the place.

Dan and Dave Bowens' gas station had closed and been renovated into something called the "Hitchin' Post Gallery." Most of the paintings were landscapes with the clearcuts and powerlines carefully colored over. The Bowens brothers had to sell out when a Californian chose to build the "Sunshine Station" gas and grub right on Highway 1. Fewer cars came into town.

Lum Wanderer's IGA was now the "Town Grocery," complete with its "Mining Company Deli." Lum was a soft-eyed, decent man who died in a way that still haunts people around here.

They call the place Pburg and go on the best they can.

The wooden street signs were still hanging in there. They were Sylvan Lutey's Bicentennial project. He even cut some of them himself at night along with bundles of survey stakes he sold to the developers. Lutey never imagined this edged up on being a conflict of interest. I knew, but kept quiet.

I dropped in on Frank Waldbillig, as always holding down the chair of the County Commissioners. He was a bit thinner is all. Still the easy smile and twangy voice. I asked how things were going. "Nothing much changes," he said, "just the players." Between commissioner work, the cows, a sawmill, and real estate, Frank was keeping busy. I asked about Sylvan Lutey. "He's down in Nevada working on gold deals: first one failed, second one came through." Then Frank got serious. "Didn't you lose a brother suddenly back when you lived here?" He meant my friend who was melding with the gravels of the Garnet Range. "No, that wasn't my brother, he just felt like one," I said. Frank nodded.

My next stop was downstairs at Daryl Goebel's office. We replayed some of the old times—the "Mr. MeOff" episode, the phone calls from hell, the night he tried to put dual exhausts on my '71 Opel. It didn't work. I ended up having to roar back to a Missoula Midas shop with the racket pouring unfiltered right out of the laser-hot exhaust manifold. Daryl was now the appraiser for two counties and wasn't thrilled with the setup. All that driving and sitting at a desk had brought on two back operations. But the jokes were still keeping him going.

Outside again, I stood in front of the county jail. Verse showed up without asking. Back in the 1970s, Dick Hugo, the large Missoula poet, strolled back from a night of beverages at the East Gate to his home down by the Clark Fork and wrote "Degrees of Gray in Philipsburg." This is the part that came to me:

You might come here Sunday on a whim.
Say your life broke down. The last good kiss
you had was years ago. You walk these streets
laid out by the insane, past hotels
that didn't last, bars that did, the tortured try
of local drivers to accelerate their lives.
Only churches are kept up. The jail
turned 70 this year. The only prisoner
is always in, not knowing what he's done.

I headed off on foot down the terrace scarp street for a look around to see what's revised.

Sarah Puyear's green boardinghouse was for sale. Nights of sex between passing strangers still scented the semi-gloss. The Stephens Hotel was the same aviary of rock-thrown windows and swallow-stained brick. The way Dick Hugo saw it. The Kaiser House had 1881-vintage French doors and Norman arches. It was now a pool hall. The Golden Rule housed the same hardware store. Huffman's Grocery, with its oiled-over floorings and straightforward vittles, was replaced by the upscale Sapphire Gallery. Gems for sale: $1,000 rings and buckets of washed gravels for the tourists to peck through on flat, chest-high tables during the brief summer season. Most actually find sapphires, some of them over two carats. Sapphires turn out to be common, just like diamonds. The money is made on controlling the supply, cutting the facets, and engineering the demand.

The Victorian-style Sayr's building was a refreshed painted lady wearing hand-applied coats of maroon, yellow, and green. "Cyndy's Broadway Clothier" went after the tourist dollar. So did "Pintler Cookies," "The Flint Creek Merchantry," and the "Blue Heron Bed and Breakfast." There are those who want Pburg to be Telluride.

The Thrift Shop next door sold the enduring truth.

The Senior Citizen Center, originally a fine bank, was still assembling the old-timers. I gave a slide show here once of the Flint Creek high country. "So that's what it looks like up there," said an elderly woman. She'd lived next to the mountains for eighty-one years and never found four hours to stroll up for a look.

I stuck my head inside the Club House Bar. A guy in a wool jacket sat where Henry Hull should be conducting his "mine bidness." Then over to the White Front for a beer. It was quiet. During the Flint

Creek Valley Days celebration in August, there had been 200 guzzlers stuffed in here.

These things sometimes get out of hand. One year, I saw a blitzed woman storm out of the bar in a state of high dudgeon. Near as I could determine her husband had cheated on her. She grabbed a can of gasoline from the back of a pickup, ripped off the cap, and poured long glurps of the stuff under a line of rigs—one of which I assumed belonged to the offending party. She was fumbling with a book of matches when three men ran out of the bar and tackled her to the pavement.

After finishing my beer, I gambled $5 at keno, lost, and headed up the street.

The Taylor-Knapp Mining Company still maintained an office in the old Weinstein Building. Weinstein was a Polish merchant back in the silver boom days. Upslope, prospects and other "diggin's" continue to measle the landscape. Miners never find their way out. Except for the Rock Creek sapphire operations, there were no active mines in the county.

I headed up Broadway to my old house at the U-Turn sign. It was now an encampment called "Montana Possibles." The offerings included a gift shop, sapphire gravel sales, chainsaw repair, and "Tru-Hone" knife sharpening. You could also buy authentic cowboy-worn secondhand Levi's. Best to keep a few irons in the fire.

Time to eat. I walked over to the Gallery Cafe. Dutch Metesh paintings covered the walls. The most expensive was $85. I was pretty sure they weren't the same ones I ate next to in 1975.

I took my usual seat at the counter and ordered the enchiladas. Merrill's stool was unclaimed, so I read the paper. The *Philipsburg Mail* had a story about a run of dog poisonings. Apparently somebody was killing them with antifreeze. No one knew why.

The door opened and I couldn't help but look. It was just a couple of woodcutters in for coffee. Their day's work strained the springs of a dented Jimmy parked out front. The men rubbed their hands—nicked, tired, and pitchy from sawing up slash.

I cleared off the last of my beans, paid, and decided to walk out to face the music. New antique street lamps were being put up along Broadway. Jerry Sullivan helped organize the rehab. He's not a fan of Dick Hugo—"You can't read that poem and have a gun in your hand."

Pburg was looking better and I was feeling worse.

I stopped at Winninghoff Ford, unsure whether I'd passed it or not.

Puritan Epic, Prohibition and Magnetohydrodynamics Party

It took a minute to get my bearings but there it was. The little building so tastefully renovated with beige faux adobe and long-grain oak was Merrill's place. It was now a psychologist's office. The old boy would not know what to make of all this. There was no sign of him: no MHD literature, no clippings taped to dusty windows, no hearse parked out back. All that emerged was a Jungian insistence on the pointlessness of flight.

I decided to head up to Granite for some air.

The four-mile road was rocky and torn by deepening gullies. Packed snow covered shady stretches as the afternoon began to wear out. I made it to the tan and orange slag heaps below the Combination Mine and parked. Snow had already claimed the road up higher until May.

I crunched uphill along Main Street. Thickening stands of subalpine fir and lodgepole pine were resuming life without all the commotion. Elk sedge, twinflower, spirea, and wild strawberry covered the few melted-out patches. Porcupine quills were jammed into a bleeding resin scar on the trunk of a lodgepole. Then I saw the dead fellow himself, curled up in a dry, sunny spot, old age quietly playing out before the finishing freeze.

A dozen shaky wood structures were about all that was left from our stay here. One large home still had remnants of a finely done fence but bear shit covered the doorstep. I went inside another building and found a mattress, propane "Trav'ler" range, barrel woodstove, and paisley curtains. The cast-iron frying pan was full of rusted nails, coffee grounds, and fossilized wads of bubble gum. A child's blue sock hung from a nail. The far corner held a card table. Locals were trying to keep the place up, probably as a hunting camp. Their firewood was a stack of old building boards scavenged from all over the disintegrating town.

Farther on was a log house with its floorboards caving clear down to grus—rotted granite turned to sand. The place smelled like packrat flatulence and used shoes. Sheets of red and green linoleum lay broken like mosaic tiles next to a tin-walled bureau gone shelves up.

Mountains to metals, rust to dust.

The roof of another collapsed house sheltered a rabbit. He stared back blankly. Or maybe he was just being patient with me.

Everywhere I walked I saw dilapidation, regeneration, and elk scat. There was a reclaiming going on.

The rounded boulders we borrowed for foundations were rolling loose again. It was getting hard to tell glacial till from freemasonry. Downhill in the red-light district, the rock rows looked like breast-works from failed battles over whiskey and ejaculation. Amateur archaeologists had dug deep into the prostitutes' cribs. Green glass bottles, silver spoon fragments, and shards of pink china were some of the things left behind here.

I followed a game trail back uphill to the Miners Union Hall. This had been the laboring heart of Granite. The old black-and-whites show hundreds of miners crowded in the street out front, hanging from the windows, fighting for a spot back when a photograph was real business. As recently as the 1960s, a working pool table complete with antique balls and fine wooden cues survived inside the hall from simple civility.

I stood alone in front of a gutted shell. Three imbeciles had burned the building down eight years before. Whatever their sentences, the crime remained unpunished. The Union Hall was dead.

The roof and upper brick walls were mostly gone. The gracefully crafted archways above every window looked absurd next to the wreckage. The front was still trussed together by the original iron framing. Each post carried the same corroding design—a cross enfolded by curving forms that resembled G clefs. The granite blocks on the corners still showed the original chisel marks from the day they were set. Sledgehammer petroglyphs. The town had come and gone so fast that oxidation and lichen growth still hadn't diminished the freshness of the impacts.

I was beginning to ache from all the losses. Not for the end of greed and extraction but for the used-up land and lives in towns like Granite and Pburg. We need to sort out the failed fictions and final truths of what goes on in places like these, to get to the bottom of it, and find our way out. Mostly, to not recoil in judgment from folks we do not know. Sometimes, they can surprise you.

The dusk had deepened to black. I remembered the last verse of "Pburg."

Eastern sky as high as Orion
brings those bandits from the trees.
Who rob all the night's potential
for finding rhythm and clarity.
We have laid low and rolled with the breakers

Puritan Epic, Prohibition and Magnetohydrodynamics Party

but we're not immune to fearless time.
So let's drink another toast
to the PreCambrian coast
and climb on out of this mine.

The snow crunched loudly under my sneakers. I walked into the Union Hall and stopped. There was a sound out beyond the far wall. A tenth of me believed that somehow it was Merrill, poking around back there, the gods of aviation and parsimony allowing him one day a year to keep linking things up.

"Merrill?" I called out softly. I had to try.

The sound stopped.

I waited.

Nothing.

Flannel mullein stalks grew out of the floor and up through a foot of snow. Roman legions used this same plant in torches to light their way home. I bent over and gathered up seven, tied them together with strands of pinegrass and lit the heads on fire. Then I knelt down and stuck the base in the snow to brighten up a few years backward.

Just in case.

5

LAND TRUSTING

I WAS STANDING boot deep in the Big Hole River when the
mosquitoes began to take effect. The sinuous world of channels
and meander-scar sloughs was the birthplace of all bugs. Hazes,
billows, veils, mare's tails of bugs. Buzzing nebulas of blood-drilling
buggish bastards. My lacquer of noxious repellent only seemed to lu-
bricate their skin-piercing equipment.

But it sure was a pretty place to be.

Cinnamon teals drifted by bobbing for plants like finicky ballerinas
at a salad bar. Great blue herons waded in the shallows poised to spear
fish caught dozing in the warming June water. Sandhill cranes croaked
out bizarre calls from nests built off beyond the willow branches. Prairie falcons, kestrels, owls, harriers, red-tails, and turkey vultures filled
the sky patrolling for rabbits, ground squirrels, fish, and inattentive

passerine birds. Pronghorn grazed skittishly up on the sagebrush grasslands. The big greenup had arrived. Idaho fescue, bluebunch wheatgrass, Richardson's needlegrass, prairie junegrass, and timber danthonia swayed in the malachite breeze. Coyotes slid between the stalks looking for any food that opportunity and guile would provide.

The valley's irrigated meadows produced some of the finest hay in the world. Back in the 1920s, Big Hole hay was so coveted it was shipped to the Bluegrass region of Kentucky to be fed to racehorses. Beaverslides—strange contraptions made of lodgepole frames, sliding baskets of teeth, and long cable pulleys—were still used to construct piles of what looked like shredded wheat. The winter climate settles in so cold and dry that the stacks can be left uncovered to cure in the frigid sunlight. The crescent-shaped structural valley is the "Land of 10,000 Haystacks." Permanent snowfields fill the high shady basins of the Pioneer Mountains and other encircling ranges. There is plenty of water for crops and creatures. A few lush, well-tended ranches work the land close to Wisdom.

The Big Hole: Montana as it was in the 1870s, achingly beautiful and unrelentingly tough. No work for outsiders, an eleven-day frost-free season and the most voracious insects this side of Alaska. Nearby, the Big Hole National Battlefield looked much as it did that morning in 1877 when U.S. military forces killed eighty-nine Nez Perce Indians as they slept in their tipis. The Big Hole—widely known for a long history of difficulty.

Despite that, in 1976, the recreational housing boom was at the valley's outer gates. Soon it might be here. Preciousness itself swam in the Big Hole River. The object of all my slogging about was to help save a relict population of an opalescent little fish called the fluvial Arctic grayling.

In 1805, Lewis and Clark saw this "new kind of white and silvery trout" all over Montana. Settlement, irrigation withdrawals, and competition with introduced trout soon began to eliminate this Ice Age fish one drainage at a time. The Missouri, Gallatin, Jefferson, Smith, and other rivers lost their grayling.

In 1970, the Sun River population became extinct. In 1975, the Madison River grayling disappeared. By 1976, the upper Big Hole River was the last place in the lower forty-eight states that still had river-dwelling Arctic grayling.

I was giving blood for a good cause.

Bruce Bugbee, Chris Servheen, and I were doing an ecological study of a 2,000-acre ranch. The place included about a mile of Big Hole River frontage. That meant maybe 100 grayling lived here, each as cherished as a rare seed. The owners were doing something I had never heard of before. Something astonishing. They were voluntarily donating away all their rights to subdivide and develop their property —forever. Ordinary people were choosing stewardship—continuing to ranch and raise food, formalizing their respect for ecologically intact agricultural land. Bruce Bugbee told me that the legal tool for doing this was called a "conservation easement." This was the first conservation easement ever received by the Montana Land Reliance, a newly formed land trust group. It was just the beginning, and it was coming just in time.

In the 1970s, Montana was enduring another round of land subdivision and real estate speculation. All over the state, subdivisions were claiming thousands of acres of prime ag land, wildlife habitat, and open space.

This was nothing new. From the beginning, Montanans have energetically supported Katy-bar-the-door land development. The Homestead Act of 1864: 160 acres free to any settler. The Timber Culture Act of 1873: 160 acres free. The Desert Land Act of 1877: 640 acres at $1.25 each. The Enlarged Homestead Act of 1909: 320 acres free. The homestead era set the tone. The land was limitless and should be filled up at once.

Railroad companies promoted Montana nationwide and sold vast amounts of land. In 1883, Northern Pacific real estate ads announced: "Millions and Millions of Acres for Sale in Montana at the Lowest Prices Ever Offered—$2.60–$4.00 per acre! The Best Homes for 10,000,000 People! They Will All Become Prosperous!"

In 1909, the Montana Department of Publicity issued a manual entitled simply *Montana*. The state was advertised as a paradise with endless amounts of inexpensive real estate. Urbanites were told they could make a fresh start away from the grime and violence of city life. "As older states have filled up, the pressure of population seeking homes has become great and the fact is realized that the only large area of land in the U.S. waiting to be peopled is Montana," the manual said. "The tide of immigration has set in from both east and west. The vacant lands are filling up . . . Many large ranches have become too valuable to be used as pasture and have been divided into small tracts and sold." Sounds like an article from yesterday's paper.

In 1923, the Montana Department of Agriculture concluded a massive boosteristic tome with this: "No effort has been made to sell Montana in brighter colors than actually exist . . . When the time is ripe, when economic conditions in the nation and the world are favorable, Montana will be ready."

This attitude was still dominant in the 1965 *Industrial Manifest of Montana*. The theme of this publication was boldly written: "Tired of Congestion, Traffic, Pollution? Come to Montana!" The manifesto went on to cheerfully inform us that "From less than 15,000 people in 1860, our population has grown to over 700,000. But our natural wealth can support far more development. In the years ahead, Montana can and should grow beyond all our present hopes."

Filling the land with more and more people was a policy that may have made some sense in the early years of the state. Yet the ideology of ceaseless expansion survived unchanged into the 1970s, despite the widening social and environmental impacts of growth.

But some Montanans were already feeling a vague sense of big trouble. In 1973, the Montana Environmental Information Center (MEIC) in Helena studied land splitting in thirty-five Montana counties. They found that over 334,000 acres had been carved into 114,000 residential tracts of 40 acres or less. MEIC put the actual total at well over 500,000 acres. It could have been twice that given the inconsistencies of recording.

Montana was being sliced up and sold.

In 1974, the state legislature responded by passing the Montana Subdivision and Platting Act. This law allowed city and county planning boards to review the environmental, economic, and social impacts of new developments. Montana landowners and speculators reacted by carving out hundreds of thousands of lots during the window of opportunity before the new law came into force. Many ranchers raced into Clerk and Recorder offices and filed plats or deeds dissecting their entire spreads into twenty-acre parcels.

It was easy. Twenty-acre tracts could be created by what is called an "aliquot parts description"—one-half of a quarter of a quarter of Section such and such of a certain Township and Range. Ironically, the new subdivision law was causing the old square-mile grid to splinter apart faster than ever. And the problems with the new law were just starting.

Planners charged with implementing the act quickly found that "exemptions" from review far outnumbered cases where subdivisions could be regulated. "Occasional sales" of one lot per year were exempt. "Family transfers" of land were exempt. Lots of twenty acres and above were exempt. Over 90 percent of all land splits were still occurring with no evaluation of their effects. Montana's new subdivision law was turning out to be a de facto homestead act. Outfits like Ski Yellowstone Inc., Big Sky Inc., and Yellowstone Basin Properties descended on Montana's agricultural valleys like Rommel on North Africa. Yet much of the subdivision came when average Montanans split off a few lots at a time. Regulatory land use planning was shaping up as a bust.

I worked as the Planning Director in Mineral County for five years, from 1978 to 1983. Before that I worked in the Planning Office in Granite County. During that entire time, about all we did was make sure that new developments had proper roads, basic utility services, and adequate waste disposal. All worthy goals. But the future of the places we lived in—the matter of long-range planning—seldom came up.

The Montana Land Reliance and The Nature Conservancy decided that a very different approach was needed. These and other land trust groups began using voluntary, negotiated, compensating techniques to save Montana landscapes from subdivision. These tools included land purchases, land exchanges, and purchases or donations of development rights—more commonly called conservation easements.

Land trusts were just getting started in Montana. In the coming years, the approach would make tremendous gains. But the idea didn't originate here. Land trusting has a long history in the United States.

Land trusts first arose in Massachusetts with the formation of the Trustees of Public Reservations in 1891. Boston area conservationists began protecting wetlands, farms, and forests from spreading urbanization. The idea proved popular. By 1950, there were 53 trusts nationwide, mostly in New England. By 1965, 132 trusts operated in twenty-six states. Ten years later, the total had climbed to 308. In 1981, there were 431. Since that year, spurred by the formation of a national organization known as the Land Trust Alliance, trusts have formed at a rate of more than one per week.

There are now over 1,250 land trusts in America. They are found in every state but Oklahoma and Arkansas, and have a total membership of nearly 1 million.

A 1995 national survey revealed that land trusts had protected over 4 million acres of private land from damaging forms of development. The 1998 total is closer to 5 million. Of the 1995 total, trusts owned

535,000 acres and held conservation easements on 740,000 acres. Trusts had also acquired 990,000 acres that were transferred to other groups or agencies for management. An additional 1,764,000 acres were protected by deed restrictions, mineral rights acquisitions, and cooperative efforts with other organizations. Today, an area more than twice the size of Yellowstone National Park has been protected.

Part of America's genius is grassroots innovation. Land trusts have been established for a wide range of purposes. The names of these groups show the range of goals and settings: the Adirondack Land Trust, Society for the Protection of New Hampshire's Forests, the Kings County Farmlands Program, Jackson Hole Land Trust, Platte River Whooping Crane Habitat Trust, Ozark Regional Trust, Tennessee River Gorge Trust, Delaware Wild Lands, Colorado Open Lands, and Trust for Appalachian Trail Lands.

Regardless of locale, it's all about saving land from development. The Maine Coast Heritage Trust has conserved over 60,000 acres of shoreline and island properties. California's Marin Agricultural Land Trust has used donated and purchased conservation easements to protect some 30,000 acres of dairy farms and cattle ranches. From coast to coast, land trusts are now being formed to secure farmland, watersheds, wildlife habitats, scenic open space, historical sites and structures, forests, and wetlands.

New England has over 400 groups; the Southwest states, only 27. Trusts originated back East and are still spreading into the West. The Rocky Mountain region has fifty-one land trusts, with thirty of those in Colorado. Montana has six groups.

It's a simple idea. Citizens gather, form a nonprofit organization, raise money, enter the real estate marketplace, and start saving land. But in practice, it's extremely hard work that takes commitment, experience, and endless patience.

Government entities are also active. In the last two years, statewide general obligation bonds have been passed all over the country to fund open space protection. Baltimore County, Maryland—a $6 million bond for agricultural land protection and parks. Long Island, New York—a $13 million bond for purchasing conservation easements. Durham, North Carolina—a $20 million bond for greenways, parks, and trails. Dade County, Florida—a $200 million bond for open space. The State of Missouri—$500 million for farmland protection and parks.

In 1996, City of Missoula voters passed a $5 million open space bond. Over 1,000 acres have already been acquired. In that same year, a $2 million bond issue was passed by Helena voters.

National organizations such as The Nature Conservancy (TNC), the American Farmland Trust, The Conservation Fund, the Trust for Public Land, and the Rocky Mountain Elk Foundation are also crucial.

The Nature Conservancy preceded most local and regional land trusts. The mission of TNC is to build an ark, to protect biological rarities. It has assembled the most extensive non-governmental reserve system in the world, over 8 million acres. Its largest reserve is the 321,000-acre Gray Ranch in New Mexico. TNC's ability to generate money is legendary. Between 1990 and 1995, its national office raised $300 million to secure seventy-five unique sites across America.

Here are just a few of TNC's projects in the Big Sky.

The 18,000-acre Pine Butte Swamp preserve near Choteau is one of the last places in the lower forty-eight states where grizzlies roam freely across the Great Plains. This Rocky Mountain Front ecosystem is home to 43 mammal species including mountain lions, lynx, bobcats, moose, and bighorn sheep. Some 185 species of birds have been sighted at Pine Butte. Egg Mountain is included in the preserve. Paleontologist Jack Horner found fossilized dinosaur eggs here. This helped inspire Michael Crichton's novel *Jurassic Park*.

The 377-acre Crown Butte site includes some of the last undisturbed prairie in the state. The 400-acre Swan River Oxbow preserve near Kalispell harbors five rare plant species. The 680-acre Dancing Prairie preserve outside of Eureka is one of the last places where male Columbian sharp-tail grouse "dance" to attract mates. TNC has done some remarkable work.

Today, there are also six local and regional land trusts in Montana. Their budgets don't match TNC's, but that just makes their accomplishments all the more heartening. The Five Valleys Land Trust (Missoula) has conserved 4,500 acres using easements and land purchases. The 1,700-acre Mount Jumbo project next to Missoula is its largest success so far. The Flathead Land Trust (Kalispell) has saved over 3,000 acres of scenic farmlands and lakeshore environments. The Gallatin Valley Land Trust (Bozeman) has secured more than 2,000 acres of ranchlands and other open space. The Montana Land Reliance (Helena) holds 217 conservation easements totaling 225,413 acres. The Rock Creek Trust has protected over 3,000 acres of riparian ecosystems, ranchlands, and bighorn sheep habitat along world-famous Rock Creek. And Save Open Space (Missoula) has safe-guarded 400 acres on the urban fringe.

But these figures are just snapshots. The good news is that the totals are rising daily. While it is true that *which* lands get protected is also critical, "acres conserved" is a fair measure of land trust success.

The overall diversity and complexity of land trust projects in the state is amazing. More than 500,000 acres are now protected by conservation easements alone in Montana, including the efforts of both trusts and public agencies. While far less than 1 percent of the Big Sky's private land, this is the highest statewide easement total in the United States.

With the increasing success of trusts, few Montana conservationists are now looking to land use regulations as a way to protect key lands from inappropriate development. There are some persistent reasons why.

Zoning is just wishing. Variances and re-zonings seriously weaken the effectiveness of the tool. Floodplain regulations mostly consist of building codes and insurance schemes. Subdivision regulations are not designed or able to conserve open space lands, only to determine *how* they will be developed. Even Montana's updated subdivision law isn't helping much. Every new parcel created that is less than 160 acres in size must now be reviewed by local government. That sounds great. But in practice, nothing is being checked but plat boundaries, septic tank permits, and access. Over 34,000 new lots have been platted in the last decade. The revised law hasn't changed a thing.

Regulations continue to be ineffective for many reasons. Planners often believe they can turn things around if a perfect new set of controls is fashioned. But the failure of regulation has little to do with the wording of documents. It comes down to this—most people don't want to be regulated. Montanans have always opposed land use planning, even when it would protect their private property values. Even when a lack of planning corrodes their real freedoms, most people would rather defend an ideological abstraction.

It's a bit of a puzzling attitude.

Unplanned growth reduces true liberty. This is widely known where growth has become ruthless. Ask people in California, Nevada, Colorado, Oregon, and Washington if they feel freer today than they did a decade ago. Ask them about their property tax rates.

Las Vegas is now America's fastest-growing city. Two or three new elementary schools are being built each month. Every measure of the quality of life has declined. The only things that have gone up are taxes, crime stats, and the number of car wrecks.

Our communities are changing far faster than our ideas. Before you know it, we'll be living in towns we don't know. In 1950, Albuquerque, New Mexico, had 50,000 residents. It was about the size of Missoula. Today, Albuquerque has 500,000 people with 100,000 more living within twenty miles of the city limits.

Curiously, Montanans have already acknowledged that more people and more growth will devalue their lives. In 1992, Governor Stan Stephens commissioned a poll and found that 63 percent of all Montanans felt the state's population was as big as it should be. Another 10 percent felt it was already too large.

Yet Montanans also continue to tote around a hefty illusion—that they live on the frontier and their individual actions have little impact on anyone else. So they oppose land use planning even though they don't want more development. That's quite a conundrum. But reality quarters out this way: you cannot address growth without dealing with land development. This is as plain as a gingham dress.

But most people still refuse to accept regulations. A friend from Colorado named Marty Zeller was hired by Flathead County a few years ago to create an innovative comprehensive plan. A Cooperative Planning Coalition was formed. The latest Geographic Information System tools were used to analyze data. The public involvement process was staggering. Over 33,000 questionnaires were mailed out, one to every household in the county. Nearly 200 meetings were held where state-of-the-art implementation tools were presented. It was an extremely professional job. In all, more than $400,000 was spent. And still the plan was widely rejected because people said it threatened their rights. As if open-ended growth wouldn't.

Real liberty in the twenty-first century will be freedom from crowding, crime, undue tax burdens, pollution, traffic jams, bad schools, concrete open space, and bad fishing. Freedom carries responsibilities. One of those is to protect and plan our communities. We plan weddings, household budgets, and Sunday barbecues—hell, we plan bowling banquets. So why is planning the future of the places we live in seen as a Stalinist plot?

Decades of time and thousands of acres will be lost before we solve that particular riddle. But one thing is obvious: opposition to subdivision control and other police power devices is unlikely to change anytime soon. To be fair, regulatory planning's often bureaucratic history

Land Trusting

is partly to blame. It has created a persistent bad taste in people's mouths. That is because regulations are sometimes misused by planners who personally oppose *all* development. Such emotional concern for the landscape is admirable, but it is counterproductive in a regulatory setting. Many planners really want to be conservationists, and they're frustrated because the day-to-day tools of their trade won't allow them that opportunity.

But let's not just pound on the planners. The behavior of average citizens is hardly above reproach. People loathe planning until someone decides to build a hog farm or metal-bending factory or mink farm next door. Then they descend on public meetings screaming for the most stringent restrictions since Mussolini.

Sometimes entire communities react this way. In 1995 in just five days, 12,500 Missoulians signed a petition opposing an in-fill development slated for a small amount of Fort Missoula land. It's a fair bet that few of those signers knew or used the land in question. Most would shriek like rabbits caught in a hay baler if anyone tried to block their own development plans. It's in our nature to lean toward hypocrisy from time to time.

So what can we do?

First, we must acknowledge something important: the level of regulation needed to save our places is unlikely to become politically acceptable until it is too late—when our communities have already become overgrown and miserable. Second, it is time to make a real commitment to voluntary, negotiated, compensating techniques of open space protection and growth management.

Missoula has completed a countywide inventory of important lands and, with the help of an Open Space Advisory Committee and land trusts, has begun conserving them. As these efforts become even more systematic, regulatory systems will be more effectively used to improve the quality of developments on non–open space lands and for other essential tasks—such as the creation of affordable housing. In many cases, conservation easements can be successfully integrated with environmentally sensitive subdivision designs.

Livable communities and valleys will only come from some version of this basic approach. It will be some of the hardest work we will ever do. And the most lasting.

That's what began to dawn on me, standing in the Big Hole River encased in mosquitoes all those years ago. Maybe it was the loss of blood, but ever since that day I have firmly believed that caring people can save a good measure of Montana.

Conservation easements are a big part of that belief. This is how they work.

We're used to thinking of land ownership as an absolute. But any legal privilege to use land—such as mineral, timber, water, grazing, and subdivision rights—can be severed from the title and given away or sold. Most of the time when we do this we convey the right to use the resource in a certain way: road and powerline easements—those sorts of things. But when the right to subdivide land and build houses is conveyed to a land trust or land managing agency, these land uses can be permanently retired. This type of transaction is what conservation easements are all about.

A conservation easement is a perpetual statement of stewardship. Each is a voluntary, free-market transaction—no one can make you grant one. Easements are based on meeting the needs of the land, landowner, and land trust. No two easements are alike; everything is negotiated. Land use practices that are typically eliminated or restricted include subdivision and development, mining, channelizing streams, and draining wetlands. Selective timber harvest for ranch purposes can be maintained. Agricultural practices are typically not changed.

The main purpose of a conservation easement is to keep the land more or less as is—to maintain the status quo. If a place is a working ranch and the wildlife are thriving—perfect. About all an easement does is eliminate potential land uses that would diminish ag yields, habitat quality, and scenic beauty. But an easement doesn't always mean no more houses. Cluster development is sometimes included in the design.

The land trust that holds the easement can never use the rights that have been transferred to its care. Its mission is to work with the landowner, and all future landowners, as a partner in stewardship. And to make an annual visit to make sure the terms of the easement have not been violated. If they have, then the trust can enforce the easement in court. No such legal actions have ever been needed in Montana. People who choose to live on conserved land tend to be good managers.

So why would anybody voluntarily give up development rights? Many feel compensated by the knowledge that they have done right by the land. The thought of their property being lost to development is too much to bear. Despite all the venom we direct at them, many newcomers have been drawn to Montana by the beauty and wish to conserve it. A large share of all easements given in the state have come from new people. But the old-timers are on board as well. I have worked with dozens of ranchers over the years. Most care deeply about the ground they work. For them, an easement is a way of ensuring a family legacy in agriculture and a declaration of the proper way to use the earth. Dozens of rancher easements have been completed in Montana.

Feeling good isn't the only compensation. There are also hard-headed economic reasons for giving a conservation easement.

The donation of an easement in perpetuity to a land trust or unit of government is a tax-deductible charitable gift much like giving money to your church or the United Way. The dollar value of an easement is set by a land appraiser who compares the market price of the land before and after the project is completed. The difference equals the amount of potential income, estate, and capital gains tax deductions that the donor is entitled to.

Norman Myers wrote in *The Sinking Ark* that "we can persuade some to protect land but ultimately we must recognize the sacrifice and compensate it." It seems a simple courtesy to thank people for being generous in ways that improve our landscapes and our lives.

Not every property qualifies for tax benefits. Congress has set up four categories of qualification. At least one of the following "conservation purposes" must be met by an easement: ecological, open space (including ag land), recreation, and historic. If fieldwork discovers significant conservation values on a property, the tax codes provide some very real incentives to the landowner who donates an easement.

The income tax deduction from a conservation easement can be written off over a period of six years—up to 30 percent of a donor's "Adjusted Gross Income" for each year. This tends to appeal to wealthy newcomers. Ranchers have enough tax deductions walking around on four legs. But for ag operators, the looming specter of federal and state estate taxes can make easements a real ally in their struggle to stay on the land.

Here's how. Let's say a ranch is worth $1 million. Under current federal law, an estate valued at $600,000 can be passed on to family members without paying a cent in taxes. But the remaining $400,000 is exposed to heavy taxation—$153,000 will be owed to the government. If a conservation easement is placed on the property—thus reducing its *paper* value by 40 percent—this drops the estate's worth to $600,000 and no taxes are due. The bottom line? The land can be kept in the family. It can still be sold at any time for whatever price a buyer is willing to pay. Easements do not freeze the market value of property.

In Montana, 24,000 ranchers control most of the private land in the state. The average age of these landowners is sixty. Statewide property values shot up 38 percent between 1992 and 1996. In heavily agricultural counties like Sanders, Granite, Gallatin, Park, Sweet Grass, and Carbon, these values skyrocketed between 61 and 75 percent.

Montana ranchers are facing an estate tax nightmare. Many families will lose their spreads unless they act. Conservation easements and other land trust techniques offer a tremendous range of new options for ranchers if they will give them a chance. Some already are.

The Montana Land Reliance (MLR) has a strong program of working with ag people. Its Board of Directors is thick with ranchers, and the Reliance's director, Rock Ringling, comes from a Montana ranch family. MLR conservation easements have helped dozens of families stay on the land: the 3,200-acre Bench Ranch in the foothills of Beartooth Plateau; the 5,500-acre Johnson Land and Livestock Ranch north of Absarokee; the 10,900-acre Whitetail and Sheep Creek ranches near White Sulphur Springs. And on and on they go.

In 1996, MLR completed forty-four easements totaling 49,509 acres. The Reliance has the highest tally of any local or regional land trust in the United States—over 225,000 acres of ecologically important ag land protected by donated conservation easements.

Dean Thorson, a rancher who gave an easement, says: "We want the next generation to enjoy this land as much as we have. There is too much natural beauty here to see it divided up into homes. They're not making any more land, someone has to look after it. We want to leave it in better shape than we found it." Simple, gracious words for an eternally kind act.

So why are these easements needed? Ranches and farms make up Montana's day-to-day open space. They comprise the cultural landscape we take for granted but surely need. Ag land is important not only as a food-producing resource but also as an ecological anchor—ground that is just as vital as wilderness. Ranches contain most of the state's big game winter range habitats, rivers and wetlands, waterfowl areas, historic sites, and archaeological treasures. The biological diversity of the entire state is canted toward private land. Yet these are the same places we covet for housing expansion.

Tom McGuane writes and ranches beside the Boulder River. He serves on the Board of the Montana Land Reliance and has put an easement on his place. "The river valleys are some of the most imperilled parts of our landscapes because that's where people settle," McGuane says. "The concept of easements has not been understood by all Montanans and many still see it as an intrusive sort of thing. I live in Sweetgrass County, [where] putting an easement on your property was once considered an act of Satan and anti-community. But now people are starting to see the good that can come of it."

Part of the ranchers' resistance comes from cases like Ted Turner's Flying D Ranch. The media magnate placed an easement on 130,000 acres—the largest such transaction in American history. The Nature Conservancy was the receiver. Some locals resented the transaction, not so much because it banned subdivision, but because Turner removed cattle and replaced them with bison. Rumor was he got a major reduction in property taxes. Other people were angry because he closed the ranch to hunting. Some harbored hatred of Turner's wife, actress/activist Jane Fonda. She didn't help matters by calling cows "fat and lazy" on national television. Not the brightest or most tolerant thing to say about your neighbor's livelihood. The Turner easement caused some bad blood around the state.

But here are the facts beyond the finger-pointing. Conservation easements do not block public access. That decision is up to the landowner, just like always. Easements do not reduce property taxes. In Montana, a ranch is taxed as agricultural land whether an easement is in place or not. Conservation easements don't cost local governments one cent in lost property tax revenues. The bison? Well, it's Turner's land, so I suppose that's his business. Private property rights are pretty sacred. So is the freedom to marry whomever you please, even if she hates cows.

The only real problem with easements is that too many people still haven't heard of them. Or if they have, they are toting around a bunch of misinformation. Ranchers hold the key in all this. The decisions of those 24,000 property owners will shape the kind of Montana the remaining 860,000 of us live in.

Bruce Bugbee has given this a lot of thought. He's worked in land conservation across Montana for a quarter of a century. His Missoula-based outfit, American Public Land Exchange Company, has protected more land than any similar firm in the West. I've been fortunate enough to work beside him on a number of those projects. Among Bruce's many land-saving accomplishments are substantial acquisitions in the Rattlesnake National Recreation Area and Wilderness, the White Cliffs corridor on the Missouri River, the Upper Mesa Falls area on the Henry's Fork of the Snake, and countless other land exchanges, purchases, and conservation easements.

Bruce Bugbee has an impressive résumé. As he sees it, "Understanding the needs of ranchers is a weakness in the land trust approach."

One sunny, 8-degree day we talked in his office. Files and folders from two dozen jobs sprawled out across the floor. "Easements have to be explained in ways that make sense to people who work out there on the land," he began. "They won't work if it's just people from the outside trying to impose changes. So far, we haven't done a very good job of addressing local ranching cultures. The entry point hasn't really been found."

"What do you think it will be?" I asked.

"That's a tough subject. One that sometimes bumps up against our image of ranching. The way I see this, those ranchers who survived all the tough times—weather, recessions, depression—handed down a culture from generation to generation that has two sides to it. One side says, if you can outlast your neighbor, you get the spoils. When they leave you get to buy their land cheap. You went through hell and the reward of hell is more land that you can use to try and make it on a broader base. The other side is hospitable and caring, ready to help a neighbor calving out his cows in a spring blizzard."

"Isn't there some kind of balance point there?" I wondered.

"Sure, an equilibrium is reached when you have enough land to grow 300–500 cows a year, a herd big enough to support a family."

"Sounds pretty Darwinian," I said.

"Yes, it's a very hard life and tough position to take. One that's the opposite of how these people are good neighbors—helping out through thick and thin, even risking their lives for each other. All that sacrifice is true and very noble. Yet the one thing you don't save another rancher from is the bank—there is a line drawn there. Not always, but I've seen it a lot. For some reason you can help your neighbor until they are going under, then you turn off that part of yourself that cares. Maybe it's too strong a reminder of their own mortality."

"So people get angry when you're saving a ranch operation?" I asked.

"Sometimes. The conflict comes when a land trust or agency comes in to solve a rancher's problem—to buy a conservation easement, to do estate planning—then some of the neighbors get upset because you are interfering with their hopes of getting the land. Suddenly, after years of waiting, a prized ranch isn't available to them at a certain price."

"They were waiting for a sell-off at a bargain," I said.

"Exactly. Problem is, ranchers seldom sell to each other at agricultural values. In the last ten years, ag values have become a myth. Everything sells at amenity price—at top dollar."

"And that's why estate planning is so important now," I said.

"Absolutely. That's probably the best place to start. The Montana Land Reliance is so successful because they realize something basic. The biggest problem most ranchers face isn't how to manage their land, it's how to survive the estate tax dilemma—the silent partner of the IRS and Uncle Sam. Once you sell some of the land to pay the taxes and no longer have a viable ranch unit, you become a victim, a modern-day honyocker that has to move on."

It was a strong image. During the wheat boom days from 1909 to 1917, several hundred thousand homesteaders rushed into Montana. A "honyocker" was German slang for "chicken chaser." It meant they were dirt poor. Media hype enticed trainloads of greenhorns into the state. Montana was promoted by a broad collection of railroad windbags as a land of bottomless wealth waiting to be liberated by the honest sweat of yeoman labor. Telling the arid truth was taboo. By the 1920s, nature and market forces intervened. Drought and a crash in grain prices quickly caused over 80 percent of these farmers to abandon the land and leave the state penniless. They'd been railroaded.

"So the ranchers who adapt will survive," I continued.

"They've got the best shot. In Montana, there are 90 million acres of private land. In the next ten to fifteen years, one-third of that may change hands. If I wanted to be where the action is, I'd be in estate planning. Easements are just one tool that can assist ranchers in facing that challenge."

"But there's still resistance to land trust work out there," I added.

"Oh yeah, the Montana Association of Counties even pushed for a state law prohibiting state agencies from buying perpetual conservation easements. It was an extremely bad bill for ranchers," Bruce said, shaking his head. "I guess some objected on moral grounds, that people living today didn't have the right to commit land to conservation in perpetuity. Others in the Association got the idea that easements will lower a county's tax base."

They actually have just the opposite effect. Keeping land in production often generates a stable economy. Rural and suburban housing is a net drag on city and county budgets. In Gallatin County, a 1996 study showed that residential developments on formerly agricultural land cost government $1.47 in services for every dollar the houses generate in taxes. Residential growth seldom pays its own way. Industry, commercial businesses, and agriculture have to make up the shortfall. This raises their tax rates and creates a poor climate for attracting new jobs.

Bruce looked over at a map of Montana. Colored pins marked completed easements. "Rancher land trusts will be a whole new direction for the future," he said. "The Reliance is excellent and works with a lot of old families, but many of their projects are still with new owners. The ag sector hasn't been totally solved. But I believe the ranchers will come around. In Colorado, we did an easement in the San Luis Valley, remember?"

"Yes, 1982, the La Garita Ranch near Creede," I said.

"When we did that job," Bruce said, "the Colorado Cattlemen's Association opposed it. Today, they have their own land trust that negotiates easements with ranchers. That's a pretty amazing change! I really believe that economic forces will drive ag people toward conservation options. Trusts need to continue positioning their ideas as a competitive choice to development. In time, the Conservation Districts and the Soil Conservation Service will begin to get into the land trust business. Then we can begin to save entire landscapes.

"But easements are not the objective," Bruce continued; "stewardship is. If you have economically healthy ag operations run by knowledgeable people, there's every reason to be upbeat. Easements are just a tool."

"How do you help make things more economical?" I wondered.

"Ranchers and farmers are beginning to think a bit more abstractly about what business they're in. They have collateral, equity that they can get paid for—open land, wildlife, beauty. They've always enjoyed it but until recently they didn't think anyone else did. Easements are one way to be compensated for providing those things.

"But there's another way," he went on. "Most ranchers don't realize how unusual their lives are. Outfitters and guides are now leading tours of ranches showing city people how haying, cow-calf operations, and horse raising work. Guest ranching, ecological tours, bird watching, hunting districts, outfitting—all these things can add revenue to a ranch's coffers."

"Ecotourism," I said. "A lot of ranchers hate the idea."

"Yes, but if it's handled locally that may change. There may be more money in showing people sandhill cranes than in trying to shoot the ones that eat your grain."

"Like in Rwanda with the mountain gorillas," I said. "Visitors are paying over $500 a day to see the animals; that's far more money than a poached carcass brings."

"We haven't even begun to imagine the ways that agriculture and tourism can coexist," Bruce said. "It won't be for everybody, but it will sure help. But as long as ranchers see things as 'us versus them,' it won't happen. Ranchers are extremely creative—they'll out-think anybody to get two more cows out of the range. When you turn that sort of mind loose on adaptation, then the future looks pretty good."

"You're not talking about closures to local hunting are you?" I asked.

"No. Leasing the right to hunt to an out-of-state outfit can be a bad idea; ranchers end up regretting it," Bruce said, frowning. "Cuts them off from the tradition of public access. But people do have the right to figure out who hunts on their land and how."

The phone rings. Bruce spends five minutes setting up a meeting up in Kalispell—habitat protection along the Flathead River.

"So ranchland is where we have our work cut out for us?" I went on.

"We sure do," Bruce said, looking off toward Lolo Peak. "The West's last wilderness is open space on private land. It is huge, unprotected, and taken for granted. You hear the same statements made like back in the early days of the wilderness movement—'Who cares about it? Why bother with it? We've got lots of that stuff.'

"But the world is shifting before our eyes," Bruce insists. "We can't put our heads in the sand and say property values won't keep going up. Land values are no longer local; they're set by national forces. People can now move into Montana from anywhere and go to work or retire.

Development will continue, it will cycle up and down, but it won't just stop on its own.

"Montana's agricultural landscape hangs in the balance right now," Bruce said, gesturing at the state map. "We need to work to save it from two directions—direct conservation and improved economic viability. Profits will keep land open as much as any land trust could."

"Save Montana—Eat More Beef," I laughed.

"Absolutely. Cows Not Condos," he laughed back.

But it's true. People who attack federal grazing leases don't understand how vital they are to the survival of ranchers. Two-thirds of all ranch operations in the West have federal leases that are essential for maintaining their economic viability. And if the leases are eliminated, the ranches will go under, taking open space and wildlife habitat with them. It's a delicate system.

"Right now the biggest message ranchers hear about easements is that you can sell one to the state," Bruce said. "Like the 21,000-acre easement bought near Helena for $2.6 million."

"That was a hell of a deal," I said.

"An amazing bargain!" he said beaming. "You conserve a huge ecosystem for $124 an acre! But there's a limit to purchasing; there isn't enough money to buy easements on everything worth saving.

"Ultimately, conserving land comes down to a personal decision," Bruce continued. "It's about stewardship and honor. Ranchers are trying to figure out how they can live on ground they're so captivated by without being forced to do it harm."

"And easements are a big part of the answer," I said.

"A major, major part. But it's caring that counts," Bruce said smiling. "And having a smart estate plan."

Sometimes ideas come around that have a practical grace about them.

Bob Kiesling agrees. I visited Kies in Helena at the "Global Headquarters" of his conservation real estate business, an outfit named "OUTLANDish." He's a tall, charismatic native of Havre with a true gift—work like mad and still have a ball. Bob ran the Montana office of The Nature Conservancy for years. Most of that group's reserves in the state were set up by his hands.

The OUTLANDish office was stuffed with memorabilia from a life spent saving land—Monte Dolack posters, dinosaur fossils, photos of friends, jackalope heads, agricultural antiques, and stacks of books on subjects ranging from tax law to trout fishing. After a shot of Tulla-more Dew, we sat down for a chat. I wanted to get the view from east of the mountains.

"So how's it going out there? Are we a prefecture of California yet?" I laughed.

"Some days it seems like it," Kies said, smiling. "But the numbers show that most of the people who move to Montana fleeing urban problems—the 'lifestyle refugees'—typically only stay two or three years. Then they realize that there is little economic opportunity here and the weather's harsh. So pretty soon they turn around and head back to where they came from. But the buyers who have snapped up many of the scenic ranch properties are different. They're using them as second homes. Montana's their summer playground. They don't need to earn even one dollar here, so most are sticking around."

"Where are the ranches turning over the fastest?" I asked.

"All the choice river valleys—the Bitterroot, the Flathead, the Gal-latin. But the demand is spreading, even to the Rocky Mountain east front. Ranchers from out there tell me that people are coming over from the Flathead Valley and knocking on their doors asking if they have any land for sale. They say, 'It's too crowded in the Flathead any-more.' Newcomers are now fleeing the latest round of newcomers. Pretty amazing."

"How are the ranchers responding?" I asked.

"Mostly they say 'Hell No!' But that won't last forever. Land trusts offer the only permanent solutions. Yet there's a perceptual problem out there. The stockgrowers' associations, the old-line, true-blue ag organizations, tend to look at land trusts as land grabbers, as a com-petitive threat. There's a big misunderstanding that trusts are enemies, not allies. Many ranchers still see them as environmentalists out to shut them down. That's a big problem and progress is painfully slow."

"So how do we break through to the ag people?" I wondered. Maybe he saw it differently than Bugbee did.

"I see a two-tiered strategy here. First, there's no substitute for case-by-case, ranch-by-ranch conservation—each one a baby step. But in a land trust, there's only so much money and time. So you tend to concentrate on the baby steps in front of you. When a rancher does an easement and the sky doesn't fall down, some of the hostility and mis-perception begins to fade. In fact, the easement giver often ends up crowing about it down at the coffee shop because their family can keep ranching. When enough people see that from across a fence line, land trusts won't be the boogeyman anymore.

"But you also have to be involved in a broader strategy," Kies went on, "one that includes media and education. Those things take years before there's a payoff. That's tier two. And you have to do them both to reach a happy outcome.

"Yet the attackers are out there," Kies said, flipping his pen like a baton. "It's tough political sledding. These attacks are emotionally driven and schizophrenic. On one hand people shout that no one has the right to interfere with private property rights, but on the other they are opposing private market transactions.

"Remember when we did a conservation easement on Mrs. Heller's property in the Blackfoot?" he asked. I nodded. I'd done the field work for the project back in the eighties. "She was a sweet octogenarian school teacher who was genuinely interested in conserving her property," Kies continued. "She had children who didn't give two hoots about that; they wanted the money and she knew it. But she chose to do the easement anyway. Now, Montana law requires local government notification whenever an easement is done. I remember vividly that when we ran it past the Powell County Planning Board, several people were loudly opposed. They said that no landowner should have the right to control the future use of land from the grave. Well, I reminded them that every time they as a planning board—as an agent of government—approved a development, they were sanctioning a perpetual change in land use. They were being hypocrites. Yet logic often doesn't matter, because many of these people operate emotionally and facts get thrown out the window."

"So there's no grandiose solution," I said.

"Nope, just a lot of hard work. But I'm somewhat optimistic. There's so much pragmatism to the conservation easement tool. Most ranchers are reasonable people," Kies said. "If they give you a kitchen table chat, you can make an incredible amount of headway."

We had another shot of Tullamore Dew and headed to the Windbag Saloon for burgers. I had an in. Kies was half-owner.

Bugbee and Kiesling, two experienced conservationists with a single message—land saving may be difficult but it is practical, proven, and fair. I've worked with both men for twenty-two years. I agree.

The Montana Land Reliance and the state's other trusts are improving their effectiveness month by month. In time, the clear logic of land saving will be widely understood. I have faith that those working the land will find it. Despite all the growth and lost landscapes, beyond all the intricacies of tax law, bond issues, and politics, there are abundant human reasons for that faith.

The Hilger Hereford Ranch is just one of those reasons.

In 1984, Bruce Bugbee and I were hired by the Montana Land Reliance to prepare an ecological study of this 5,500-acre property on Upper Holter Lake near Helena. The owners were four elderly, unmarried siblings—Bryan, Dan, Susan, and Babe Hilger. The property had been in their family since before Montana was a state.

It was a magnificent ranch covered with a mosaic of cottonwood bottomlands, hay ground, bunchgrass prairies, and conifer forests. Elk, deer, and antelope depended on it. Mountain sheep and goats lived up on the rocky slopes. Mountain lions, coyotes, black bears, and badgers hunted the meadows. Waterfowl covered the lake each spring and fall. The Missouri River passed through—a national class fishery right out the front door.

Nomadic Shoshone, Blackfeet, and Flathead had originally used the place as a hunting and fishing ground. Pictographs and abundant artifacts have been found in the Gates of the Mountains, the Missouri's steep limestone canyon.

In July 1805, Lewis and Clark paddled up the Missouri toward what would become the Hilger Ranch. Through the din of a July hailstorm, Meriwether Lewis watched as the bedrock wall appeared to part like the gates of a fortress as the river entered the ridgelines. Lewis observed:

> The rocks approach the river on both sides forming the most sublime and extraordinary spectacle. We have entered the most remarkable cliffs that we have yet seen. These cliffs rise from the water's edge to the height of 1200 feet. The river appears to have forced its way through this immense body of solid rock for the distance of 5¾ miles. From the singular appearance of this place, I called it The Gates of the Rocky Mountains.

Then Lewis described the vicinity of the future Hilger Hereford Ranch: "Here the perpendicular rocks cease, the hills retire from the river and the valley widens to a greater extent than it has done since we entered the mountains." Lewis also noted a large spring issuing from the ground. This was the site of a homestead cabin built in 1867 by a twenty-year-old immigrant from Luxembourg named Nicholas Hilger.

Hilger ranched the place and thrived. He even found time to serve as a Justice of the Peace in Helena. In 1886, he had a solid steel steamboat built to haul tourists and freight through the canyon. This $4,800 boat, the *Rose of Helena*, was a fifty-five-foot-long sternwheeler built at the Iowa Ironworks in Dubuque. Small by Missouri River standards, the *Rose* drew only sixteen inches of water. She was designed to operate upstream of Fort Benton, the usual head of navigation for what the Indians called "fire canoes."

Tourists flocked to see the Gates of the Mountains on Hilger's boat. He could carry about sixty people at a time. His customers were mostly locals, but he was hired by European tourists, Californians, and on one occasion President William Henry Harrison. But the tour business eventually faded. By 1906, the *Rose* was beached and left to rust. All that remains today is the boiler, whistle, and a few scattered shards of metal.

In 1908, Hauser Dam was built across the Missouri upstream of the Hilger Ranch. This first attempt at an earthen dam broke before it was completed, unleashing a 30-foot-high wall of water. Dan Hilger told me that he, his mother, and the other kids jumped into a buckboard and slapped leather for high ground. They barely escaped. Their house was picked up by the surge and floated out into a large whirling eddy. The structure eventually circled back and was dropped just 100 feet from its foundation. When the Hilgers re-entered the house by rowboat, they found a fencepost sticking through the kitchen floor, a lighted lantern floating in the hall, and a full sugar bowl somehow perched in a wall-mounted candleholder. The Hilgers shrugged, shoved the house over to where it should be, cleaned it up, and moved back in. While the dam was being rebuilt, the family constructed a stone house away from the rising lake.

Nicholas Daniel Hilger, Jr., began operating the ranch in 1904. Everyone just called him "N.D." A herd of 400 cattle was grazed on the property. His children—Bryan, Dan, Susan, and Babe—acquired 640-acre homesteads and purchased land from adjacent ranchers who sold out during the droughts of the late teens and early 1920s. N.D. started the boat tours back up with a vessel called the *Rose of Helena II*. The Depression halted the tours for good. Then even the ranch business got hard.

For one brief stretch, N.D. lost the ranch to the bankers, but the four kids quickly got it back. After N.D. passed away, the Hilgers turned their energy toward the raising of purebred polled Herefords. They were good at it.

They bred superb Benchmark Dams like Hilger Mode Sara and Coppertone Sara F—Herefords capable of producing the finest calves in America. Dozens of their bulls, like Hilger Special 415, became Grand Champions. The Hilgers raised and sold about thirty solid bulls a year. It provided a steady and sufficient living. Ranch debt became a thing of the past.

The property supported three generations of Hilgers. The family had toughed it out through everything imaginable—drought, flood, fire, Depression, and loneliness. And still the land was in superb shape.

This is the way I found it in 1984. Bruce Bugbee and I hiked all over the ranch making lists of plants and animals, studying the geology and soils, taking pictures of the way things were. The Hilgers soon donated a conservation easement to the Montana Land Reliance, then sold the place to a neighbor. A "life estate" was held back so they could live on the ranch until they died. Without heirs of their own, the Hilger family decided to move the operation into trusted, younger hands.

I later spoke with Dan Hilger out in the stone house. It was crowded with ox-yokes, horseshoes, butter churns, farm equipment, photos, and old buggy harnesses—decades of stuff too sentimental to toss and too worn out to sell. It gave the day a scent of history. After my tour, we walked outside. Dan looked over at the dry shoulders of rolling hills:

"The Indians come through up there on what they called the Beartooth Trail; it went past that three-cornered peak [Baldy Mountain]. On the trail, they made a lot of tipi rings and little coulees with travois that dragged behind their horses. Some of them coulees were worn down three or four feet into the soft, shaley rock. You can still see them . . . they'll be there a long time before they wear out."

The Hilgers had left their own mark by keeping the ranch open and productive. In a memoir entitled *Building the Herd*, Bryan Hilger spoke about the choice they made: "We was gettin' too old to do all the ranch work. Dan couldn't help with the cattle. Babe was gettin' too old and I couldn't do it all myself.

"People were coming out of the woodwork," Bryan wrote. "Long-lost, shirt-tail relatives showin' up, letters from interested buyers, real estate agents; everyone wanted to buy the Hilger Ranch. But we didn't want the ranch spoiled. That's why we threw in with the Montana Land Reliance people. The conservation easement guarantees that Hilger land'll never be subdivided . . . and whoever buys the ranch down the line, is still covered by that deal.

"The land across the river ain't under a conservation easement," Bryan said. "There's several houses on it now, and it's gonna get worse; about seventy lots are laid out. They call 'em estates or something."

But that can never happen on the Hilger Ranch. It will produce beef and beauty forever. So will the ranch next door. The 4,620-acre Carrie Hilger Ranch is now also protected by a conservation easement with the Montana Land Reliance.

Today, only Bryan Hilger is still with us. Dan, Susan, and Babe have passed on. But their wishes are still being honored. Drive by the Hilger Hereford Ranch these days and you'll see good grass and thick cow bellies. Eagles fish the waterways. Elk drop down in the winter and find forage and cover. It will always be so.

A family with deep Montana roots faced down the threat of estate taxes and the harsh designs of developers. And they chose another way.

Much obliged.

6

THE REAL RIVER THAT RUNS THROUGH IT

S OMETIMES THERE are stories that challenge your heart, ones where good sense is at risk to nonsense, where the endurance of strong people begins to falter but will not give way. The remote Blackfoot River Valley is a landscape with one of those stories.

It starts out there in the Big World.

Papua New Guinea has always been mapped as big trouble. Headhunters, cannibals, colonialists, and politicians have lived in a constant state of quarreling over territory. Conflicts have usually meant lost land or a sudden shift in food chain position for somebody. My friend, geographer Tom Eley, lived in Papua back in the 1980s and saw evidence of the old ways still being chased up in the highlands. The rainforests of the Bismarck Range carry urgent secrets.

To make matters worse, a shooting war is now taking place in Papua along a border claimed by invading forces from Indonesia. Half of this island country is occupied by a foreign army, and West Papua has been renamed Irian Jaya in most atlases. The Indonesian government demands it. Call yourself a Papuan there and you go to jail or die.

Papua is not a place most of us know. Or if we did, we might not choose to go there. That's why multinational corporations have moved in to mine gold. Nobody's watching. A huge cyanide heap leach gold mine is now contaminating the Ok Tedi and Fly rivers with acids, arsenic, cadmium, and a spoiled sauce of other toxins leaking from mine tailings. The Fly empties into the Torres Straits just north of the tip of Queensland, Australia.

On three occasions in recent years, massive sodium cyanide spills have occurred in Papua's river systems. One of these choked the Ok Tedi's channel with dead fish, crocodiles, and turtles. Another time, during a heavy rain—not uncommon in rainforests—the mine's filtration system failed. Hundreds of tons of contaminated sediments poured into the river. Dead fish were seen 540 miles downstream. A few days later a barge carrying 2,700 two-hundred-pound drums of cyanide overturned in the Fly River estuary. Only 128 barrels were recovered. Two people died from the poison. Salt water crocodiles, barramundi, shrimp, riverine fish, and rare Fly River turtles were killed. The Australian press reported fourteen more human deaths from eating poisoned fish.

Not surprisingly, the fishing villages along Papua's south coast have seen their catch decline. It isn't their fault. Tom Eley lived inside the coastal Kiwai culture for a year. He found that local people had evolved some of the world's most sophisticated systems for conserving marine species. They used closed fishing seasons, size and total catch requirements, restrictions on equipment, sacred ocean sites, and marine tenure regulations to maintain both biological diversity and a full belly. Dugongs (manatees) are the keystone species here, the form of life that must be preserved for the entire marine web to survive. The Papuans have learned this from centuries of fishing life. Dugongs are caught only for special feasts and other ceremonies. Resource greed is considered a significant crime. The Kiwai have seen what happens when more is asked of the water than it can provide.

The Kiwai's stewardship came from long recognition of an unadorned fact—intact, well-managed environments are necessary for personal health and cultural survival. "They think it would be crazy to destroy the fishery and the water," Tom told me. "It would tear apart everything they need and will ever care about." The Ok Tedi mine is now doing exactly that.

Gold and cyanide—the contaminators of worlds.

And in exchange for all this toxicity and imbalance, we get jewelry. Eighty-four percent of the world's production of gold is for decoration.

Papua is just one front of a global rush for gold. When U.S. gold prices were decontrolled in 1976, the market price rose from $35 an ounce to a record high of $875 in just four years. Since then it has hovered in a range of around $300–$500 per ounce, a figure that is more than sufficient to empower the boom. America's production increased from 970,000 ounces in 1980 to 10,587,324 ounces in 1995, a tenfold increase. The use of sodium cyanide has now made it commercially viable to dissolve gold from extremely low-grade deposits. Some mines have no true veins or lodes at all, just a few flecks of gold scattered throughout the fabric of ordinary bedrock. Miners call this "microscopic gold." Some sixty to seventy-five tons of mountain must be mined, crushed, heaped, and spritzed with cyanide to leach out enough gold to make a single wedding ring.

In the Amazon, deforestation is often followed by gold operations. In Brazilian states like Acre and Rondônia, many branches of the Amazon are now so contaminated with cyanide that aquatic species are disappearing before they can be catalogued. Local people who had sustainably harvested fish must turn to canned goods and starchy vegetables raised in the brickish latosols of clearcut landscapes.

In Alaska, USMX is developing a huge cyanide gold mine beside the Yukon River near Galena. The site is located between the north and south units of the Innoko National Wildlife Refuge, one of the U.S. Fish and Wildlife Service's gems in the north. At peak production, 400,000 pounds of sodium cyanide will be floated down the Yukon River on barges each month.

Tom Eley works as a biogeographer near Innoko. Gold mines seem to follow the guy around. "The company shrugs off most environmental concerns," he says. "Their attitude is 'We can do it; it's easy.' But there's a lot of risk and some basic chemistry involved. When you mix cyanide and water you get hydrogen cyanide—that's the stuff they use in gas chambers. And that's if we get lucky and the spill happens in the open air. I've seen what happens when it goes into water; the Fly River showed me that. It doesn't come highly recommended for anything alive."

In Nevada's Carlin Trend, an unprecedented gold rush has ripped open huge expanses in the Tuscarora Mountains region. Over 4,000 mining jobs have been created in the last ten years. Mines with names like Goldstrike, Bullion-Monarch, Bootstrap, and Genesis are now producing 60 percent of all U.S. gold.

It's a bizarre sight—cyanide mist in the aridity of the Great Basin Desert. The Betze Mine alone is expected to suck 85 billion gallons of water from Ice Age aquifers by the turn of the century. The delicate hydrology of the Basin and Range is little known. Many ranchers fear that the creeks, springs, and seeps needed for cattle raising will go dry. The cone of depression from groundwater pumping already measures 350 miles across.

Nearly all of the Carlin Trend's cyanide gold comes from public land. In conformance with the General Mining Law of 1872, this land costs the companies $2.50–$5.00 per acre and no royalties are paid to the taxpayers. Zero. When the minerals are used up, the companies just leave.

The Environmental Protection Agency guesses that there are 557,650 inactive metal mines across the country. These abandoned hard rock holes and active mines have contaminated over 10,000 miles of America's creeks and rivers. The Mineral Policy Center estimates that cleanup would cost between $32 and $71 billion.

Trouble is, most of the companies no longer exist or have gone bankrupt. If EPA Superfund cleanup ever actually occurs, it will be paid for mostly with taxpayers' money. Just one example. In 1992, Galactic Resources, a Canadian corporation, declared bankruptcy and left behind a $105 million cyanide gold cleanup problem high in Colorado's San Juan Mountains. The U.S. taxpayers are paying all the costs.

People certainly seem willing to put up with a lot to wear gold chains.

Despite all this contamination, demand continues to outpace production. We keep buying the stuff. That's why gold mines are consuming more and more of the world's fine places. The Gold Institute reports that even in China—population 1.4 billion—"gold jewelry is the third most important purchase after a color TV and a refrigerator."

The media, which could effectively inform the public about the true costs of cyanide gold, tend to get sidetracked. In the fall of 1995, NBC News *Dateline* ran a two-part series on gold. But for some reason they focused an entire hour of prime time network air on the "under-carating" of gold jewelry. The crisis came down to this: sometimes when you buy 14 carat gold you get only 13.2 carat. That's it. While I suppose this robs people of millions of dollars, jewelry buyers seldom melt down their wedding rings for cash. The value of gold is ultimately a matter of perception and belief. People glide blissfully along never knowing their pendant is a few grains shy. So the "crime" of under-carating seems a bit esoteric compared with the tangible habitat dev-astation from cyanide gold.

I e-mailed *Dateline* and pointed this out. No response. Then I asked them to at least look into the giveaways of federal land to gold mining companies. I told them about the 1872 Mining Law. I told them about the federal sale of patented mining claims—land ownership—to mul-tinational corporations for a farthing. Between 1994 and 1996, the government sold 2,701 acres of Western public lands containing $15.8 billion in minerals for $13,095. I asked *Dateline* to contact Phil Hocker of the Mineral Policy Center in Washington, D.C., for the full story.

I never heard from NBC. Neither did Phil.

It seems to most people, gold is about jewelry. Even as the mining frenzy spreads to more watersheds every day, gold is still about fashion statements and the economics of ornamentation. It gets very simple here: if we didn't buy it, they wouldn't mine it. So why do we?

Partly because people don't know the environmental costs of gold. We're also just enraptured by it. This has been so for a long time. Some of the blame for this bewitching goes to Heinrich "Shady" Schliemann, President Grover Cleveland, and King Tut.

Back in the nineteenth century, the search for Homer's legendary city of Troy kept a posse of scholars, treasure hunters, and other ego-maniacs out of more serious trouble. The *Iliad*'s tale seized the imagi-nation of a young German boy named Heinrich Schliemann. He dreamed of walking where Helen and Agamemnon did, of proving Homer's epic true. As an adult of sorts, Schliemann made archaeology a sideline of his black marketeering, war profiteering, and smuggling. The man elevated falsehood to genius. He was clever enough to raise thousands of marks for repeated expeditions to Turkey, where he dug for Troy. Then he surprised even himself by actually finding the place.

Schliemann gouged through the layer of the Homeric Period (1400 B.C.), destroying as he went. He finally bottomed out at the first incar-nation of Troy. It dated back to 2500 B.C. "Shady" then fanned out, ripping through all nine levels of the city, desperate for artifacts, es-pecially those fashioned from gold. He found plenty, and thousands of pieces were carted off to Germany. There were crowns, beads, bracelets, saucepans, perfume flasks, rings, pins, belts, brooches, earrings, necklaces, vessels, and bowls—all crafted from some of the finest gold ever seen. The discovery of this glowing treasure captured the world's attention. Gold, it was said, was the metal of the enlightened and worldly. Silver was tasteless slag.

Fast forward. In 1893, President Grover Cleveland, influenced by heavy lobbying, moved the country off silver-gold bimetallism and onto the gold standard. Silver prices crashed and have never recovered. Now gold was not just stylish—it secured our currency. The dollar was "as good as gold."

Nineteen twenty-two. The discovery of King Tut's tomb in Egypt: tourists swarmed in by car and camel for one look at all the gilded loot. Cycles of Tut mania have swirled around ever since. The image of golden caskets, birds, cats, bulls, and horses still stirs the imagination. The golden face of the Boy King has graced more magazine covers than Madonna. Lines of Tut-inspired jewelry now fill cases all over the world. I was in London when the Tut road show hit the British Museum. The lines trailed out the wrought-iron gates clear down to Gower Street. I decided to hit a pub and watch rugby.

The story leads everywhere, but one elemental fact pans out— people have a voracious hunger for gold. Green gold, white gold, red gold, gold foil, gold leaf, gold plate, filled gold, gold alloy, gold cloth, gold thread, rolled gold, gold wire, gold lace, gold tooling, mosaic gold, dead gold, Egyptian gold, Assante gold, Roman gold, Etruscan gold, Alaskan gold, Black Hills gold.

Cyanide gold is now its true name. And the Blackfoot River watershed is the next place to be sacrificed to mine it.

"In our family, there was no clear line between religion and fly fishing." That was Norman Maclean's opening to "A River Runs through It," a novella composed to the four-count rhythm of fly fishing. But he cared for much more than trout. The Big Blackfoot was Norman's bone country, his landscape of spirit and blood. In telling his family's story of closeness and loss he figured a way to tell our own.

It started with the water. He was "haunted by water." Over the decades, fly fishing quieted Norman's head and heart. His writing proves he could hear the watershed. The voice without words spoke to him of sensitivities and strengths, of delicate endurances of pine, rock, fish, and belonging—of the right scale of our presence here. "Eventually all things merge into one, and a river runs through it." When Norman

Maclean wrote that clear and perfect sentence, I am certain he heard that voice.

So did the Nez Perce. They called the place Cokalarish, "the river of the road to the buffalo." The Blackfoot was a meat and medicine trail leading to the Great Plains. Tipi rings, projectile points, awls, and other artifacts from many tribes still grace the riversides.

Meriwether Lewis traversed the valley in 1806 on his journey east to reconnoiter with William Clark toward the end of their astounding expedition. Lewis loved the beauty of the Blackfoot, its moose, deer, elk, eagles, and trout. He noted "much sign of beaver in this extensive bottom." He called it one of the most peaceful landscapes of his entire trip.

That would slowly begin to change.

Trapping, homesteading, and logging operations began in the coming decades. Yet it wasn't until 1880, when a robust Irish entrepreneur named Marcus Daly arrived in Butte, that destructive exploitation of the Blackfoot seemed inevitable. Daly worked for a California mining syndicate headed by George Hearst, father of the newspaper magnate William Randolph Hearst. This outside capital would physically and socially transform Montana. And eventually break its heart.

The first property Daly bought was the "Anaconda," a rather bereft silver prospect on "The Hill" in Butte. The silver came to nothing, but by 1882 copper sulfide ore was hauled out which assayed 55 percent pure. Red metal became the principal deal. Daly began ramrodding all over the city and soon assembled the immensely powerful Anaconda Company.

In 1884, the massive Washoe Smelter was built at a new company town east of Butte called Anaconda. Mine acids and heavy metals slunk into the Clark Fork River and were carried as far downstream as the mouth of the Blackfoot River and beyond into Lake Pend Oreille in Idaho. Poisonous fumes from the smelter's gigantic smokestack killed forests over hundreds of square miles. Astonished scientists from Princeton University called the millions of dead trees "grey ghosts."

When Montana gained statehood in 1889, the Anaconda Company demanded that the new Constitution exempt mines from taxation. The voters dutifully obeyed, and the Constitution was ratified by a vote of 26,960 to 2,274. The Company then began to set the ground rules for other details of Montana life. A copper collar began to tighten around our necks. John Gunther wrote that during this long heyday "Montana was the nearest to a 'colony' of any American state."

The Real River That Runs through It

The Anaconda Company began stripping timber from the Black-foot, Big Hole, and Clark Fork drainages for smelter fuel and mine timbers. By 1910, the Anaconda subsidiary—the Montana Improvement Company—owned a million acres of Montana forests and was the state's largest timber producer. The Company's logging headquarters was at Bonner, where the Milltown Dam had been built at the confluence of the Blackfoot and Clark Fork rivers. Heavy metals from the Anaconda smelter flowed downstream and built up in the sediments at the base of the dam. The Clark Fork sometimes ran red and orange through Missoula, a trout stream turned to a caustic ribbon of grunge.

The steep, unstable mountainsides along the Blackfoot River were logged as fast as men could whip crosscut saws through the bases of 400-year-old Douglas firs, western larches, and ponderosa pines. By the 1930s, timber cutting and log drives were taking a toll on the river but the impacts hadn't crested. Norman Maclean crafted another novella, "Logging and Pimping and 'Your Pal, Jim,'" about life in these tough-skinned logging camps. It was mostly about Jim Grierson, "The Bull of the Woods," and about The Company. Maclean wrote: "The lumberjacks were registering their customary complaints about The Company—it owned them body and soul; it owned the state of Montana, the press, the preachers, etc.; the grub was lousy and likewise the wages, which The Company took right back from them anyway by overpricing everything at the commissary . . . all of a sudden I heard him [Grierson] break the quiet: 'Shut up, you incompetent sons of bitches. If it weren't for The Company, you'd all starve to death.'"

The tradition of shutting up and taking what The Company gives you runs deep in Montana.

The log drives eventually gave way when railroad and truck hauling proved necessary to keep up with chainsaw gangs fanning out through the woods. With the Washoe Smelter switched over to coal and other fuels, a sawmill and plywood plant were built at Bonner to process the trees. Hundreds of millions of board feet were cut. Yet, as recently as the 1960s, the forests were still holding their own and the Blackfoot's sediment burden was not extreme.

Mining had been taking place in the drainage since the 1860s, most of it in the Heddleston District upstream of Lincoln. The Mikehorse, Carbonate, Paymaster, and Midnight operations extracted lead, zinc, silver, gold, copper, and molybdenum. In 1919, a concentrating mill was built at Mikehorse Creek and things got serious. During the 1940s, the Anaconda Company sold its Mikehorse holdings to ASARCO, which over the next fifteen years processed 385,000 tons of ore. Heavy metals and toxins mounded up in slag piles and filled runoff containment structures. By the mid-1950s, the Heddleston District was inactive and it seemed that the watershed was off the hook.

But a threshold had been crossed. The upper Blackfoot was now the stuff of miner's lore. In barrooms and boardrooms, a notion crystallized out: there is still a fortune lying unclaimed beneath the overburden. When the time is right, we'll come back and take it.

The passage of stringent clean water laws during the 1960s and 1970s began to make this boast sound hollow. Getting a permit to mine was more trouble now. Things like the National Environmental Policy Act, the Clean Water Act, and Montana's Major Facility Siting Act threatened to make ecological responsibility a required part of doing business.

In 1975, a disastrous washout of a dam on Mikehorse Creek swept 300,000 tons of toxic tailings down the length of the tributary. The plume contained acids and a dozen lethal metals with pretty sounding names: antimony, arsenic, cadmium, chromium, copper, lead, mercury, nickel, selenium, silver, thalium, and zinc. All creatures need most of these in small amounts. But not this much. The toxins poured directly into the Blackfoot River, killing thousands of rainbow, cutthroat, brown, and bull trout. It wasn't just a one-time event. Bacterial action kept these acids and toxic materials mobilized as continuous pollution.

Public support of mining hit rock bottom in Montana. Then it went lower. In 1976, ARCO bought the Anaconda Company and soon shut down all mining and smelting operations in Butte and Anaconda.

It looked like the public was beginning to get it. The most common outcome of hard rock mining appeared to be lost jobs and toxic landscapes. Superfund sites began cropping up like chancre sores wherever the corporate hand of mining had touched.

It seemed there was a chance things would work out differently now. But in the Blackfoot, the threats just kept escalating. By the late 1970s, large portions of the former Anaconda Company forest lands along the Blackfoot had been sold off to the Champion International Corporation. The Connecticut-based outfit drastically increased timber extraction. Clearcutting of excessively steep slopes in tributaries like Gold, Blanchard, and Belmont creeks sent slurries of sediment into

The Real River That Runs through It

the Blackfoot. The 130-mile river system began to choke on mine toxins and clearcut mud.

The trout fishery crashed. The reach below the Mikehorse spill was the worst. Whitefish, squawfish, and sculpin ruled the river all the way down to Lincoln. A friend of mine called this reach "the Cuyahoga water" after the river in Ohio that caught fire back in the sixties. But the legendary Blackfoot troutwater was hurting all over, from Rogers Pass to Bonner.

Despite it all, people kept moving into the valley. Ranchlands and riverside holdings were being split up at a gallop for residential and recreational homesites. It had been this way a while.

Back in 1972, Dr. Arnold Bolle, Dean of the School of Forestry at the University of Montana, made a trip to New York City to save 1,500 acres of subdivided inholdings within the Blackfoot's Lubrecht Experimental Forest. Arnie met with Charles Lindbergh (whose son Land ranched along the Blackfoot), actress Myrna Loy (a native of Helena), and other prominent conservationists. This and other efforts raised the $150,000 needed to buy these vital lands. The sensitive center of Lubrecht, a 28,000-acre ecological treasure, was sheltered forever.

But one-time land-saving efforts wouldn't be nearly enough. Subdivisions were claiming thousands of acres. Even with the new Subdivision and Platting Act, most developments were exempt from Planning Board review. In the Blackfoot the proportion was more like 100 percent. At the same time, pressure by floaters also rose dramatically. On summer Saturdays, rafts were running bumper to bumper through the rapids. The solitude and stillness of the Blackfoot just might disappear.

By the mid-1970s, local ranchers figured they'd seen enough. Over cups of coffee at the Lindbergh Cattle Company, the Lubrecht Forest, the E Bar L, and the Sunset Hill School, a list of choices began to take shape. About all everyone knew was that the valley needed to be saved.

Having the Blackfoot declared a Wild and Scenic River was rejected. No one wanted a heavy federal hand involved. And they certainly didn't want to attract more recreationists. Zoning and other land use regulations were seen as cumbersome, ineffective, and plain awful. Ranchers won't be told how to run their land.

Finally, a thirty-mile corridor from Johnsrud Park upstream to the Scotty Brown Bridge was mapped out for voluntary conservation easement donations. Public use would be dealt with through a separate

Recreation Management Agreement signed by all the main public agencies and private landowners. Access points on ranchlands would remain open as long as people acted responsibly. Signs would be erected listing what that meant. "Walk-In Only" hunting regulations were also set up for much of the central watershed. The State Department of Fish, Wildlife and Parks would enforce all the special restrictions. It was an innovative gamble, and it worked.

At first it was thought that all the conservation easements would be completed in one grand simultaneous closing. The idea was this: each easement would be negotiated, prepared, and held by an escrow agent. When all the properties were assembled, the agent would file them together. Some landowners figured, "I'll only do it when everyone else does." The escrow system would watch everybody's back.

It didn't turn out that way. The easements ended up coming in one at a time.

Edna Brunner went first. In 1974, she and her son Paul rescued a ranch from the hands of Watergate conspirator Herbert Kalmbach, President Nixon's personal attorney. Others soon began ponying up. Bruce Bugbee and I began working a lot in the Blackfoot—studying the nature of things, working with The Nature Conservancy and the Montana Land Reliance people, designing conservation easements, filling in the corridor. We did more than a dozen over the next few years. Each stays with me more as verse than science.

The 5 Star Double R Ranch, 320 acres on Arrastra Creek. Moose and elk country. Active osprey nests along an intermittent stream— you don't often see that. Spring grizzly use, weasels, kestrels, sharp-shinned hawks, harriers, long-eared owls, sieges of great blue herons along the waterlines, golden eagles working the thermals, a single blue berry of queen cup beadlily in the deep, frozen shade. This was Fanny Steele's guest ranch. Fanny was a champion bucking horse rider and an aunt to the four Hilger offspring. She'd been in movies with Rudy Vallee and Monte Montana. Her specialty was standing up on the rump of a galloping horse—looking backward—twirling lassos in both hands. Old movie posters and flyers from sixty-year-old rodeos covered a long splintered table in a tumbledown shed.

The Blackwood Ranch, 386 acres. Glacial ice potholes and curved gravel terraces. Wetland mosaics and rough fescue prairies. Buck-wheat, biscuitroot, and shrubby cinquefoil. Sharptail grouse sightings. Long-billed curlews using downcurved beaks to shunt through wheat-grasses searching for bugs. Bats foraging like swallows through the thickening dusk. The owners, a young couple, would be murdered for no reason at all. Out here among the griz and mountain lions, death came on two legs.

Monture Hereford Ranch, 3,656 acres—Cora Barbour's place. A rare plant: Howell's gumweed (*Grindelia howellii*). Cyndi McAllister found the first colony. I mapped two more. Bobolinks nesting in the meadow grasses. Sandhill cranes too. Goshawks, merlins, northern pygmy owls, red-tailed hawks, and four kinds of teals. Killdeer down by the water. Towhee songs all day. Cora ran the best outfit in the valley.

Landscapes stay with us. So do the people.

Otto Edder and his Salish wife ran a 1,280-acre spread alone. Their equipment was stubborn and their yields average. The developers began circling, carrying hefty checks. The Edders just smiled and gave up a fortune. The small house was filled with the kindest silence I've ever heard. Their pack of ranch dogs pried the screen door open with sharp, intelligent muzzles and walked in wagging their entire bodies with the certainty of well-loved children.

The endangered Blackfoot is full of such land-saving stories. Today, over 10,000 acres are protected by conservation easements in the watershed. The Nature Conservancy, the Montana Land Reliance, and the Five Valleys Land Trust are active in negotiating more. The Recreation Management Agreement has been expanded from annual contracts to a ten-year term. And the Walk-In Hunting regs are working—except for a recent increase in spotlighting and drive-by poaching.

Hank Goetz, who runs the Lubrecht Experimental Forest, calls the whole thing "a rare good marriage of public outfits and private landowners."

Land Lindbergh has lived and ranched in the valley for over thirty years. He simply says, "We were just trying to adjust to the changes that were coming. The whole valley is worth saving, so that's what we decided to try." The Lindbergh Cattle Company ended up donating conservation easements on 763 acres of key lands, including more than three miles of Blackfoot River frontage. One parcel has an osprey nest that the same mated pair used for sixteen years. Land and his wife Susie personally gave another easement on 260 acres beside a nice stretch of riffles and rapids.

By the late 1980s, it seemed that the Blackfoot landscape had turned a corner. Local people had figured out some lasting and fair ways to hold their place together.

But the troutwater was still going bad. The Big Blackfoot Chapter of Trout Unlimited (TU) was formed to figure out why fish numbers were down and help fix it. The state had done plenty of "butt counts"—census tallies—but getting at the exact reasons for the crash was harder and more politically dangerous. In 1988, a fellow named J. Monroe McNaulty gave an unsolicited donation of $4,000 to TU to find out the answer to one question: "Why are there so few fish in the river?" McNaulty had fished the Blackfoot for twenty-eight years and seen the decline from hip-deep in the current. He noticed that "there were few stoneflies left, [and] the caddis population seems to be a sparse one—there is less feed now by far than there was five years ago." McNaulty wrote to Dennis Workman of the State Department of Fish, Wildlife and Parks cataloging the falloff. He told it straight: "I caught and released a single cutthroat trout in the head of the Cottonwood Creek pool and had short strikes from two good sized browns and no other fish. After Labor Day I went fishing alone and walked up river from the old railroad shack about a mile below Cottonwood Creek. I forded below the pool and fished it, using both wet and dry flies. I rested it and tried again with different flies. Not one damn fish."

A five-year $220,000 study of the fishery was begun with funds from the Big Blackfoot Chapter of TU and the state. The Environmental Protection Agency funded a watershed project for the Blackfoot that used remote sensing of satellite images and a Geographic Information System (GIS)—a computer-based form of environmental analysis and mapping. A watershed group called the Blackfoot Challenge Coordinating Committee was set up to address issues such as mining, logging, grazing, and recreation.

The people of the Blackfoot were once again coming together to face things head-on.

Based on results of these studies, new "catch and release" and size regulations were established. The fishery began to come back. By 1991, Don Peters, a fisheries biologist with the state, said, "We're starting to see some nice improvements in numbers of adults and good numbers of larger fish." The number of twelve-inch rainbow trout in some reaches had tripled to 150 per mile. A recovery was under way.

But it wasn't just the new fishing regulations in the main stem: the tributaries were also getting better. Spawning trout had returned to Nevada Creek after cattle were fenced off from the water. Flow agreements were reached on Blanchard Creek and the spawners came back. Culvert barriers were removed on Belmont Creek and trout redds (nests) were being seen for the first time in years. One mile of Rock Creek was restored. Long stretches of Elk Creek were put back together. Over sixty-four miles of the North Fork of the Blackfoot River on national forest land was slated for inclusion in the National Wild and Scenic River system.

The Blackfoot watershed, the catch basin for all we have done, was still alive, still capable of healing given half a chance. We were beginning to pull back, rebuilding the generous margin of nature itself, saving ourselves from a future of certain craziness.

Then cyanide gold changed everything. Cyanide gold allows no such margin.

In the early 1990s, Phelps Dodge, a multinational company with a single-minded view, decided that what the Blackfoot watershed really needed was a massive excavation on the scale of Butte's Berkeley Pit. They proposed to operate a heap leach gold operation on the banks of the river. Its name—the McDonald Mine.

Exploratory pits and test holes have been torn into the headwaters of the Blackfoot upstream of Lincoln. The company's application for a state permit was 9,000 pages long and still managed to be insufficient. The company's position was that the mammoth enterprise would have no impact. That seems a bit fanciful. An Environmental Impact Statement is being prepared to discern the truth. The proposed site is right next door to the disastrous Mikehorse Mine, one of the most perplexing, contaminated, and unresolved of all the state's Superfund sites. The sick mystery is this: the McDonald Mine would be built within view of its toxic outcome.

Cyanide gold in the headwaters. You don't need a hydrologist to know which way the river flows. If you kill the head, the body follows. The mouth of the river is already part of an EPA Superfund site. Residents near the Milltown Dam have been told that 6 million cubic yards of contaminated sediments sit at the bottom of the reservoir. It is estimated that $700 million may be needed to clean it up if a safe way can be found. Fish kills have already occurred whenever the guck is disturbed and swept downstream in the Clark Fork. Tests show that local drinking water has four to ten times more arsenic than is considered "safe." The American Rivers organization has now listed the Blackfoot as one of the country's most threatened waterways.

The long-winded name of the McDonald Mine is the Seven-Up Pete Joint Venture. Phelps Dodge and Canyon Resources Corp. of Colorado would jointly manage what, if allowed, will become the largest gold mine in Montana history. This won't be pick-and-shovel quaintness out here.

The scale of the proposed thing is almost unimaginable. The pit will be 6,000 feet long and 1,200 feet deep, covering almost a square mile. Some 980 million tons of mountainside will be moved. That works out to 10,000 freight trains with each one pulling 100 cars of Blackfoot bedrock. The "deposit" may yield only 0.025 ounce of gold per ton, some of the lowest-grade ore ever mined in Montana. The crushed rock will be heaped into stacks and sprayed with cyanide mist. The gold will seep as an aggressive acid extract to the bottom, where a liner theoretically will keep the caustic broth from leaking into the groundwater before being pumped off for finishing treatment. The gold is then precipitated out and the cyanide reused. The "waste rock" will then be put into two 600-foot-tall mounds flanking the pit.

The mine will be nearly surrounded by the Blackfoot River, the Landers Fork, and Hardscrabble Creek. Floodplains all around. Each year, 15.8 million gallons of acidified groundwater will be pumped to keep the pit dry. Each year, 3.2 million gallons of diesel fuel and 7.6 million gallons of gasoline will be used. Millions of pounds of cyanide will be applied to the land. Phelps Dodge will mine for only fifteen years; then the 400 workers will be fired.

All this will be very profitable for the Seven-Up Pete Joint Venture. By the end, the company expects to extract about 3.7 million ounces of gold. At current prices that would gross the company about $1.5 billion.

Then they will leave.

I ate lunch with Land Lindbergh trying to make sense of this. "Aside from the technical and ecological problems, which stun me, I keep wondering what this will do to the valley forever," he said. I'd never seen Land so baffled by something. Everything else the Blackfoot had ever had to contend with could be worked out through patience and honest good sense. Land is as reasonable as it gets.

He shook his head. "With most changes we felt we could somehow slide things around and work it out. But with this . . ." Land was downcast. "There's no way you have that immense an amount of change, that fast, without having tremendous impacts on everything we care about. It's not going to be just the river but the entire Blackfoot, the way of life in the towns and ranches, the schools, higher taxes, more crime. Most of the workers, you mark my words, will come in from out of state and they'll bring their troubles with them. With a few exceptions, locals here aren't miners; they're ranchers, loggers, and store owners. They're being fooled if they think this thing means jobs for many of them."

Land finished his hamburger and stared out the window of the Old Town Cafe. "It will never be the same," he said softly. "You just can't adjust to this."

But true to one side of Montana's nature, stout opposition has organized against the mine. When the proposal was made, the Clark Fork–Pend Oreille Coalition, TU, and other conservation groups began working on all fronts. Mostly the job was to provide the public with basic information and to make sure the review of the mining plan was competent and professional. There was a chance that good sense would still prevail.

Then, in 1995, Phelps Dodge and other mining companies ambushed reason. With the Republicans in control of Montana's government for the first time in memory, mining lobbyists collaborated with the state legislature and Governor Marc Racicot to gut Montana's clean water laws. Twenty-five years of environmental progress was wiped out in ninety days.

"This was where they lost me for good," says Land Lindbergh. "When they went into the 1995 legislature and got the water quality standards lowered on 100 toxic and carcinogenic substances, they showed their true colors. They just went in and said, 'This is the way we want it, so if you want the jobs, give it to us.' It was ridiculous!"

When the session was over the companies had eased away with extensive rights to pollute Montana's world-famous waterways. The standard for arsenic alone was relaxed by 1,000 percent.

Good things come to those who wait—crap comes quickly.

People across the state read the news in shock. Montana was supposed to be the last best place. The legislature and governor were treating it so it wouldn't last at all.

In 1996, a citizen initiative (I-122) was drafted to counteract what were widely viewed as corrupt shenanigans. At best, the weakening of the clean water laws was seen as a case of full-frontal stupidity.

I-122 would shift *where* water quality standards must be met. For years, samples had always been taken downstream of a point source like a mine. This use of "mixing zones" meant that surface waters could be used by companies to dilute the gunk before testing took place. I-122 would change the point of measurement from the river to the pipe leading out of the mine. While some other complexities were involved, this was basically all the initiative would do.

Governor Marc Racicot immediately lashed out at the public initiative and called it "an unfair, inflexible, and inappropriate way of conducting policy." Critics of the Governor's pro-mining position quickly figured out why he threw a tantrum: much of the McDonald Mine is on state land. The state will receive a 5 percent royalty on all gold taken. That could add up to as much as $75 million. This may also help explain why the Montana Department of Environmental Quality reviewed the cyanide operation and concluded it would have no significant environmental impacts. None.

Gary Buchanan, Co-Chair of Montanans for Clean Water, responded. "All of us would agree that the best place to leave water quality laws is in the hands of the professionals," he said, "but the Legislature and the mining industry opted to take it out of the hands of the professionals and politicize it. The companies who were breaking the laws started writing the laws. I think the laws are much better written by Montanans."

The mining industry quickly raised some $2.5 million for a campaign to crush I-122. The name they chose for their front group was "Montanans for Common Sense Water Laws." Cyanide gold is a stealth industry. These "Montanans" turned out to be out-of-state corporations. In the first six months of the counterattack, 98 percent of all their money came from the mining companies.

The cyanide gold companies had a lot to lose, and they spent like it:

Phelps Dodge: $500,000, McDonald gold mine, Blackfoot River
ASARCO: $150,000, Rock Creek gold mine, Cabinet Wilderness
Golden Sunlight: $100,000, GS gold mine, Jefferson River

The list of mining company contributors was long and their ad campaign was Orwellian. They told Montanans that if I-122 passed, 2,300 mining jobs would be lost. Unsubstantiated and untrue. They implied we wouldn't be allowed to pour a cup of tea down our sinks without

The Real River That Runs through It

a permit. Silly. Pamphlets bore the slogan, "In mining, *every* day is Earth Day." Doublespeak.

There was more.

Industry literature showed a snowcapped mountain range and well-ranched valley with a caption reading, "The most pressing consideration facing the mining industry in the next decade will be the availability of land to explore for new minerals." Terrifying.

The industry's television ads showed a woman taking a drink of water from German Gulch, a stream below a mine—*that's* how clean we keep our mine water. She was later admitted to a hospital for what was described as "an intestinal problem." Really, really dumb.

We were told that the provisions of I-122 were "unmeasurable and extreme." Chemists have had the ability to measure minute amounts of pollution for decades. The State of Montana sat on a report from the Denver EPA office for months showing how I-122 *was* measurable. Extremely unethical.

The companies ran ads with a police chief saying we would be in great danger from crime if I-122 passed. The taxes from the mines would keep us safe. Unprofessional.

In the last two weeks of the November 1996 election campaign, the mining industry spent more on ads against I-122 than any other group or individual spent on any candidate or issue. The word had come down from the boardrooms: "Beat this damn thing no matter how much it costs!" The industry had one intention—to make voting for clean water seem like a thoughtcrime.

Amidst all the turmoil, a long-held dream came true in the Blackfoot. The Plum Creek Timber Company sold 11,730 acres along a 10.4-mile stretch of the Blackfoot to The Nature Conservancy for $18.1 million. Conservationists had been negotiating for the protection of this vital stretch of river for twenty years, back when Champion International owned the land and Ernie Corrick tried his damnedest to make the company do the right thing. At least now the *land* from Johnsrud Park upstream to Ninemile Prairie was safe. The Nature Conservancy then resold the acreage to the Bureau of Land Management with easement-style restrictions to safeguard it.

A brief signing ceremony was held beside the water. Land Lindbergh confided, "I suspect that on my way back up the valley, I will hear the river give a sigh of many thanks and much relief." Governor Marc Racicot attended the celebration, hailing the project as proof of the "civil existence we share here in Montana." Many were stunned that he showed up. Racicot was attempting to claim credit for saving a resource he was condemning to death from cyanide injection.

Montanans for Clean Water, the real citizen group, could muster only about $375,000 to combat the governor's support and the industry's ad blitz. Clean Water's strategy was direct—inform the public of the true record of cyanide gold.

The Zortman-Landusky mine in the Little Rockies near Malta was fined $3 million in 1996 for leaking cyanide and other contaminants into the Milk and Missouri rivers. Despite this fine, the state still approved the company's application for a 126 percent expansion.

The Pony Mine in the Tobacco Root Mountains was leaking cyanide. Livestock had dropped dead from drinking the water. Of the $130,000 cleanup cost, only $10,000 had come from the bankrupt, out-of-state mining company.

In the Sweetgrass Hills, a Minnesota company called E. K. Lehmann and Associates was proposing to mine cyanide gold in land sacred to the Chippewa-Cree nations.

Near Yellowstone National Park, the New World cyanide gold mine was such an environmental threat that the federal government bought out Crown Butte's claims for $65 million. These claims had been staked on public lands for pennies.

The story of the Rock Creek cyanide gold mine under the Cabinet Mountains Wilderness was recounted. As was the litany of problems with the McDonald Mine in the Blackfoot. The public was told how the company had canceled several tours of the site by the press and members of the State Environmental Quality Council. They were reminded of the failed water well tests at the mine: of shutdowns, mechanical breakdowns, and a pipeline blowout. Bill Snoddy, Public Relations Director for the venture, dismissed these problems as "unexpected unpleasantries"—as if a spring shower had fallen on a church picnic.

Geoff Smith, Staff Scientist with the Clark Fork Coalition, spoke out. "The Seven-Up Pete Joint Venture says they can de-water entire aquifers in the Blackfoot without affecting flows in the river and they can spray millions of pounds of cyanide solution annually without having spills," he said. "Yet they can't even run a simple pump test without having spills and major equipment failures."

The nationwide record of Phelps Dodge was publicized. Thirteen of the company's mine sites were being evaluated for inclusion in the "National Priority List" of the Superfund program. At the Chino Mine in New Mexico, the company has had twenty spills of highly acidic, toxic water since 1987. One of these released 180 million gallons into a creekbed. Phelps Dodge seems to view waterways as a conveyance for waste.

Many people believed that given these facts, logic would prevail over empty promises on election day. The straightforward wording of I-122 on the ballot gave even more reason for cautious optimism. The voters would be asked to choose whether they were "FOR" or "AGAINST"

124

> requiring the removal of specific levels of carcinogens, toxins, metals and nutrients prior to dilution or release of mine discharges into state waters.

Then the results came in—57 percent voted "AGAINST" clean water. Around here this passes for wisdom.

Money can buy public opinion. This is widely known. But in Montana, a state with a long history of mining contamination, the result was tragic. It was the ultimate corporate takeover.

Curiously, the voters passed another initiative that banned corporate spending on future citizen measures. It was as if Montanans were saying, "Stop me before I vote stupid again."

Only five counties voted in favor of the Clean Water initiative: Missoula, Sanders, Gallatin, Big Horn, and Roosevelt. Each is being remade by the mining industry. But in my old home of Granite County and Pburg, 71 percent of the voters were against the measure. The ghost dance drums along.

The mining companies had won. They had achieved their goal—lower expectations and raise hell.

Land Lindbergh was Treasurer of Montanans for Clean Water. Two weeks after the election, I headed up the Blackfoot for a visit. He lives near the troubled water on a place with big pines called "The Homestead."

"People feel hopeless," he said. "They don't know how to influence this thing anymore. What is amazing is that the Farm Bureau and the Montana Stockgrower's Association—the folks who need clean water the most—came out against I-122. They tend to resist things out of habit. And their paranoia was that they'd be next in line for some sort of regulation.

"The company told us they'd be good citizens, use the best available technology, run a clean operation," Land said. "Then they screw around in the legislature, run a deceitful ad campaign, and back off

MONTANA GHOST DANCE

from using the best methods they can. The whole thing is about production—about dollars and the short-term view."

Mergansers swam by on the river, working the bank heading upstream.

"When I sort out my priorities between the river, the fish, the beaver I saw this morning, the elk and eagles, the people in the communities that will drop everything and come help you when you're in trouble—when I sort all that out, gold is at the bottom of the list," Land said. "That's just where I draw the line. I can't buy that it's worth the gamble."

The river washes by, cascading over quartzite boulders.

"The irony is the gold's not going anywhere," he said. "I like gold. But Montanans have the right to make sure it's mined responsibly. If the companies can't do that yet—and their record seems to show it— then we have the right to say no. If they can't meet our standards then they shouldn't be here. But time after time we just give our landscapes away."

"Why don't Montanans feel they can stand up to these companies?" I asked.

"You go over to Butte, with all that trouble, and people are proud of getting taken advantage of. I mean they got sick and many of them died. And now they're living with the health and economic consequences. If mining meant long-term prosperity then Butte would be the richest place in the state. Instead, what they've got is consistent hard times and mined-over country. And yet they're proud of it; they still want more mining. Maybe the old-timers figure, 'We've suffered so you have to suffer too.'"

Land leans gently against a Doug fir, staring out over the water.

"Jack, I guess it comes to this. Change is coming in from the outside, we don't want it, it will undo a lot of our conservation work, it will affect our health and ways of life, but that doesn't seem to matter. And in the end, when Phelps Dodge is off mining somewhere else, we will be the ones who have to try and live with the mess they've made. I know that we need mining, that we're going to have mining—we have to have mining. But it doesn't have to leave us with all these problems. The standards don't have to be determined by the mining industry. Those of us living here should have something to say about what we are left with."

Anger and disbelief are what come from this. Sufficient emotions to turn a conservationist back into an environmentalist all over again.

The Real River That Runs through It

I drove slowly down the dirt lane, turned onto Highway 200, and headed upstream toward the mine site near Lincoln, a strung-out little town of 530 souls named for the Great Emancipator. Locals work in the woods or over at the jerky factory or make do with cattle and a couple of side jobs. If the McDonald Mine is allowed, there will be 700 workers during the construction phase, 400 when things settle down. Some local people will actually get hired on. Most will not.

Mining engineers are social engineers. Lincoln will need new schools, police officers, fire stations, and road equipment. Taxes will rise, hunting spots will get crowded, the bars will turn nasty, crime will increase, and doors will get deadbolted. In gold mining towns, the only things that turn out positive are urine tests. Many locals will regret that the mine ever opened, and they will regret it for the rest of their lives.

Out on Stemple Pass Road is Lincoln's main tourist attraction—what is said to be the Unabomber's place. Ted Kaczynski, a former math professor at Berkeley, allegedly engaged in an eighteen-year letter-bombing campaign targeting bioengineers, mathematicians, airline executives, timber industry lobbyists, and others representing the uncontradicted march of modernity. He is charged with murdering three people and injuring several others. The government is deadly serious about the case. No stray Unabomber artifacts lie out in the grouse whortleberry bushes. Even Kaczynski's cabin has been helicoptered away by the FBI as evidence in his prosecution. Bombs, detonators, triggers, and a copy of his rambling 35,000-word "Manifesto" were found inside.

There wasn't much to see, but I lingered, letting the wind work through the trees. Out here in the larches and pines a highly rational person lost his mind. He just couldn't seem to solve the calculus of environmental change. So he lashed out with a serial killer's cowardice and forfeited compassion to rage. Ted Kaczynski's mind broke. It's hard to know all the reasons why. But here in the valley of the shadow of cyanide I guess he feared the evil.

I turned the pickup around and headed back downriver. There was a place I needed to be.

As the truck rolled over the bridge above the Roundup Bar Rapids —the "rock garden" is what we call it—I remembered when Phil O'Connell and I wrapped a Mad River canoe around a submerged block of maroon Belt Rock downstream of here. The canoe stayed there two days before a come-along popped it free, gunwales and thwarts snapped but repairable.

I drove my friend Jim Parsons along this road several times for a look around. A Berkeley geographer for sixty years, Jim helped re-shape our thinking about the pre-Columbian population of the Americas. The numbers he scratched together on the backs of envelopes have stood up. He was a field guy fond of good maps and clear thinking. Parsons traveled the world and wrote about whatever seemed to be "the best story." Usually that meant agriculture, forestry, grazing, and mining—the human role in changing the face of the earth.

"So what should we do about this gold mine?" I once asked him. Maybe he'd part with some arcane secret out of highland Guatemala. Parsons had studied gold operations there back in 1955. I was still drooling onto my jammies in those days.

"Well, just look at the landscape, use maps, and think it through," he said. This was the Parsonian approach. I should have remembered. I will never forget.

Farther on, the Big Blackfoot turned hard against argillite cliffs. Ponderosa pines scented the air vanilla. This is the place I go to feel things out. I've come here when I nearly lost a girlfriend to a heart attack, when I lost my dad to cancer, whenever a hurt gets overwhelming and must be released.

The ripple-marked slab of purplish rock has felt the same for most of Earth's memory. Fresh ripples are being remade three feet away in soft silt at the slowing margins of the channel. The Blackfoot is a place with a billion years of continuity.

I sat down tiredly on the wavy bench of rock and leaned back against the cinnamon-barked trunk of a leaning tree. The Blackfoot rustled by in dark pools and tropical green shallows. I watched an osprey make a try for a trout and miss. The quiet rolled in from everywhere.

A standing wave rose forever across a humpbacked river ledge. The water moved through; the wave form remained. As a boy I watched the ocean in Maine. It was the opposite there. In the sea, the waves pass through; the water abstains.

The thought of the Blackfoot being poisoned brings me here over and over. Hell already has four rivers—Acheron, Cocytus, Phlegethon, and Styx. Why are we making one more? Then a familiar pain told me.

Beyond Montanans' need for work and tough talk is something else—a deep aching secret abuse. Abuse brings a pathology that's hard to shake. Torment and poor treatment are what we believe we deserve. Our rational mind says otherwise, but somewhere the notion persists: hard life is what we have coming; this is all we can expect to ever see. Things will never get better so shut up and take it.

Montana has got this one bad.

Since the first years of this place, mining companies have felched the land and people here. The exploiter's Faustian bargain has been this: "Put up with whatever we want or you'll have nothing—no job, no home, no future. We'll just abandon you." And like terrified children we go along. That is the disordered tradition that makes Montanans vote in favor of self-destructive, dangerous development. It is all we think we deserve.

Mining doesn't have to mean chaos. We're just afraid to say we won't take that kind of treatment anymore. This Third World attitude of dependence allows Montana to be treated like a colonial possession, not a landscape we need. There is a strange and persistent nostalgia for the false glories of an extractionist past in this state. We can't seem to free ourselves from it.

The McDonald Mine is only one ghost dance. In early 1997, a Canadian company, Big Blackfoot Mining Inc., began seeking state and federal approval to explore for minerals a mere ten miles from the McDonald operation. Paul S. White, president of the company, said it simply: "What attracted us to the area was gold." Nothing else—gold. One day, the entire Blackfoot watershed may be dissolved away.

Across the state, Montanans are dancing against reason for other projects, for a return to the bliss of an imagined metallurgical age. One whose earthly ruins surround us, warning how poisonous this path can be.

It's human nature to want simple answers, but here are the real ones:

Developmental extremism will not save Montana.

The economic elitism of corporations will not save Montana.

Rough Rider colonialism and cyanide will not save Montana.

They never have. Making a good life is more complicated and democratic than that.

Karl Wittfogel wrote about hydraulic societies, places where the centralized control of water controls people. Freedom and economic health only come from stewardship, from reclaiming sovereignty and the sound management of water and other resources from those who abuse.

We're writing checks the land can't cash. In our hearts we all know it. The time for deferring to those who do not believe this is well over. I believe one thing completely. The bone-deep courage of Montana people will inevitably prevail—but not until we stop chasing ghosts.

That can be tough. The Blackfoot is both fiction and true terrain. Robert Redford's movie version of *A River Runs through It* wasn't even filmed in the valley. The Blackfoot was too over-mined, over-cut, over-fished, over-recreated, and overlooked to play itself. What you saw was actually filmed hundreds of miles away on five other rivers we have treated with gentler hands.

The real river that runs through it is the tired heart of a true place. It is the decision ground where Montana's twin urges are engaged in something epic.

The wreckage confounds.

The salvation redeems.

I jumped down from the rock, stretched my aging hide, and started walking back to the truck through a dense regrowth of Douglas fir. In a few weeks I'll bring Beth here. We'll cut our Christmas tree. Things will open up a bit for the others.

An old road always leads me back to the water. I paused beside snowberry bushes for one last look. A breeze passes upriver like a low steady breath.

As mist starts to rise around a sharp breaking meander.

The Real River That Runs through It

7

THE CURSE OF CHARLOT

I REMEMBER HEARING the news on the radio. Vince Swann, a Missoula television weather forecaster, was dead at a ridiculously early age. He died of a sudden wracking fever.

Rocky Mountain spotted fever.

A tick bite had done in a good friend. A tick from a canyon in the Bitterroot Mountains. His wife Renee and daughters Bridgett and Michelle watched delirium collapse into coma and silence. He died right there in front of them. Somebody at the ER had sent him home. They said it was probably just the flu.

A few days later we buried him in coarse alluvium next to his favorite water. Rough ropes lowered the unvarnished wooden box into a hand-dug hole. Then we covered him up forever.

The Bitterroot has seldom been easy.

Lewis and Clark camped in the valley at the mouth of Lolo Creek, a place they called "Traveller's Rest," on their way to and from the Pacific. They almost died on their westbound crossing of the Lolo Trail. Only the elk meat and kindness of the Nez Perce saved them. On their way back, Meriwether Lewis traded with the Salish for "a few articles of merchendize" and what William Clark called "ellegant horses." Lewis listened to the Salish talk and concluded that, despite the nation's ardent wish, these people were not descendants of "Prince Madoc and the Welsh Indians." In 1805, the world was still so magical that we actually thought a lost tribe of swarthy Welshmen lived out there just beyond the margins of our cartography.

Meriwether Lewis gave the valley, river, and range their name—the Bitterroot. The word came from a small, pink-flowered plant that grew on wind-swept prairie hillsides. The Latin name is *Lewisia rediviva*. *Lewisia* for Lewis, *rediviva* for the plant's ability to appear reborn after winter's seemingly complete destruction. The Salish and other tribes dug the bulbs from the ground with sharp sticks. The soft inner tissue was used in soups and mashed into meal.

The Bitterroot may be bitter but it has sustained life.

It wasn't until 1841 that Montana was settled by whites intent on more than skinning fur pelts from mammal carcasses. It all started in the Bitterroot. The valley has had a sequence of occupants ever since.

In 1841, Jesuits came to the Bitterroot Valley and established St. Mary's Mission at the far edge of the known world. Two years before, the Salish had sent a delegation to St. Louis to request Black Robes. By the spring of 1842, grain and potatoes were planted by Father Pierre DeSmet and five other priests. About 1,000 Indians were baptized as instant Catholics. In 1845, Father Anthony Ravalli, an Italian missionary, underwent an arduous trek to the Bitterroot. He sailed around Cape Horn to Chile and on to Fort Vancouver. From there Ravalli traveled overland to the Willamette Valley and across the Cascades to the mission. He arrived bearing gristmill stones carted all the way from Belgium. The man was serious. Ravalli was also skilled at medicine, mechanics, art, education, and transmitting his abundant faith.

But it was tough going. Harsh weather, isolation, and conflicts with the Blackfeet and fur trappers forced the fathers to sell the mission to Major John Owen. He promptly renamed it Fort Owen and began trading with anyone who asked. The Salish people returned to hunting, fishing, and digging up starchy bitterroots from the foothills.

In 1854, the Jesuits came back. But instead of reactivating St. Mary's, they established the St. Ignatius Mission up north beneath the maroon peaks of the Mission Range. The fathers urged the Salish to come up and join their kin, the Kootenai. Few accepted the invitation.

Whites coveted the Bitterroot Valley. It had a mild climate, reasonably fertile soils, abundant river and creek water for irrigation, and vast forests of tall trees. The settlers felt that the valley's future should come from homesteading and logging, not from poking around for plants with digging sticks. The federal government decided to parley with the Salish and make a treaty to remove them.

On July 16, 1855, the Hellgate Treaty was sort of worked out. Eighteen chiefs from several nations marked a pact with the United States that handed over ownership to most of western Montana. The Flathead Reservation was established in the Jocko country surrounding the St. Ignatius Mission. In exchange, money, food, equipment, and other aid would be provided to the tribes. Great promises were heard. But not much came and nothing was really over.

Chief Victor of the Bitterroot Salish (part of the larger Flathead Nation) insisted on retaining the entire valley south of Lolo Creek as a reservation. But Articles 9 and 11 of the Hellgate Treaty left it up to the President to determine whether such a reservation was needed. The matter would be "studied." In the interim, whites began rolling in to farm the valley bottoms and benchlands. These settlers from Missouri, Georgia, and the Carolinas soon screamed for the complete removal of the Indians.

In 1871, General James A. Garfield (who later would become President), ordered the Salish to leave. No real assessment of a possible reservation had been made. No teachers, blacksmiths, carpenters, or farmers had been sent to help the tribe as pledged. Garfield simply broke the treaty.

Congress appropriated $50,000 to pay the tribe for their removal and as "reimbursement for their improvements," as if a homeland was appraisable property. The Indians initially refused but were worn down by a lack of options. The never-ending trail of whites could not be stopped. On August 27, 1872, the so-called Garfield Agreement was signed by most of the Salish.

Charlot, son of Victor, the First Chief of the Salish, refused to sign.

His "X" was forged on the document. While many Salish trudged off to the Flathead Reservation, Charlot and 360 of his band remained behind. Indian Agent Peter Ronan offered 160 acres in the reservation to every family that came north. They all said no.

Charlot told Ronan that he wouldn't leave alive: "your Great Father Garfield put my name on a paper which I never signed and the renegade Arlee [made "First Chief" in Charlot's absence] is drawing money to which he has no right. How can I believe you or any white man?"

Government reports would later confirm that Charlot never signed. Despite this, word of the "resolution" of the Bitterroot situation spread and even more whites flooded in to homestead the Salish Land. Charlot's band erected tipis along Lolo Creek and watched the transformation of their world.

In 1877, Chief Joseph and the Nez Perce entered the Bitterroot in flight from the U.S. Cavalry. Charlot offered no aid since the Nez Perce had killed whites. The Salish wanted their land back but had no spirit for war.

In 1884, Charlot traveled to Washington, D.C., to argue with men in suits for the promised Bitterroot reservation. Charlot's actual name was Slem-Hak-Kah ("The Kittle Claw of a Grizzly Bear"). With him were Callup-Squat-She ("Crane with a Ring around Its Neck"), Li-coot-Sim-Hay ("Grizzly Bear Far Away"), Ta-Hetchet ("Hand Shot Off"), Swam-Ach-Ham ("Red Arm"), and Chim-Coo-Swee ("The Man Who Walks Alone").

It was a collision of worlds. This was the time of French Impressionism, gas streetlights, trolley cars, photography, Coca-Cola, and baseball. The Salish felt emplaced in an ancient way that the suits could not comprehend. Instead of providing a Bitterroot homeland, the U.S. government offered each Indian family a 160-acre tract in the Flathead Reservation, a house, two cows, a wagon and harness, seeds, a plow, and food for one year.

Charlot glumly carried the offer home. Only twenty-one families went along. Even though the federal government came through on its promises, most of Charlot's band — some 342 people — decided to stay in the Bitterroot and endure its hardships.

But life along Lolo Creek became unbearable. There was real hunger. Many grew lonely for friends and families. Finally, in 1891, Charlot and what remained of his band rode north onto the Flathead Reservation. The removal was now complete. This was one year *after*

Wounded Knee, the massacre often thought of as the end of Indian resistance.

Not until 1967 would the U.S. Indian Claims Commission acknowledge the wrongful taking of the Bitterroot. The Confederated Salish and Kootenai Tribes accepted a settlement of $4,016,293. The land was valued at 1850s prices. The check came in devalued 1960s dollars. More than a century of anguish was not factored into the equation.

Charlot's story tells a larger tale. Over the course of U.S. expansion, the federal government entered into some 800 treaties with Indian nations. Of these, 430 were never ratified by Congress or even put up for consideration. The nations did not grasp these political intricacies and felt betrayed when words meant nothing. Of the 370 treaties that *were* enacted, significant provisions of every one were violated by the federal government.

As a result, only 4 percent of the United States is now Indian land; 96 percent was taken. Over 90 percent of the Indian people died in this process. Today, the number of Indian people in the country has rebounded to about 4 million. This may be what the population was at the time of Columbus. But the land is gone forever.

Some Indian nations don't believe that.

The Western Shoshones still have a pending claim to much of Nevada and parts of California, Utah, Idaho, and Oregon. The tribe calls this immense country "Newe Sogobia." They never signed the Ruby Valley Treaty, so as they see it, we have been trespassing since 1859. The U.S. Indian Land Claims Commission agrees. They offered a $26 million settlement in 1967. The Western Shoshones rejected it. The case is now in the U.S. Court of Appeals. The tribe wants a $118 million "lease fee" for the past decades of white occupancy. And they want the land back.

Drive through parts of Nevada and you'll see homemade Western Shoshone license plates. A friend of mine attended an international parks conference in Venezuela a few years ago. Western Shoshones traveled there under Newe Sogobia passports. The Caracas customs people shrugged and stamped them.

But back in the Bitterroot, the land is no longer Salish. Charlot left and he left angry. For years, it was as if a painful incantation echoed up and down the valley.

After Garfield's 1872 extraction of the Salish, Bitterroot settlers reported scattered outbreaks of a strange, usually lethal fever. Following Charlot's eviction, things only got worse. By 1901, over 200 cases of fever were being reported each year. The mortality rate was 80–90 percent. In some areas, everyone who suddenly sweated and ached died within six to fourteen days. Locals called the plague by many names: "black fever," "black measles," "spotted fever," and "blue disease." No one knew what caused it. The fever would spike to 107 degrees and plummet into ice shivers. A red mottled rash rose on the arms, chest, and neck. With time it darkened to a blue the color of decay.

People living on the logged-over West Side of the Bitterroot were getting the fever far more often than those on the grassy East Side. Marcus Daly, the archduke of copper, had bought up thousands of acres of West Side timberlands and cut heavily to supply his Butte-Anaconda mining enterprise. Loggers fell in scores to the fever.

Theories abounded on what caused the die-off. Some people wore masks because they thought it was communicable. Others felt it was a kind of malaria from rotting pine needles. Perhaps it was waterborne. Maybe it came from mosquito bites.

In 1907, a researcher named Howard Ricketts saw tick bites on infected people and theorized that the arachnids were transmitting the death. Ricketts was right, but left for Mexico to work on the typhus epidemic before he could isolate the microbe responsible. He died three years later in Mexico City, brought down by the disease he was working to eradicate.

All anybody knew at this point was that the fever came from ticks and was more common on the West Side. So a group of investors from Chicago figured that the valley's future lay on the tick-safe eastern benches. They financed the construction of the "Big Ditch," a sixty-mile-long irrigation canal from Como Lake in the south end of the valley to Florence in the north. Tomorrow's better fate would come from land subdivision and the growing of red, crisp McIntosh apples.

The valley's first fruit trees had been set in the ground back in 1869 by the Bass brothers. The root stock was freighted by stagecoach all the way from Plymouth, Massachusetts. By 1907, apple trees were being planted in huge swaths at the Thousand Acres Orchard east of Corvallis and the Sunset Bench Orchard southeast of Stevensville.

In 1909, the Montana Department of Publicity began aggressively promoting the state nationwide. "Why come to Montana?" they asked. "Some move to get away from drouth or floods or cyclones ... some remember the fortunes that have been realized by the rise in values of land in states which have become settled and wish to get into a new country where the same thing will occur again . . . men with capital know that their money can be put to work more profitably . . . many feel that they could better their condition in a less crowded environment. To all such . . . Montana extends a hearty welcome to the Treasure State—the land of opportunities unequalled." Sounds faintly familiar.

The first rule of Montana land speculation: never mention aridity, cold weather, isolation, or ticks.

The fruit orchards of the Bitterroot were being hyped as the certain path to shining health and gently earned fortune. "Land set aside in fruit or orchards soon doubles in price. Irrigation makes the crop as certain as the rotation of the earth," the state literature bragged. "The industrious horticulturalist can work a few years to take care of the orchard until it produces fruit, and then sit in the shade while the fruit grows and his money comes in . . . [this] is proof that the old times have passed away."

"From a ten-acre tract in the Bitter Root Valley planted to an apple orchard," the state promised, "the investor can secure a livelihood, a life of independence and competence. The apples can never be produced in quantities to glut the market."

The Bitterroot was promoted as the "Garden Spot of Montana," the "Favorite Child of Montana," and the "Home of the McIntosh Apple." Cherries, pears, plums, and Transcendent crabs were also grown, but Macs were the premium ticket.

The Bitterroot apple boom swept over the landscape. By 1910, the Big Ditch was completed all the way to Stevensville where 14,000 acres were split into ten-acre plots and sold to greenhorn Easterners. The land had been bought by the Bitterroot Valley Irrigation Company for $2.50–$15 per acre and resold as apple orchard tracts at $400–$1,000 per acre. The outfit was quickly getting rich.

Architect Frank Lloyd Wright designed the Bitter Root Inn for the fruit speculators. The fine structure was erected six miles north of Stevensville. The apple boomers were not the honyockers, scissorbills, and nesters of the eastern Montana wheat bonanza. These were refined, often wealthy urbanites seeking a rural escape. And they wanted things easy.

The land developers sure made it seem that way. Potential investors were given free rail passage to Missoula. A chauffeured car would then roll them past Charlot's old camp and on to the Bitter Root Inn. Lodgings and the use of a golf course were free. So were the tender steaks garnished with local produce and washed down with French wine. Once you signed on the dotted line, you were driven to your remote patch of sagebrush and dropped off to sober up.

A great rush of investors lunged into the Bitterroot and more than 100,000 acres was quickly platted. Once the Big Ditch water started flowing, apple orchards actually began to rise. The East Side bench-lands were a plausible setting: above the late spring and early fall frosts, west-facing for warmth, modest soils from basin fill sediments. The early yields were excellent, but things soon came crashing down. There wasn't enough water for all the tracts, the soils played out, and the distance to market proved to be extreme. The Bitterroot was unable to compete with Yakima and Wenatchee. Washington apples won out.

In 1918, the Big Ditch Company went bankrupt and its officials fled back to Chicago. Some of the investors were wiped out, others lost expendable capital on a risky adventure, and a few stuck it out. Their names persist along the East Side crossroads.

The apple trees rotted or were cut for firewood. The Bitter Root Inn burned to the ground. Much of the land was turned over to grazing, and knapweed quickly covered the landscape. Once this pink-petaled exotic takes over country, it's pretty much there for good. Evolutionary scientist Alfred Russel Wallace coined the phrase "indefinite departure" for a turn of events that is unlikely to be undone. Knapweed and the law of indefinite departure.

Over on the West Side, it was ticks that were keeping things grim for the settlers of Charlot's homeland. The deaths were increasing. Tick researcher Thomas McClintin died from a bite. Terrified ranchers ran out and killed 3,500 porcupines, skunks, squirrels, and other tick-carrying animals. Nothing changed. In 1921, State Senator Tyler Warden and his wife Carrie died of spotted fever after a May picnic near Charlot's old camp up Lolo Creek. Governor John Toole immediately authorized the establishment of the Rocky Mountain Lab in Hamilton to find a solution. Locals called it the "Tick Lab." A large sign on the front door read "Enter at Your Own Risk!"

A scientist named Roscoe Spencer began studying ticks on dead deer. He found that one infected tick carried enough deadly rickettsia to kill 15,000 guinea pigs. The stuff was so aggressive it could breach unbroken skin and spawn infection. The Bitterroot was found to be the world's vortex for the disease.

Spencer's work lead to the development of a preventive vaccine. Ravalli County school kids were inoculated against Rocky Mountain spotted fever until 1967. Then the shots were stopped because of adverse physical reactions and a strange ebbing away of cases. Fever still came, but it was rare.

The drop-off could have been caused by many things: fewer people working in the woods, greater care taken to do buck naked body searches during the spring tick season. Maybe the vaccine had worked or people were gaining natural resistance as the Salish had. But the timing makes me think of Chief Charlot. It was also 1967 when the taking of the Bitterroot was finally paid for. Maybe at last the curse was lifted.

I first saw the Bitterroot a few years later. People were still leery of canyon hikes when the ticks were feeding. The valley developed its own gyration. If you find a single tick working its eight legs across your body, you'll feel phantom crawlies for days and contort yourself trying to itch away the menace. I once saw a guy drop his pants in broad daylight in downtown Hamilton to inspect the tangles of his crotch. None of the shoppers seemed offended. They all knew it was a tick panic. They'd all been there.

By the 1970s, despite occasional deaths like that of my friend Vince Swann, the most powerful danger wasn't bugs anymore but subdivisions. The Bitterroot Valley has been repeatedly strafed by realtors for most of the twentieth century. Most have been simple brutes and bandits, others creepy, coifed privateers. A few have been responsible folks trying to make tangible lives for people in a place they're willing to share. But all agreed on one thing: the relentless hyping of the Bitterroot was the correct order of things. Despite this, little growth came after the initial apple boom. Ravalli County had 11,666 people in 1910 and 12,241 in 1960.

But the decades were far from benign. Settlement had a biotic price. In 1956, the last Bitterroot Range grizzly was shot. The great bear was gone from 6 million acres of Montana and Idaho wilderness, an area of prime habitat larger than Vermont.

During the 1960s, growth returned when a new generation of lifestyle migrants began foraging for rural homelands. The Bitterroot Valley grew to over 15,000 residents by 1970. Then things really took off and survey crews raked the valley into vast subdivisions. The Environmental Information Center in Helena found that 50,267 acres of

Ravalli County had recently been split up. Apple orchard tracts covered far more. By 1973, you could see the signs of our presence everywhere. The Highway 93 corridor was lined with new houses and businesses. Hidden Valley near Florence, the Threemile country, even Charlo's Heights were rapidly going residential.

The 1909 State of Montana publicity had been prophetic: "As older states have filled up, the pressure of people seeking homes has become great . . . the tide of immigration has set in from both east and west . . . the vacant lands are filling up . . . many large ranches have become too valuable to be used as pasture and have been divided into small tracts and sold."

But most of the newcomers were not wealthy. Most lived in trailers or managed to put together homemade houses. My friend Dave Odell moved up the Bitterroot in those days and built a log house on fifty-six acres next to Smith Creek. He hauled in loads of granite, gneiss, and quartzite in a dented Ford pickup he called "the Bomber." They made a nice foundation. One lower wall was made into a mountain scene using dyed concrete and polychromatic rock.

Lots of hippies, artists, and university students had discovered the still abundant joys of the rural Bitterroot. There was time for hikes, mountain climbs, ski trips, floats, and hot pool soaks at Sleeping Child. There were topless, coed riverside volleyball matches, mass saunas, parties with live bands, and more days of freedom than life usually cares to provide. The ranchers harrumphed and kept baling hay.

Dave Odell held epic gatherings at his log place. When he turned thirty, he threw the "Over the Hill in Margaritaville" bash. Over 200 people showed up. We knew about half of them. Folks were coming in off the street. Dave filled his bathtub with a massive margarita and used a chainsaw to properly blend up the severely alcoholic mixture. I was pretty sure he'd cleaned the porcelain beforehand. We didn't really care.

He met Ms. Right that evening. I met Ms. Right Now.

Dave and I became good friends, watched our relationships with wives and sweethearts ebb and flow, and somewhere along the line decided we were something called Kinte Brothers. Suffice it to say, *Roots* had a big effect on us, but the total story is a bit hazy now. Dave became Odeo Kinte. I was Cosmo Kinte. Over the years we've sort of fallen back on just "Kinte." We use the same name with each other to keep things simple. We're both pretty lucky to still be walking around.

There was a time when Dave was seriously into chainsaws. He

ended up tearing the spinning scalpel teeth of a Stihl right across his shin. The blade augered straight down to bone turning skin, muscles, and ligaments into human hash. His wife Jane tied a rag around the erupting wound and rushed him to the hospital. Two surgeries later he was OK—just a slight limp is all.

Sometime later, we climbed Borah Peak in Idaho's Lost River Range. Borah is 12,662 feet high and straight up. No preambles or foothills—just 6,000 feet of instant vertical. The summit came easy enough but going down we turned brainless. You're supposed to descend a peak side by side so that any rocks kicked loose will fall harmlessly away. Somehow Dave got directly above me or I got below him. All I heard was Kinte yelling "ROCKS!" I turned and saw boulders the size of Orson Welles tumbling at me, gaining acceleration with each increment of gravity. I managed to spin away from the worst of it, but enough of the rockfall impacted to knock me over a cliff. Dave later told me that his first thought was "How am I going to tell his parents I killed him?" But instead, I was able to friction-bounce down thirty feet of escarpment, land on a foot-wide ledge, and scurry out of danger. Below was a quarter-mile of empty air. After a well-deserved case of the adrenal shakes, I hiked back down, leaving bloody handprints all over the limestone ridgeline. We soaked out the weirdness at Challis Hot Springs and laughed all the way back to the Bitterroot listening to reggae music. Zion train is coming our way.

Montana friendships tend to be like that.

In comparison, Ravalli County isn't quite as friendly these days. Its 1997 population had climbed to more than 32,000—a 100 percent rise in less than twenty years. The median cost of a home in the county rose from $61,500 in 1990 to $110,000 in 1996. About 70 percent of local residents can no longer afford to buy an average home. Millionaires have built 7,000-square-foot palaces in sight of hand-to-mouthers bouncing along the East Side Highway in 16-year-old Chevy 4 × 4's. The 1990s boom is driven by wealth.

Growth and change are all anybody seems interested in talking about anymore. During the 1990s, between 1,500 and 2,000 people have moved into the Bitterroot each year. About a third of those are disgruntled folks leaving Missoula's air pollution and traffic jams. Many of the rest are West Coasters. County Planner Tim Schwecke says, "The schools are just getting hammered." Corvallis had 852 students in 1989. By 1996 the school system had 1,270 kids. Predictions show an enrollment of 1,638 in just eight more years.

The Curse of Charlot

During the 1990s, the Bitterroot has seen a land rush on the scale of the apple boom. Even Marcus Daly's 2,600-acre Bitterroot Stock Farm has been subdivided. You can still tour the forty-two-room Georgian Revival mansion, see the Italian marble fireplaces, and walk the spiral staircases. But the land, bought with copper dollars, is now being sold off.

The Bitterroot is seeing phenomenal subdivision activity. New electrical hookups are increasing by 6 percent a year in the county—a doubling time of about a decade. The County Planning Office doesn't have the time or the budget to plan for the long term. It's just a daily grind of moving paperwork and granting permits. "We're definitely behind the eightball," says Schwecke.

The Bitterroot Valley, once a place so lovely that Chief Charlot spent twenty years trying to reclaim it, has now become one of Montana's fastest-growing and most plundered provinces. Route 93 is being rebuilt as a four-lane interstate highway through a nearly continuous swath of development at the valley's heart. A javelin runs through it.

The 1990s boom has turned an apple and dairy farming valley into a cultural melange of isolated ranchers, California trustifarians, unemployed loggers, tick PhDs, Missoula commuters, Second Amendment cranks, and dry fly fishing guides all pushed closer together than they'd prefer.

The valley has always leaned toward redneck, but now the place is taking on water. A militant "Constitutionalist" named Cal Greenup recently got into an armed confrontation with law enforcement over his failure to pay his taxes. Greenup called local officials "stinking, dope-headed fornicating bums." He sizes up his imagined persecutors as "pukeheads." When a helicopter passed near Greenup's ranch the call went out and thirty members of the "Patriot Movement" militia showed up hefting heavy caliber weapons.

The Bitterroot also has a polygamous Mormon town called Pinesdale. These excommunicated LDS followers mostly lead peaceful lives, but some crank out inflammatory rhetoric. Former Pinesdale Mayor Loran Herbert sees gunplay ahead. To him, the government "puts a couple of plants in an area, and they get people stirred up." "Like the Christians and the Muslims, or the Chechnyans against the Russians, or the patriots against the politicians," he says. "They get a conflict going among the people, and then the U.S. troops show up, and then there's slaughter by the thousands and the hundreds of thousands."

Herbert seems convinced all this will come to the Bitterroot. "I think they've probably got a plant or two in the Sheriff's Department and I think maybe they've got someone in the County Commissioner's office. They're taking orders from somewhere else. I see these things coming. I see bloodshed."

Bitterrooters tend to be conspiracy buffs.

Ravalli County Judge Jeff Langston recently received a letter from the North American Militia warning: "We are prepared to defend with our life, our Rights to Life, Liberty and Pursuit of Happiness. We number in the thousands in your area and everywhere else. How many of your agents will be sent home in body bags before you hear the pleas of the people?" Another local judge, Nancy Sabo, has received death threats and been forced to use bodyguards.

Cal Greenup seems almost hungry for a showdown. "If [Ravalli County Sheriff] Jay Printz comes on my property, I will give him one chance. I will turn my back, and he'd better shoot me in the back of my head," Cal advises. "Because if I get back into my house, Jay Printz, you are not going to take me alive. And I will do whatever I have to do to stay alive." He concludes, "The Bible is clear on that. 'There can be no cleansing without blood.'"

In 1996, faced with this and other real threats of violence, Sheriff Printz decided that the prudent thing to do was challenge the Brady gun control law in the U.S. Supreme Court. Printz proudly told the Washington, D.C., media: "I carry those Brady [background check] forms straight from the fax machine to the shredder. Some day, I want to hook 'em up together so they'll go automatically." Around here we call this colorful.

But like most of Montana, despite all the edgy strangeness, and rampant development, the Bitterroot still retains ample reasons for elation. Most of this comes from its robust geology, passionate hydrology, and the work of conservationists holding fast to the stubborn chance that things will come out right.

Not much is subtle about the Bitterroot landscape. The valley is a deep, fault-bound structural basin running north-south for ninety miles. You could fit Massachusetts into the graben. To the west, the thick-necked mass of the Bitterroot Mountains rises 6,000 feet above base level. The range is made up of hardened plumes of granitic magma 50–70 million years old. Geologists call it the Idaho Batholith. This liquid rock blurped up beneath a block of billion-year-old quartzite and argillite laid down when Montana was a shallow tropical sea. These semi-sedimentary strata are called Belt Rocks after the Big Belt Mountains of central Montana. When these strata were forming, the only life on the planet was stinky algal colonies—stromatolites—and rogue self-replicating molecules.

With the emplacement and cooling of immense granite blobs, the overlying stack of rock began to slide eastward along a low angle thrust fault. The bottom of the mass was metamorphosed to mylonite, gneiss, and schist—baked rock—with feldspar and quartz crystals re-aligned into stripes and swirls like vanilla ice cream melting into chocolate sauce.

The traveling heap now has a name: the Sapphire Gravity Slide Block. It traversed the Bitterroot Valley and smashed into the rocks of the Pintlers—folding, faulting, and overthrusting as it went—before running out of tractive force and settling down as the Sapphire Mountains. Sparkling blue and pink gems are found in some of its drainages. The Sapphire Mountains frame the east margin of the Bitterroot Valley.

For the next 65 million years, sediment washed into the lowlands. The East Side's basin-fill deposits are a layered pile of sand and gravel, clay pans from intermittent ponds, and eruptive horizons of volcanic ash. Small seams of lignite coal exist in a few carbon-rich pockets.

Things turned gigantic during the Ice Age. Glaciers formed in the Bitterroots and merged into a 3,000-foot-thick ice cap atop the range. Off and on for 2 million years, ice sheets scoured and flowed down every canyon. There were at least seventeen episodes of glaciation and deglaciation.

A massive continental glacier damned up the ancestral Clark Fork River downstream near present-day Sand Point, Idaho. A lake the size of Erie backed up into western Montana. Geologists call it Glacial Lake Missoula. Water filled the Bitterroot, Clark Fork, and Flathead valleys to a maximum elevation of about 4,400 feet. The future sites of Missoula, Kalispell, and Hamilton were submerged in frigid water turned the color of spoiled milk from glacial rock flour. But the lake didn't just sit there. Every so often the ice dam bobbed up like a cork from the pressure of the rising water and a gargantuan torrent poured westward. The emptying took only about twenty-four hours. This flow was equal to the combined discharge of all the world's rivers combined. Repeated flooding carved the "Channeled Scablands" terrain of eastern Washington, including the Grand Coulee and Dry Falls.

The lake drained and refilled more than three dozen times. You can still see the old lake shorelines on the sides of mountains like Sentinel and Jumbo in Missoula.

In the Bitterroot, the canyon glaciers south of Hamilton advanced onto dry land and built coarse, bouldery moraines. North of Hamilton, the sheets floated out into Lake Missoula. Icebergs calved off and sailed across the valley before grounding on beaches at the base of the Sapphire Mountains.

When the Ice Age quieted down, the glaciers shrank back. Roaring creeks then reworked all the morainal dumps into sorted outwash plains. The Bitterroot River, liberated from its choking load of lake sediment and glacial goo, began downcutting into the valley fill. This created a staircase of terrace scarps down to its present channel.

I've walked the valley scores of times letting myself go adrift in all that time. The Bitterroot reveals its geology without artifice. It's all right there. You just have to squint and the snowdrifts morph into moving ice, creaking and booming through canyons we now call Sweathouse, Tin Cup, Kootenai, Blodgett, Boulder, Bass, and Bear.

On the East Side, you can hike the basin-fill slopes through prairies so fragrant with sagebrush that even your hair gets sacheted with alkaloids. During the summer, the sunny aridity sucks the juice right through your cell walls. If you don't take in water, you faint. But even here, the time of the ice is just a few paces away.

One scorching June day, I hiked up Chaffin Butte hoping for badger sightings. The valley was a mirage of heat columns and for a moment I could imagine the lake. Ice was tacking against an eastern headwind—Bitterroot bergs bleaching white in the Pleistocene sun. I could envision a top-heavy mass rolling over, dumping its cargo of rocks into the murky porridge. I walked all over Chaffin Butte until I found the barest tip of a granite boulder just emerging from thousands of years of burial. A quick thundershower doused us down and more overburden was washed clear. As the sun returned, I sat and watched liberated grains of crow-black mica steaming beneath a freshly rainbowed sky.

Down below, the Bitterroot River was flowing high, roiling away what the ice had brought. In a few weeks, the snowmelt would ease back and the water would clear to full transparency.

Despite Charlot's curse, despite all the land development, irrigation rustling, and apple orchard rip-offs, that boisterous stretch of water

The Curse of Charlot

was still the pulsing liquid heart of a fine valley. Its survival is mostly due to the astonishing quality and quantity of water entering the river from dozens of tributary creeks. Much of the watershed is in the Selway Bitterroot Wilderness. There are no active mines in the drainage. The 2,700-acre Lee Metcalf National Wildlife Refuge near Stevensville also helps. This reserve is named for a wise U.S. Senator who walked the wetlands as a boy. It has thirteen lakes, countless waterfowl, wintering Canada geese, scores of nesting ospreys, and a sacred Salish site where annual singing and drumming keeps the whole place properly aligned.

Conservation easements have tamed the development rush in a few places. This keeps down the sediment load. Wynn Rainbolt and others have protected hundreds of acres along Camas Creek. Otto Teller's 1,280-acre refuge secures riverside lands. Ken Siebel placed an easement on 1,080 acres near Bell Crossing that includes long reaches of river and spring creeks. The 1,750-acre Trinity Ranch at the confluence of the East and West forks of the Bitterroot was salvaged from an aggressive splicing into "twenties" by a new owner who had the spirit to conserve. More easements are being completed each year.

But the perseverance of the Bitterroot River also came from the efforts of people like my friend Dave Odell. Odeo Kinte. Dave can read the cold tiny minds of trout. There is little doubt here. He has an M.S. in Environmental Studies from the University of Montana. He pretty much majored in troutwater. Beyond the books, he has fished wherever it seems worth trying: the Rockies, Alaska, Canada, New Zealand, South America, Belize, Europe, and Tasmania.

Most years Dave spends over 200 days with a fishing rod in his hands. His outfit, Anglers Afloat, makes this addiction affordable. He rows an Avon raft and takes people down the Bitterroot or wherever else they'd like to wet a line.

Stream restoration is Dave's other line of work. As "Stream Solutions," he fixes damaged channels by scouring out choking shrouds of silt, building islands for waterfowl nests, cabling-in cottonwood logs for overhanging trout cover, remaking meanders, and planting willows and grasses. Water repaired by his hands produces more and larger trout within a year. There's something miraculous in that.

But Kinte prefers to keep things down to earth. He's a solid six feet, two inches of Swedish Fu-Manchu and direct thinking. His troutwater tales come from a quarter-century of wet-footed experience.

Dave lives in a tall brown invention built along Mitchell Slough at the core of the valley. With all the aquatic hatches happening out back, the eaves and window casings of the house are often encased in spiderwebs. The Addams Family should be living here.

One fall day I drove up the Bitterroot for some river talk. Dave was going to show me how the river was doing. No one knew more about its history. He began the tour with a stop at the main channel near Bell Crossing. Snow had already claimed most of the world but the beaches were still bare. Cold water slid by burbling toward Missoula.

Dave's got a lot to tell about conserving his home drainage. "The thing that distinguishes the Bitterroot from other rivers is the instability," he said, pointing at the flow. "The Army Corps says it's the most unstable river in the entire Columbia drainage, so constant change is normal. If you happen to find a fishing or swimming hole you like, well, you'd better get out there and enjoy it, 'cause next year it may be gone. In this country you're only one high-water event away from the river shifting a half-mile. Your special spot can turn into a riffle or a back eddy right before your eyes. It's like living next to a glacial stream in Alaska."

We walked along a gravel bar, checking out the chaos. On this day there was a floatable amount of water coursing by in the main channel. It hasn't always been this way. Back in the 1970s, the irrigators took so much water you could easily step across the river during the summer. In dry years, it was two feet wide and two inches deep.

"The dewatering used to be pretty grim along here," Dave remembered. "But the Bitterroot is a funny river," he said with a twinkle returning to his eyes. "Even though they sucked it dry, the groundwater kept coming into the deeper holes. The Bitterroot turned into a chain of ponds with a little trickle between them. The surface of the 'river' sometimes reached 75 degrees on hot afternoons. That temperature would kill a trout. So the fish hung out at the bottom of the pools. I dove down with a thermometer into dozens of them and the bottom water was usually about 55 degrees, perfect. Of course when the river was low you lost a lot of aquatic insects; being less mobile, they tend to die in desiccated gravel. The ponds became the trout's last stand. With nothing else to eat, the big fish ate the little fish, so we had fewer individuals but many of them were humongous."

"Was there any attempt to get in-stream flows reserved?" I asked.

"Fish and Game tried to add in-stream flows about thirty years ago from the Painted Rocks Reservoir up the West Fork," Dave said. "It didn't really work out. The ranchers just took all the water the state released."

"Then you characters decided to revive the whole thing," I said smirking.

"We were troublemakers for sure," he laughed. "My idea was that this middle reach was the bottleneck for the whole river system. This was the limiting factor on the ecological productivity for the entire drainage. We needed water right here!" he said, pointing to the channel emphatically. "And all things being equal . . . the more water, the more aquatic productivity. It's not rocket science."

"With all those variations in flow, the fishery must have gotten pretty erratic," I said.

"You bet," Dave said, tossing a rock into the current. "In those years the Bitterroot fishery was extremely cyclic, just like many other Montana rivers, only more so. The Big Hole—with its rare fluvial grayling—might have been worse. They completely dried it up at Melrose most years. The state spent money to study the Big Hole's problems and proposed building a dam on Pattengail Creek to retain flow for late summer. Problem was, this was going to cost about $15 per acrefoot of water. That was the end of that."

"But here in the Bitterroot, the Painted Rocks Reservoir was already built and paid for," I said.

"Exactly, my Kinte brother!" Dave bellowed. "Lots of water was available at only $1.50 an acre-foot! I mean the answer was right in front of us!"

"So you went after it," I said.

"Right, but there were some uncomfortable realities for locals to face before we got there. Here we were with a massively diverted stream and most of the water wasn't even being used efficiently. A lot of it just flowed down ditches onto knapweed-infested fields or was returned to the river unapplied. It seemed a weak reason to destroy this beautiful, wild, living thing. I had this foreign notion that the Bitterroot was here long before irrigators arrived and that it had the ultimate right to its own water. Basically, the fish and other wildlife had a right not to die.

"But," he continued, "the Bitterroot is what is called an 'overappropriated river'—by the end of summer, there's more water rights than water. TU [Trout Unlimited] was confronting the old consumptive-use doctrine. Use it or lose it. The first water right in time is the most senior and most legally defensible. Then we came along talking in-stream flow. In-stream flow was a communist plot to ag people around here.

"Yet," he said, smiling, "I located some computer runs at the University of Montana that showed that even though the river got dried up, there was no shortage of water—even in drought years! It was just that people were getting greedy and pouring on as much as they could, more than their crops even needed. Some ranchers over on the semi-arid benches were flood-irrigating so heavily they had cattails growing in their fields! They were hurting their own operations! On the West Side, they were diverting entire creeks onto piles of porous gravel and watching it seep away. So greed and hardheadedness was the basic problem, not a lack of water in the drainage."

Dave and the tiny TU chapter were taking on big trouble.

"So how much water was available in Painted Rocks?" I asked.

"Plenty!" Dave boomed. "We did some research and found out that the Fish and Game owned 5,000 acre-feet in Painted Rocks and there was 26,000 acre-feet of unpurchased water just evaporating away up the West Fork—even in years when the river disappeared!"

An "acre-foot" is enough water to cover an acre of ground with a foot of water—about 326,000 gallons.

Dave kept after the story. "We figured that at $1.50 an acre-foot we could save the Bitterroot for ten cents on the dollar compared to the story over on the Big Hole. I charted out decades of river flows and figured that if about 25,000 acre-feet of Painted Rocks water were released just right, we could maintain a minimum flow of 250 cubic feet per second [CFS] at Bell Crossing in 95 percent of the years."

In nineteen out of every twenty years, the river flows would be fine.

"Why Bell?" I asked.

"Because this is the low point," he said, "the bottleneck below the last of a dozen major diversions. With 250 CFS here we were sure to have at least that amount both upstream from flows and downstream from groundwater recharge and returns."

We took a break for a rock skipping contest. Dave won. Never bet on rock skipping with a river guide.

"So how'd you find the money to buy all that water?" I asked. "That's about $37,000 a year."

"I decided to start by stirring up the Conservation District," Dave said, tossing a victory stone across the current. It made eighteen hops. "I put together a slide show of all the outrageous things they allowed to happen to the river. I hit the road with hard evidence. These were the people responsible for issuing what are called 310 Permits for channel modifications. Minor cleanup jobs around headgates were usually exempt from permitting. But some Bitterrooters routinely stretched that to mean driving D-9 Cats upriver, cutting off entire channels, and building 100-yard-long dikes to try and sluice the entire river into their ditches! That's how far they went! Hell, the Conservation District wouldn't even allow the Army Corps into the valley to check things out!"

"What happened?" I asked.

"Nothing," Dave grunted. "Then Ron Marcoux of the State Fish and Game told me what we needed was 'a media event.' So we got six rafts full of government types, biologists, state senators, the press, and went on a float trip. We put in at Woodside where there was still halfway decent flow. Everybody was smiling and catching fish, even this 350-pound guy. Of course I knew that in two hours that poor man would be dragging his boat over dry gravel. It was all kind of a setup."

"How'd it go?" I asked.

"It worked beautifully," he said beaming. "All of a sudden we passed three big irrigation ditches and the river all but disappeared. Poof! We had to yank the boats out. It was grueling work. I thought we were gonna lose the big guy to a coronary. But from that day on even some of the real conservative legislators recognized we could do better."

The Bitterroot is just one stem of the highly dammed Columbia River drainage. During the early 1980s, the Northwest Power Planning Council began evaluating the effects of hydroelectric development on riverine ecosystems. Ron Marcoux saw this as an opportunity and worked with Dave and TU to find the money to buy Painted Rocks water.

Dave remembered that "the feds told the power companies they had to mitigate the impacts of their dams. Back before the big hydro push, bull trout and cutthroats from Lake Pend Oreille in Idaho used to run clear up the Bitterroot to spawn. These were huge, genetically stunning fish that migrated hundreds of miles to and from the lake. That was their ocean. Once the three dams were built at Noxon and Thompson Falls, the migrations stopped. So we decided that 'off-site mitigation' money could be used to buy Painted Rocks water and undo some of their damage to the regional river system."

After some initial shrieks from Bitterroot irrigators, that's what happened. A total of 25,000 acre-feet of water from Painted Rocks was purchased. The State Department of Fish, Wildlife and Parks used off-site mitigation funds to buy 10,000 acre-feet of it. The irrigators bought some. Landowners like Ken Siebel, Huey Lewis, and Charles Schwabb bought a share to make sure their river frontage stayed wet. Dave Odell bought 200 acre-feet for the fish.

"It felt pretty good to help out in such a basic way," Dave said. But it's a complicated system.

"Everybody's water is turned loose together," he explained. "Our notion was that enough would stay in the channel to do some good. The water gets released in increments. Some on August 1st. Then some more in the middle of the month. It varies. Whatever a particular flow year demands."

"Who enforces it?" I wondered.

"One key part of the system is the river commissioner," Dave said. "He drives around and makes sure that nobody is poaching water. One year Fish and Game even put measuring gauges in every ditch mouth to keep people honest. This sent shudders through the old irrigators. After decades of rustling water, they figured they'd had it now.

"But it's running incredibly smooth," Dave said. "Enough water is on the fields and in the river. With the added flows, the river's doing much better." Dave smiled at the thought.

"In what ways?" I asked.

"I've noticed that since we got the Painted Rocks water, the number of geese and ducks have increased tenfold, the fish have improved in size and numbers, and the ospreys have made a dramatic recovery. The more of the river channel that stays soaked—we call that the 'wetted perimeter'—the better the entire riparian ecosystem does." Dave holds out his hands like he's carrying something. "We've got a bigger aquarium now, more habitat. Sunlight feeds the algae, insects eat the algae, trout eat insects, and we, the apex predators, catch the fish.

"Of course, then we release them," Dave laughed.

"How much of the river has catch and release regulations?" I asked.

"About half of it: Darby to Como, Tucker Crossing to Florence," he said.

"Is that new?"

Dave grew serious again. "When I first came here, the fishing regs said that each angler could catch and kill ten trout or ten pounds of trout *each day!* I mean you could fill up a gunnysack full of trout, throw

The Curse of Charlot

them in your freezer, go back the next morning and do it again. But the saving grace was that not nearly as many people fished back then. Fly fishing hadn't gotten cool, so bait dunkers and lure danglers were pretty much it. So even with all the problems, the fishing was pretty good—when we had a wet summer. In dry years, the trout got hammered in those shrinking pools. Some of these potholes were no bigger than a hot tub. You could dump bait right on a trout's head. Hell, you could name each fish if you felt like it.

"Catch and release has really helped," he continued. "But not everybody was in favor of it. I remember when we went to a Fish and Game Commission meeting to argue for the Darby to Como stretch. They hadn't even been considering the issue but we talked them into it. Back in Darby, one guy heard the news and went nuts! This character was a classic fish hog—he absolutely loved to kill the troutero. Rumor was he got caught dynamiting the river to protest the new regs! So the state backed off a little and reopened the Darby Bridge to catch and kill.

"But overall, folks are pretty used to using small-barbed hooks and not TNT," Dave said wryly.

Those explosions were nothing compared to what Bitterrooters felt on June 24, 1992. A summer rainstorm hit the Overwhich Creek watershed up the West Fork of the river. An inch of rain fell in one hour onto Bitterroot National Forest slopes that had been extensively logged, roaded, and burned off. The land couldn't take it. A 250,000-cubic-yard slurry of mud, boulders, slash, trees, and road culverts charged down several small tributaries and buried four miles of Overwhich Creek. That's equal to 28,000 dump-truck loads of gunk. Thousands of trout were buried like Pompeii in Vesuvian ash.

A few days later, Dave and I gave a tour of the devastation to a reporting team from the *McNeil-Lehrer Newshour*. Prior to the disaster, Overwhich averaged 1,500 fish per mile, including rare bull trout spawners. When the mountainsides came down, about 10,000 fish in the creek and the West Fork were smothered to death.

McNeil-Lehrer got their footage: Dave looking in vain for trout and aquatic insects, the wreckage-strewn quicksand stream channel, Painted Rocks Reservoir turned into a huge mud puddle. Then they left. We never heard whether they aired anything.

The Bitterroot National Forest issued its official explanation in a press release. The debris flows were not caused by any flaws in its management, the agency said, but were a natural disaster made worse by "last October's fire."

Dave Odell calls the coverup "horse pucky."

He remembered the story as we continued our walk beside the Bitterroot. "Here you had very fragile lands that the Forest Service had either clearcut, roaded, skidded, dragged, or burned," he said angrily. "When the rains hit, the culverts clogged and everything came down like a wall of chunky cement. Little streams were ripped fifteen feet down into solid bedrock. Twisted culverts were hanging twenty feet up in trees. I had only seen this kind of demolition in the Cascades before this. Now it was in Montana."

When it comes to forest management, comparisons with the Cascades are not what you're after.

"Painted Rocks didn't trap the sediments as we'd hoped," Dave said. "Cold mud flowed right through the lake and reached the outlet at the dam; then the stuff just charged downstream. The West Fork of the Bitterroot got so funky you couldn't see two inches into it. This was a stream that always had four to ten feet of visibility. The entire Bitterroot, famous for its gin-clear water, ran muddy all the way to Missoula—seventy-five miles downstream!"

The Painted Rocks water, the vital discharge that saved the river, was now at risk.

"I got angry!" Dave shouted. "Here we were doing everything in our power, spending years of our lives doing sensible things to bring the Bitterroot back to its full potential, and the Forest Service let this happen!

"At first, I thought that something good would come of it," he said, calming a bit. "Maybe the agency would realize that you can't over-road and over-cut steep, unstable country. But unfortunately, they had the opposite reaction—denial. They called it an 'Act of God.'

"Right after this catastrophe," Dave remembered, "the Forest Service sent out people to find anywhere in the region where some dirt had moved. And they found it—a small slump over in Idaho someplace in an area that had not been logged.

"They felt like they were off the hook," he said disgustedly. "But in Overwhich, the slopes only came down where the forests had been cut and nothing was left to bind the soils together. None of the adjacent unlogged slopes failed. It's pretty obvious what happened up there."

Mountainsides collapsing is pretty strong evidence of failed forestry.

"Have things recovered?" I wondered.

"Overwhich was trashed," he said. "It took two to three years for the West Fork to come back. Even the realtors trying to sell trout

The Curse of Charlot

cabins suddenly sounded like environmentalists. But with so many healthy side streams, the mud has been fairly well washed away now. If a stream dies, its tributaries will eventually breathe life back into it. We got lucky: the Painted Rocks water is now back to what it was.

"What really concerns me," Dave said soberly, "is the long-term picture. Rivers can heal if we give them a chance; the Bitterroot proves that. Give them enough water and sensible fishing regs, and Nature will restore herself.

"Yet how much logging and roading can happen before occasional events like Overwhich become common?" he asked. "How long before we get a constant succession of slides and mudflows like over in the Olympic Peninsula and the Cascades? When that happens, a watershed unravels and it takes hundreds of years to recover. That's if we left it alone, which of course we wouldn't. I mean, people are dying in Oregon from debris flows in logged-over landscapes. Yet they still call these 'Acts of God.' Not a lot of sense in that.

"They can log in the Bitterroots if they use a little common sense," he continued. "We all use wood. But in places it's gotten out of control."

How can we tell when we've cut too much? Dave closed with a simple reminder. "All we have to do is listen to the river."

We walked back to the Bell Crossing Bridge. A stream gauging station was on the other bank. It had an electronic relay system that continuously broadcast the flow of the Bitterroot to state biologists down in Missoula. People were listening now.

More than a century ago, John Wesley Powell set up the country's first gauging instruments on Embudo Creek where it spills into the Rio Grande north of Santa Fe. Powell knew both sides of the Western coin—aridity and high water. And the necessity of recording and remembering both.

When Mark Twain visited Missoula in 1895, he walked out for a look at the Bitterroot River. He was completely fond of rivers. "You cannot tame that lawless stream," he once said of the Mississippi. "You cannot save a bank that it has sentenced." The unstable Bitterroot raised no contradictions for the man.

Rivers are about endurance and equity. If we are fair, they survive. If we are not, we get stranded—shipwrecked on the banks of nothing.

Dave and I jumped into the truck and soon we were back at his house beside Mitchell Slough. Dave went inside and I stood looking up at St. Mary's Peak. The feds want to reintroduce grizzly bears into those deep mountains. Biologists say the range could eventually support 200–400 of the great ones. Some of the locals are damned aggravated about the plan.

But I figure it this way. We should return griz because we messed up badly. Because we owe it to the natural world to restore what we have damaged—land and water. Griz belong up in those mountains digging for roots, scarfing huckleberries, and chowing down on carrion. It's wilderness, and common sense tells you that the bears have a basic right to their home. We'd all wish to be treated with that sort of fairness and respect.

People are plenty scared of bears and that's good. Wilderness ought to have an element of risk. Keeps the heart and lungs tuned up. Granted, being devoured whole is a pretty cringeworthy way to die. But it's awfully uncommon.

I watched a banner cloud trail off the summit of St. Mary's. On Easter Sunday, people hike up there for Mass.

Taken whole, the Bitterroot seems to have three simple, interwoven needs: troutwater in the river, wildness in the mountains, and well-managed forests. Sounds proper.

Maybe even Charlot would agree.

Dave and his daughter Ellyn walked outside. We played three games of "Kinte" at a basketball hoop hung from the garage. It was our version of "Horse." Ellyn was only twelve but already stood five feet, seven inches tall. Strong "Scandahouvian" genes. In a few years, she'd be posting up and schooling us with baseline moves. But for now, we each won a game.

We fired up the barbecue and laid huge onion-burgers on to cook. All this talk of troutwater made Dave antsy to try his hand on the slough. Downstream he'd restored a mile of this spring creek on Huey Lewis's place. Here on the homewater, he'd made overhangs and brought back the meanders. Some of the browns were now reaching twenty-five inches. Hall of Famers.

Dave used a dry fly—a small dun—that he'd tied himself. He used a barely barbed hook. The rod was waved a few times to stretch out the line. Then he made his cast with a smooth and practiced touch. The fly landed softly on a gentle curve of downflow at the margin of a promising riffle.

Ellyn and I watched. The whitetail deer feeding on the marsh grass relaxed, their shoulders calm and sure. It was just Dave fishing again.

Suddenly Kinte got a strike and quickly raised the bending rod overhead to set the hook. A minute later the trout was played up into the shallows. Ellyn and I walked over for a look.

It was a twenty-inch brown, mottled with spots and slick as oil. Dave gently stroked the sides of the fish to calm it down.

"A real beauty," he said smiling at his daughter. "But we'll let it go so you can catch it next year."

Dave eased the hook out and turned the fish upstream to fill its gills. Then he released the trout back into water as clear as newborn light.

8

THE CHURCH LADY
IN PARADISE

IN THE SUMMER of 1988, Yellowstone National Park caught fire and America went kind of loopy.

Lightning strikes and human carelessness sent massive fire fronts roasting across the Yellowstone Plateau. Each night for weeks the press updated how many acres had been "destroyed" or "lost" to the burns. We were told the park was "ruined." Even Tom Brokaw, who owns a nearby ranch and might have known better, duly reported the conventional wisdom of death.

I conned my way into Yellowstone while the fires were still uncontained. Two cameras slung around my neck and a quickly flashed video rental card got me past the security post. I stopped at Madison Junction. The National Guard had erected a tent city where the fine waters of the Madison and Firehole swirl together. Hundreds of troops carrying shovels and Pulaskis were being loaded onto trucks and driven off to the fire lines.

"What's your mission up here?" I asked one brushcut.

"Aw, we're just moving dirt," he said eyeing my cameras. "What paper you from?"

"The *Brushy Fork Prevaricator*," I slurred back quickly.

He stared blankly but was a nice kid.

I kept talking. "So what do they tell you about the fires?" My notebook and pen seemed to reassure him I wasn't a complete loon.

"We're told that the park's being hurt and we need to help stop it," he said earnestly. "But I don't know with all the smoke how anybody could really tell what's goin' on."

This young National Guardsman had scooped the networks. Indeed, with all the smoke how can anybody tell?

"Say, will you take my picture for your paper?" he asked cheerfully. "I'll give you my address and you can send me a copy when it comes out!"

I felt like a duck turd. Rather than burst his youth, I took several shots and accurately wrote down all the information I would never use. Tim from Casper, I'm sorry.

The next spring, I went to the Greater Yellowstone Coalition's annual meeting at the Old Faithful Lodge next to the priapic geyser. By now the real story of the fires had been resolved.

Instead of most of the 2.2-million-acre park being "destroyed," it turned out that about 1.4 million acres had experienced some fire. A few stands were incinerated down to volcanic ash, but most burned in a mosaic of intensities. Many areas felt only light ground fires. Driving through the park, I photographed broad terrains with only scattered blackened spots. The 1.4-million-acre figure came from drawing the boundaries of "burns" rather generously.

Despite all the hysteria, Yellowstone lost relatively few animals: 246 elk (of a total population of 32,000), 32 deer (of 2,000), 9 bison (of 3,000), and zero bears. Griz, coyotes, ravens, and eagles quickly devoured the carcasses in an impressive display of what biologists call "hyperphagia"—porking out. Ferruginous hawks were seen moving from smoke to smoke nailing rodents fleeing the scorch.

After the snows came, hundreds of elk died from a lack of food in winter range habitats. Elk populations were at record highs and the range had become overgrazed. The fires just speeded up an inevitable dieback. Within just five years after the burn, the elk would return to their former numbers.

And of course, lost in all this reported gloom was an obvious fact: geysers, waterfalls, rivers, and mountains are pretty much fireproof.

The forests and grasslands of Yellowstone were destined to burn. Lodgepole pine dominates the park. It has closed cones—serotinous cones—which only open and shed their seed after a fire has burned through. Therefore, lodgepole pine is a fire-dependent species. No fire, no reproduction.

Fossil pollen grains and charcoal samples from Yellowstone Lake show that fires on the scale of 1988 have occurred every 130–400 years since the end of the Ice Age: 10,000 years of natural fire. Burning is the truth. Decades of fire suppression and pine beetle kills had created artificially high fuel loads. Two years of drought cooked these fuels to tinder. Then the ignitions came.

Over $126 million was spent fighting the Yellowstone fires. Some 9,500 firefighters and 4,200 military personnel were involved. There really was no way to stop the conflagrations. The onset of fall finally did the job.

Ultimately, fighting fires in Yellowstone is like asking rivers not to flood. Of course we do that too, with about equal success. There is a prime lesson here. Without fire, Yellowstone's forests die. Decomposition is too slow in the dry, cold climate to keep nutrients cycling throughout the park's ecosystems. Fire kills so that life may proceed.

The park is dead, long live the park.

Tom Brokaw was the keynote speaker of the meeting at Old Faithful. He took some heat on the media's mishandling of the story. "Well at least we ended up getting it right," he concluded.

True enough. Science eventually won out over superstition. John Varley, Chief of Research at Yellowstone, put it bluntly: "Nature does not destroy herself." Park Superintendent Bob Barbee told the media: "I'm not trying to celebrate the fires, but people over the years will be able to watch the forest and recognize that the fires were a classic event . . . scenery doesn't have to be greenery."

The press now stampeded all over each other to say how perfect and good the fires were. They were over-reacting again. Fire is a force of nature; it is neither good nor bad.

Today, roadside exhibits have been erected in the park to explain the role of fire in natural ecosystems. Uncounted billions of pine seedlings now mantle the ground. Wildlife populations have rebounded. Yet there are still those who argue that fires should be put out in the park.

Senator Malcolm Wallop of Wyoming has scolded the National Park Service for its handling of the 1988 fire. He predicted economic ruin for the portal towns that cater to tourists. Instead, the flames have caused a boom. Visitation in Yellowstone has increased by more than a third since 1988, to 3 million people a year. The same thing happened at Mt. St. Helens after it exploded.

While the Yellowstone fires have gotten a lot of press, the genuine threats to the park receive far less notice.

In 1872, Yellowstone was set aside as the world's first national park. Ferdinand Hayden's scientific party traversed the plateau studying the geysers, mud pots, cataracts, and wildlife. Hayden wrote, "we pass with rapid transition from one remarkable vision to another." The establishment of the park displayed the most stunning vision.

But Yellowstone Park was mapped out when the surrounding terrain was unsettled by whites, when the land was open. Today things are closing in.

The park is just the core of a 28,000-square-mile region conservationists call the Greater Yellowstone Ecosystem (GYE). From the Crazy Mountains on the north to the Wind River Range on the south, the GYE embraces some of America's last remnants of the wild world. The ecosystem includes portions of three states (Montana, Wyoming, and Idaho) and the jurisdictions of twenty-eight public agencies. The Greater Yellowstone Coalition, based in Bozeman, has been established to defend this remarkable treasure.

The Greater Yellowstone is home to a spectacular assemblage of species: 316 birds, 94 mammals, 24 reptiles and amphibians, 22 fish, and an uncountable diversity of invertebrates—including 128 flavors of butterflies. Nineteen animals are very rare. Six of them are officially "endangered": bald eagle, peregrine falcon, whooping crane, gray wolf, black-footed ferret, and the Kendall Warm Springs dace. In the spring, wildflowers fill our eyes with complete beauty. Some 1,700 vascular plants grow in the GYE: 120 are rare; 16 are being considered for listing as endangered species. And there is water and beauty enough to quench our thirsty souls.

Problem is, wildlife ranges, river basins, and the patterns of plants, rocks, and climate resist administrative mandates. Political and ecological boundaries are not the same. As a result, America's first national park, the essential core of the Greater Yellowstone, is now an island under siege. Fire will not harm Yellowstone. Ten years after the big burn, the forests are regenerating, the troutwater is refreshed, and the wildlife are busily procreating. What will harm the park is happening on its edges—places that conservation biologists call "buffer zones," "corridors," and "linkages." Yellowstone is wider than it seems, and the external threats to the park extend in every direction.

To the west, the Targhee National Forest has clearcut hundreds of thousands of acres. The cutover border of Yellowstone can be seen from space. To the south, the Falls River Dam proposal, a Jackson Hole housing boom, and oil and gas development. To the east, more hydrocarbons and hard rock mines. To the north, geothermal development and land subdivisions. Some 12,000 active or inactive mining claims exist in the Greater Yellowstone. Over 7,500 miles of logging roads exist within the region's national forests.

The Greater Yellowstone Coalition and other conservation groups have kept track and have had some success dealing with the threats. The Clarks Fork of the Yellowstone has now been secured as a Wild and Scenic River. Some Forest Service timber sales have been redesigned. A few developments have been scaled back. The Jackson Hole Land Trust has protected over 8,000 acres from subdivision. Progress is being made on many fronts. But the problems just keep coming, and conservationists can never rest easy.

Bison who wander from the park into Montana are being shot by the Montana Department of Fish, Wildlife and Parks. About 10–15 percent of Yellowstone's bison are thought to carry brucellosis—a bacterial disease that causes sterility and abortions in cattle. During the winter of 1996–1997, over 1,000 bison were killed as they strayed out of the park. That's more than one-third of the total herd. Wildlife management may be needed to control their numbers, but bison are being shot out of fear. Montana is a certified "brucellosis-free" state. Naturally, the ranchers want to protect that crucial status. However, no cases of bison-cattle transmission have ever been documented. Elk and deer also carry the same disease. Strangely, ag people tolerate the presence of big game herds just fine. Maybe the ranchers are really scared of the unintentional creation of little baby beefalos. In any case, a national boycott of Montana has been launched by animal rights advocates because of this senseless slaughter.

Grizzly bear numbers in the Greater Yellowstone are holding semisteady at about 200. Today only 1,000 griz roam in all the lower forty-eight states. In the early 1800s, there were about 100,000. The great bear is a federally threatened species, and the Yellowstone Ecosystem is one of its last refuges. Available habitat is shrinking. About 60 percent of it is found on national forest lands where significant acreage is being logged, mined, or explored for oil and gas. Although "cub explosions" happen (fifty-seven were born in 1990), human-caused mortality is sometimes high. In that same year, nine adult females were killed, four by hunters in Wyoming. Griz survival seems likely, but the numbers are no cause for complacency. Development continues to erode prime bear habitat each year. Grizzly bear biologist Frank Craighead says, "Somewhere we must draw the line." The lands around the park seem the best place to start.

Gray wolves were extirpated—made locally extinct—from Yellowstone in 1927. The federal policy of extermination by paid "wolfers" caused more than 100,000 American wolves to be poisoned, trapped, or shot between 1883 and 1942. After the bison and elk were cleared away, Western rangelands were stocked with heavy, slow-moving, dehorned cattle. The wolves began eating what we put in front of them, and their numbers exploded. This set up the slaughter and created a genetic predisposition in Westerners to hate, fear, and shoot wolves.

No cases of wolves attacking people have been documented. Unlike us, they don't seem to hold a grudge.

For years, conservationists argued that wolves belonged back in Yellowstone, that they were the missing piece of the ecological puzzle—a large efficient predator. In their absence, elk, deer, and bison numbers had grown unnaturally high. Genetic resources were being compromised. The prime directive of national park management, the conservation of intact biological communities, was being violated. Yellowstone is a World Biosphere Reserve. So it seemed sensible to find a way to reintroduce the gray wolf.

Many people disagreed.

Hank Fischer's excellent book, *Wolf Wars*, tells the tale from the inside. Hank works for the Defenders of Wildlife and has set up successful grizzly bear management systems in Montana. The key to making peace with the ranchers was paying them for any cattle killed by bears.

The main opponents to wolf reintroduction were also ranchers and farmers. Ag operators in the Greater Yellowstone were told that in Canada, with 50,000 wolves, livestock losses to predation average less

than one cow per thousand. The ranchers sued to stop the reintroduction anyway.

In *Wolf Wars*, Hank describes what happened at a pivotal court hearing in Montana: "The Farm Bureau presented five witnesses—all
ranchers. Although they were sincere, forthright people who elicited
sympathy from the judge, they presented only fears, not facts. I wonder if they realized that the Farm Bureau had paid more money in legal
fees in this lawsuit than Defenders had spent compensating Montana
ranchers for grizzly predation over the past seven years?"

The final obstacle to getting the wolves back was the establishment
of a Wolf Compensation Fund. Ranchers would not lose one cent to
wolf predation. No solid arguments were left.

On March 21, 1995, the National Park Service released fourteen
Canadian gray wolves into Yellowstone. Howls echoed across the Lamar Valley for the first time in sixty-eight years. The Lamar pack began killing elk and deer, fending for themselves in an environment
evolved with the cyclical motions of predator and prey. The wolves
were adapting, making a home. But the reintroduction drama was far
from over.

In 1995, Red Lodge resident Chad McKittrick was convicted of
knowingly killing a large male wolf. The female mate—known as #9
(or "Murphy Brown" to biologists)—soon had a litter of eight pups to
raise alone. This was an impossible burden. Biologists brought in
road-killed deer as food.

"No one declared a truce in the wolf wars," Hank Fischer wrote,
"even after the wolves had returned to Yellowstone and central Idaho.
In fact, the battle grew shriller than ever. The Wyoming legislature,
dominated by agricultural interests, welcomed the wolves with a $500
bounty for anyone who managed to shoot one straying outside the
park boundaries. The governor vetoed the bounty but not the senti-
ment behind it. Montana's legislature responded with a resolution
calling for the government to stock New York's Central Park with
wolves. Idaho's new governor threatened to call out the National
Guard to drive the wolves from his state."

Hank gets to the bottom line: "Bringing wolves back to Yellowstone
certainly shows our nation's good intentions. But the test of our wisdom will be whether we allow them to flourish." The good news today
is that the most frequently asked question from Yellowstone visitors is
"Where are the wolves?" That outpouring of interest and affection

will be crucial in the coming decades as Westerners readjust to the presence of these astonishing animals. Yellowstone Park is the heritage of all Americans, not just people living along the borderlines.

In 1996, President Clinton signed a bill that reaffirmed this status. The federal government agreed to buy out the Crown Butte mining company and put an end to the New World cyanide gold mine on the edge of Yellowstone. It will cost $65 million. The President said, "I'm not willing to gamble a national treasure for short-term economic gain."

But not every threat can be resolved with a check. The Yellowstone River flows north out of the park through one of Montana's most contested valleys—the Paradise. The place is well named. The valley is a fault-bounded basin framed by high ridgelines. Serrate peaks of the Absaroka-Beartooth Wilderness lift the eastern sky. The west is held up by the Gallatin Range. Volcanic rocks from the time of Yellowstone's explosive birth dominate the bedrock. Ancient petrified trees stand beside living spruce and fir.

Ice Age glaciers descended from the highlands excavating bedrock as they went. Stream-cut canyons were widened and smoothed into U-shaped valleys. The Yellowstone Glacier spilled down from an immense ice field that encased what is now the park. This 3,000-foot-thick tongue of ice pushed north into the Paradise for thirty-five miles. Erratic boulders and terminal moraines, reworked tills and outwash gravels now form stair-stepped topography that extends from the river to the fault-line escarpments that raise entire ranges higher each year.

Gallery forests of black cottonwood parallel the Yellowstone River. These are perfect places for whitetails, eagles, and otters. The river is a long reach of trout heaven—meander bends and gravel bars, riffles and pools, all thickly sweatered in dogwood, willow, and rose.

Wetland stringers trace the path of each tributary stream up into the peaks. The cottonwoods are joined by juniper, ash, alder, and mountain maple. The mosaic of moisture fetches a fine diversity— mosses, rushes, sedges, starry Solomon's seal, and the finest blue in flowering nature—forget-me-nots.

Away from the water, the valley raises prairies of fescue and wheatgrass, prairie junegrass and danthonia, sagebrush and fringed sagewort. Ground squirrels, voles, and rabbits are preyed on by the wings of the air—golden eagles, red-tailed hawks, rough-legged hawks, kestrels, and great horned owls. Badgers emerge from deep warrens to take their share of the rodent crop. Rabbitbrush and squawbush grow here and there, but bitterbrush is the plant devoured by deer and elk like a sugar treat.

Higher up, the prairies turn to parklands—open woodlands of Douglas fir, juniper, and the small five-needle fascicles of wind-stunted limber pines. Meadowlark calls are everywhere. The yellow, fist-sized flowers of arrowleaf balsamroot dazzle the steepening meadows. The blues and maroons of lupine fix nitrogen from the air. More lapis comes as bluebells, monkshood, and pasqueflowers. There are pink shooting stars, yellow stoneseed, purple asters, and deep cerulean pockets of larkspur. Natural rock gardens grow in dry spots where bedrock stays close and wind whips away moisture. Delicate mats of rockcress, rose pussytoes, biscuitroot, and prairie star brighten the rocky ground.

Thickets of ninebark and chokecherry rise up from depressions where springs make the surface or snow lies in late. Aspen groves reveal the groundwater trends. Never reproducing by seed, their age is unknown. The aspen of Paradise may be 10,000 years old. Whenever fire, avalanche, or senescence prevails, the roots send up shoots to remake the stand. Beneath the fluttering leaves, moose or elk sometimes bed down in serviceberry, snowberry, gooseberry, and brome.

True forests fill in upslope where the climate allows. Above the semiarid basin, Douglas fir, lodgepole pine, subalpine fir, and Engelmann spruce grow atop swards of pinegrass. Where the shade gets thick, fewer species find home: grouse whortleberry, buffaloberry, and prince's pine. Bobcats and lynx hunt the stands with strong caution. The grouse react differently: the ruffed are on guard, the blue stand out in the open. In winter, weasels and wolverines drift down from the snowpacks to feed on deer carcasses. Mountain lions pad through the forests like hungry shadows. Grizzlies and gray wolves complete the pure circle.

This is the Paradise.

The first whites to set foot on the place were fur crazies and explorers like Jim Bridger and John Colter. Colter had been on the Lewis and Clark Expedition and seen a lot of country. Nothing matched up to the Paradise and Yellowstone. His accounts of boiling mud, hundred-foot geysers, countless Niagaras, and firehole rivers raised widespread suspicion. Yellowstone was called "Colter's Lie" until Jim Bridger owned up to having seen the same things. It was rumored that Bridger could draw a map of the entire Rocky Mountain

West in the dirt with a stick. His word helped. But it wasn't until the Washburn-Langford and Hayden expeditions of the 1860s and 1870s that Colter's reputation as the West's biggest liar was fully reversed.

The phenomenal landscape was real. Early settlers had a hard time with that one. Some of the newcomers still do.

Mining began in the Paradise in the early 1860s. It never amounted to much. Typical of the West, the craving for instant wealth gave way to more modest and longer-lasting intentions—raising cattle and crops.

That's the way things stayed until the 1960s when dam-building enthusiasts proposed building a plug at Allenspur, a narrow constriction in the valley just south of Livingston. The reservoir would back up water for miles, flooding out ranchlands and prime wildlife habitats. The dam people figured that Allenspur was suddenly critical for flood control. The water was actually wanted for processing eastern Montana coal.

An alliance of ranchers, environmentalists, and leaders from downstream states fended off this concrete nightmare. In 1974, the Yellowstone River Basin Moratorium was signed. This created a sensible system of water reservations and set aside over 6 million acre-feet of water annually for in-channel uses. The Yellowstone still remains the last undammed major river in the lower forty-eight states.

Today, the Paradise is both stable and shifting ground. The valley has been discovered, not as a place to ranch in peace, but as a retreat. Celebrities such as Meg Ryan, Dennis Quaid, and Peter Fonda have moved in. But most of the in-migrants have industrial wealth and unfamiliar faces. Still others are working people fleeing cities to live a rural life on horseback.

Over 124,000 acres of the Paradise have now been subdivided for residential development. Most of these survey lines are still invisible on the land, but houses are beginning to fill up the small angular spaces in a valley that twenty years ago looked like Tibet.

In that Himalayan country, mountains are seen as signs of God's proximity. They remind us to exist in the moment, to breathe in every second of life, even the one that brings our death. Mountains let go of parts of themselves and the beauty only deepens. We can watch the unneeded rock fall away.

Mountains tell us what is true about where and how we live. Horeb, Sinai, Fuji, Olympus, and more. The four sacred mountains of the

Navajo Nation define the border of a world called Dinetah. *Hozro*—a balanced way of being—can only be felt within this spiritual geography. Traditional Navajos still wear a "four mountains bundle" around their necks. Inside this small leather pouch are stones and other earthly reminders of lessons gained along journeys to the summits.

The lesson mountain of the Paradise is called Emigrant Peak. An emigrant is someone who leaves another place—a refugee, the displaced, a pilgrim.

In 1983, a California-based religious group called the Church Universal and Triumphant (CUT) bought the 13,000-acre Royal Teton Ranch from billionaire Malcolm Forbes. Then they bought up more of the Paradise. A 30,000-acre land base was assembled beside the Yellowstone River that included trout spawning tributaries, forested mountains, prairies, and irrigated hay meadows. Elk, grizzly bears, and scores of other animals from the park had historically used the ranch's diverse habitats. Park County residents watched as an unknown group began building a strangely utopian settlement at the threshold of Yellowstone.

Conflicts between this secretive religious sect and locals were immediate and intense. Over the years, a looming specter of violence and environmental impact has cast a lengthening shadow across the Paradise Valley.

I first visited the CUT compound in 1987. You could just drive in back then. The main living areas consisted of modular homes packed together next to some sheet metal buildings. I asked a young woman where they got all the trailers. "Oh we bought them from the Bhagwan Shree Rajneesh," she responded with a smile. This wasn't going to quiet anybody's fear down in Livingston.

Nearby, a gravel pit was being excavated. School buses ferried workers to a commercial carrot operation and destinations farther inside the ranch. It all seemed a bit odd but pretty benign. That would change. Over the next few years, the Royal Teton Ranch would be transformed into the Vatican City of a worldwide religious movement.

The Church Universal and Triumphant is the current name for a sect that originated in the 1880s under the direction of Madame Helena Blavatsky on the East Coast. In the 1920s, the belief in "Ascended Masters" was taught by Baird T. Spaulding as part of the "I AM" movement. Guy and Edna Ballard expanded this faith during the 1930s. The "Mighty I AM" craze claimed 3 million members before entering dormancy during World War II.

The Church Lady in Paradise

In 1958, Mark Prophet established the "Summit Lighthouse" (near Washington, D.C.) based on these teachings. In 1961, Prophet married Elizabeth Claire Wulf of New Jersey. Upon his death in 1973, Elizabeth Claire Prophet took over control and soon renamed the operation the Church Universal and Triumphant. The church was moved to Colorado, Idaho, and Los Angeles before descending on Montana.

CUT claims 300,000 members worldwide in over forty countries. However, Montana is where the "Heart of the Inner Retreat" has been established on the Royal Teton Ranch. This CUT enclave is home to some 1,000 of the sect's most ardent believers. Over the years, there has been persistent talk of CUT guerrilla maneuvers, environmental vandalism, and brainwashing. These sorts of things tend to get people's attention.

In the summer of 1996, I drove over to the Paradise Valley for a look. It was lunchtime, so I went into a small restaurant at Corwin Springs called the Ranch Kitchen. It was a CUT business. The food was nothing unusual: chicken, potatoes, and really good pie.

Next door was a small store selling health foods, mandalas, crystals, holy books of every conception, and dozens of CUT publications. I picked up three of Elizabeth Claire Prophet's books: *The Lost Teachings of Jesus #3*, *Saint Germain: Prophecy to the Nations*, and *Lords of the Seven Rays*.

I drove over to LaDuke and sat on a hillside reading the pages. The Devil's Slide, a vertical red slash of shale, was across the river. This outcrop used to mark the early entrance point into Yellowstone, but now, the CUT ranch extended as far as I could see. A guy walked up and took a few pictures of the vista. He told me that CUT had renamed the Devil's Slide the "Angel's Ascent." Isn't that special.

I went back to reading.

The CUT theology seemed to be a miasmic blend of New Age mysticism, astrology, Christianity, reincarnation, theosophy, Confucianism, kundalini yoga, sun worship, anticommunism, and the legends of Atlantis and King Arthur. Elizabeth Claire Prophet serves as an all-powerful charismatic leader who "dictates" the spiritual teachings of various "Ascended Masters" through a form of channeling. CUT believers follow the revealed wisdom of the "Lords of the Seven Rays": El Morya, Lanto, Paul the Venetian, Serapis Bey, Hilarion, Lady Master Nada (formerly a lawyer on Atlantis), and Saint Germain. Each of these Lords is assigned a chakra, color, gemstone, emotional quality, talent, day of the week, and geographical retreat. Lord Lanto's retreat is the nearby Grand Teton Mountains.

CUT literature "quotes" from these spirits as well as from Christ, Buddha, and essences known as Mighty Cosmos, Sanat Kumara, and K-17 (who heads the "Cosmic Secret Service of the Great White Brotherhood"). Elizabeth Claire Prophet's writings are engorged with cryptic terminology such as solar hierarchies, electronic belts, ascension dossiers, triangles of initiation, dispensation of the violet flame, and etheric retreats.

Reincarnation is used to link Sir Thomas More and George Washington with Ascended Master El Morya. The Statue of Liberty is believed to embody a spirit once residing on Atlantis that gave birth to Paul the Venetian.

The pantheon also includes Hercules and Snow White.

Prayer comes in the form of "decreeing"—the practice of repeating spiritual chants up to five hours each day at hypnotic speed. Some call this mind control. Journalists have written of CUT members being captured by their parents and "deprogrammed" to reverse the effects of spiritual mesmerism. However, most church members appear to stay involved of their own volition.

I drove over to the ranch to find out. There was a gate now. They meant business. I pulled up and leaned out my window. A calm, expressionless man walked out of the guardhouse.

"Hi, I've heard you have some sort of religious community here," I said.

"Yes" was all I got back.

"Well, I was wondering if I could come in and have a look?"

This was my best strategy—be direct. It usually worked.

Guardman sort of frowned and picked up a phone. "Yes, I have a man here who would like to come over," he said evenly. Then I heard a bunch of receiver garble.

He hung up the phone, and moved the gate up. "They say you can go down—it's the blue house to the left."

"Thanks," I said with a real smile. I was in.

The CUT "visitor center" was a modest home converted to the purpose. I walked in through a screen door and was greeted by a pleasant thirty-five-year-old woman who actually appeared glad to see me.

"Hi, what can we do for you," she offered.

"I would like to talk to somebody about your church." It was the truth.

The Church Lady in Paradise

"Sure," she said. She rose and showed me over to a small room with a television and VCR on a rolling table. Several folding chairs were set up facing the screen.

A tired-looking elderly man greeted me with a soft handshake. I was his only visitor.

"Hello—would you like to watch a video of Mother?" he asked.

Oh my.

"Yes, yes, that would be fine," I said, "but maybe you could tell me about the church while we're watching."

"Sure," he said softly. "But it's best from her."

He switched on the set and soon I was watching Elizabeth Claire Prophet "dictating" in a channeled monotone. A sentence at a time it was fine. Taken as a whole—incoherent.

"So how long have you been in the church?" I asked, hoping for a better sense of it all.

"For about three years. I used to live in California," he said. "But I needed to make some big changes, so I moved here. The church has showed me how."

We talked for half an hour with Prophet droning on like Thorazine in the background. Several other members drifted in and out of the room. They were smiling and busy with church projects: conferences, Summit Lighthouse University business, ranching. Nice people. I hadn't expected that. But there was an eeriness simmering just beneath their skin that I couldn't name. I suddenly felt overloaded.

"I guess I've seen enough for now," I sighed.

"Yes, it's a lot to try and get all at once, isn't it?" my older friend said.

"You bet," I responded.

I thought about my visit on the long drive back to Missoula but came up empty. There was something going on here. Something much more than I had seen. The mystery demanded solving.

My legwork led all over: the clipping files of the Livingston *Enterprise* and the Bozeman *Chronicle*, interviews with locals who did not want to be named, library stacks in three states. I made many trips back to the valley.

The story of CUT's environmental impacts began to come together. The church's development plan had been the subject of an Environmental Impact Statement back in the mid-1980s. While some of the feared damage never materialized, significant destructive exploitation occurred.

CUT has stored as much as 600,000 gallons of gasoline and diesel fuel and 300,000 gallons of propane in underground storage tanks. On one occasion, 31,000 gallons of fuel leaked into Mol Heron Creek, one of the prime spawning streams for Yellowstone cutthroat trout.

In the 1980s, the church began pumping water from the LaDuke Hot Spring to heat greenhouses for carrot production. Environmentalists feared this would harm nearby Yellowstone Park's geothermal features and sued to stop the pumping. The issue remains unresolved.

A regional wildlife official calls the CUT property a "black hole for grizzly bears" and says that "griz go in and they don't come out." Some conservationists allege that the church practices "shoot and shovel" wildlife management. However, the church did sell the famous 3,265-acre OTO Ranch to the Rocky Mountain Elk Foundation for big game winter range habitat.

Despite this record of impact, an even more powerful threat kept emerging. I found that paranoia and the anticipation of Armageddon define the CUT way of life. Church holdings are being developed as a refuge from an approaching apocalypse. CUT has constructed a bomb shelter that can house 756 people for seven years.

Two massive subdivision projects, totaling 4,000 acres, have been platted for church members. These are known as Glastonbury North and South. It's a harsh version of the Arthurian myth. Miles of roads have been bulldozed into the prairies of Paradise. Bold signs warn non–church members to stay out. I've driven in anyway and seen a mix of log cabins, frame houses, and trailers. The restrictive covenants of these housing developments are on file in the Park County courthouse. My hands shook when I read them. These strange standards require the construction of bomb shelters. CUT's development scenarios also tend to shake you up. As many as 6,000 more people may be moving in.

Millennialists tend to make poor conservationists.

In contrast, CUT's neighbors have performed stunning acts of stewardship. Len and Sandy Sargent placed a conservation easement on their 1,960-acre place up Cinnabar Creek to protect griz. Like the CUT holdings, these easement lands are adjacent to Yellowstone National Park.

I kept looking deeper into the CUT. The acquisition and stockpiling of guns is also part of the group's doomsday planning. In 1989, Edward Francis, the husband of Elizabeth Claire Prophet at the time, was arrested and pled guilty to federal firearms charges. Twenty CUT members were implicated. A complex scheme was revealed dating back to the early 1970s that involved the purchase of $100,000 worth of semiautomatic rifles. A group known as the Rocky Mountain Sportsmen's Survival Club was allegedly used as a front for church firearms training. In 1992, the Internal Revenue Service revoked the tax-exempt status of CUT over this little matter of gun running. In 1993, it was discovered that the church had purchased two Saracen armored personnel carriers (APC's) from a New Jersey company known as "Tanks A Lot."

John Sullivan, publisher of the *Livingston Enterprise*, figured that "Waco, Texas, is Mr. Rogers' Neighborhood compared to what we've got here." When the Branch Davidian compound was destroyed in March 1993, CUT officials quietly removed the APC's from Montana and shipped them away for storage.

By 1994, the IRS had reinstated the tax-exempt status of CUT in exchange for a $2.6 million settlement and a promise from the sect to disarm. Locals say they can still hear weapons being fired on church land. One nearby rancher remains deeply suspicious: "If those people don't still have an underground warehouse of weapons, I'll kiss that cow."

CUT continues to profess peaceful intentions, yet maintains an ene-mies list of people deemed to be "Malintents and Burdens." The church has official forms for "decreeing" against its critics. These have included members of the media, the local county planner and planning board, U.S. Forest Service officials, neighboring ranchers, and the Episcopal, Catholic, and Methodist churches. The forms read: "I de-mand a bolt of Blue Lightning in through the cause and core of all criticism, condemnation and judgment from (Insert Name)."

At the core of this faith seems to be a right-wing Aquarian belief— peace through superior firepower. The church's veiled threats of re-taliation, legacy of armaments, and smiling anticipation of a post-nuclear Camelot have tended to make locals a tad ill at ease.

The people of the Paradise Valley have reluctantly accepted Holly-wood newcomers because they lead quiet lives. The Church Universal and Triumphant seems destined to remain a feared outsider as it strives to transform a conservative rural landscape into a singular, militantly secretive domain.

On one trip to the valley, I hiked up Bassett Creek as high as the Rigler Bluffs. From there I could see much of the Royal Teton Ranch. The landscape spread out like a lucid dream. I could imagine most of the problems of the Greater Yellowstone finding resolution in the coming decades. It would be hard work and a violent ride, but the griz, wolves, bison, and elk would be OK. Eventually, the country's commitment to the park would prevail and the ill-considered mines and overzealous timber harvest would tail away. As land trusts and land trades took effect, the subdivisions would quiet down. All the pieces would fall together in a fair fashion. Not perfect, but fine enough.

I sat down on the soil and tried to understand the strange utopian business going on down below. A magpie flew by. They've always looked like an Archaeopteryx to me—the first reptile to lean toward birdness. The hipbone of a mule deer lay nearby. I remembered meeting the great physical anthropologist Loren Eiseley decades before. Bones always brought him back. We corresponded briefly when I lived in Pburg.

That grand, somber man could see through time the way the rest of us see through sky. Eiseley wrote to me about paleo-humans, bone-hunting trips, and dinosaurs before they were movie stars. He described the thick browridge of a quiet farmer's daughter south of the Sand Hills. Loren felt that she was a glimpse back. He found some of his best answers looking in that direction. I lay back on a Montana ridge, head resting on humus and watched the atmosphere.

That same sun had warmed the haunches of our hairy little relatives back in the tropical woodlands of Ethiopia. If I'm not mistaken, we've been searching for a way back to that lost paradise ever since. This impossible longing is woven into our brain stems.

It's been there awhile. Fossilized human skulls from 2.5 million years ago have eroded out of hillsides in Ethiopia's Hadar region. The little skeleton of "Lucy" came from the Afar country. She was an Australopithecine, not really human but close. A cousin.

A warming climate thinned the woods to open savannahs. We left the trees, stood upright, and used tools. An irretrievable gulf seemed to open in back of us. We evolved, spoke, spread, and differentiated. *Homo erectus* to *Homo sapiens*. Africa to Europe, Asia to the Americas. Colors and cultures splitting from the stalk, but still kin.

Some of us began to see animals, land, and water as separate things. Not us anymore. The Other. Gods were chosen to lift us from the burden of mammalian death. Afterlife was born and soon began to overshadow actual life. For many, nature was no longer perfect enough. So we invented paradise in many formations, every one a hazy human dream of returning to what we knew back in the trees.

The Church Lady in Paradise

Loren Eiseley died in 1976. The last thing he ever wrote to me was this: "I will retire soon and have hopes of making a high elevation. I may not make my mountain, but if I do I'll think of you far off doing the same thing."

Utopia—the perfect place and way of being. For some of us, mountains will do. But there's a world of opinion here.

I shifted position and watched clouds flow and eddy toward the Beartooth highlands. Grizzlies eat frozen grasshoppers up there every August where a small glacier melts out. Perfection.

Most people seem to prefer metaphors for the ideal—Eden, Zion, the Elysian Fields. There are plenty more.

In the *Epic of Gilgamesh*, the legendary King of Uruk made a dangerous journey to Dilmun—the Sumerian land of eternal life.

After surviving trials by darkness, mountain firmaments, and wild beasts, Gilgamesh arrived in a region of leisure, health, contemplation, and ageless youth. One of our most ancient surviving stories reveals our fond desire to somehow find heaven on earth.

The English cut the imaginary Land of Cockaygne from this same cloth. Cockaygne was a place rumored so perfect that cooked birds flew into your mouth, rivers ran with wine, sleep produced wealth, sex was abundant, and no one ever died. Shambhala, El Dorado, and scores of other promised lands have inspired a global cartography of the imagination.

However, as these regions went unfound, some pushed the ideal back to a time untainted by the sweat and corruption of the present. The Jews thirsted for the lost Kingdom of Israel, the English for the Saxon Golden Age, the Chinese for the Taoist Age of Perfect Virtue. Plato, Virgil, and Ovid warmed up the crowd for Dante's *Divine Comedy* and Milton's *Paradise Lost*.

Immaculate places did not just lie out in remote, inaccessible lands—they had passed, and our calling was to return to the clarity, righteousness, and balance of antiquity. Since we couldn't time-travel, we began crafting new cities, communities, and landscapes as replacements. Flawless geographies would arise from the intellect and spirit; from the interplay of philosophy, economics, theology, and planning.

Thomas More's book *Utopia* named the construction of paradise. The traveler in "Utopia" was Raphael Hythloday, a name that means "a distributor of nonsense." More conjured a utopia lying in the New World, off the coast of "Somewhere," out beyond America. The geographic elusiveness of the place was a social shot at the unkept promises of the ruling class to reform English society. The title reveals More's sarcasm—"utopia" translates as "no place." He didn't use a related spelling, "eutopia," because it means "a good place." Words often define worlds.

Yet many have ardently believed in the perfection of life. The Shakers—dying out because of celibacy. The Mormons—more than making up for it. The followers of Bhagwan Shree Rajneesh practiced free love and Hindu-scented meditation and chanting in the wilds of eastern Oregon until their spiritual master was deported for tax fraud. The drive for utopia has also seen the falling of Karl Marx's communism and the dissipation of Charles Fourier's smokestack dreams.

Farming has often been seen as the paradisiacal way. Agricultural colonies in Colorado became Greeley, Longmont, and Colorado Springs. The Amish, Mennonites, and Hutterites, the Amana Colonies, the Essenes, the Ephratians, the Israeli kibbutz. All based on stirring the soil.

Writers have spun endless visions: H. G. Wells' cautionary *Time Machine*, Huxley's sobering *Brave New World*, Orwell's terrifying *1984*, Skinner's ghastly *Walden Two*.

New Age beliefs in harmonic convergences, power spots, lei lines, and crystals have taken shape in Santa Fe and Sedona, the stylish promised lands of a relentlessly mellow New West.

Feminist utopias, Le Corbusier's architectural "Radiant City," the domes of Biosphere i and ii, the rambling eco-concrete of Paolo Soleri's Arcosanti.

Disneyland.

Every version of paradise has fallen short for a perfect reason. Fallible human beings cannot imagine, let alone create, a faultless world. Sometimes this clumsy fact gives way to virulence and the creation of landscapes layered with fear and death—dystopias.

The "Pax Romana" of the Roman Empire came from conquest and mass killing. The Third Reich's "Final Solution" to the perceived imperfection of a world containing Jews led to the murder of 6 million people. Genocidal attacks by Turks on Armenians, Serbian Christians on Bosnian Muslims, and Hutus on Tutsis in Rwanda are just a few of the mad outbreaks of "ethnic cleansing"—the creation of a clean geographic slate, free from those deemed unfit to share an "ideal" world.

Apocalyptic utopias evolve when religious visions are contaminated by insanity. These "cults" always have a single charismatic leader whose slide from paranoia into madness is interpreted by followers as the arrival of a prophet. As an imagined Armageddon grows nearer, the mental pathologies of the leader infect the membership. Guns are accumulated and a siege mentality cuts the group off from leavening contact with the outside world. Conflicts with government agencies and neighbors increase. Finally, the utopia built on anxiety and automatic weapons explodes in a dystopian hail of death.

176   In Jonestown, Guyana, poison and gunfire claimed 912 people in a serial suicide.

In Waco, Texas, eighty-six succumbed when David Koresh's Branch Davidians went up in flames.

In Switzerland, fifty-three members of the Temple Solaire cult died in a ritualistic circle.

In South Korea, thirty-one followers of Park Soon Ja gave up their lives rather than live on in a flawed world.

Apocalyptic groups come from millennialism and the anticipation of a divine advent when they, as the chosen people, will live on in a peaceful Kingdom of God on Earth. However, for those doomed by dementia, this optimism is replaced by a hungering for the seamless perfection of death.

It isn't always easy to tell the difference between visions that are merely marvelously kooky and those that have the potential to enrapture and kill. But warning signs are filling the Paradise Valley. The Church Universal and Triumphant may be on a path toward tragedy.

Elizabeth Claire Prophet has written more than fifty books containing an expanding arc of bizarre, often contradictory teachings. The message keeps shifting. It would take a cutting horse to keep it all herded together. Studies of cults show that members are often wounded from traumas and have low self-esteem. The best way to maintain control is by constantly fuzzying up the doctrine.

To challenge Prophet's placid smile appears unthinkable. Members quietly listen to her speak and write down the words on legal pads. They seem to think, "If I don't understand it yet, it must be my fault. I'll just have to work harder until I am worthy." Ms. Prophet appears to be increasingly intoxicated by the power of her position. This same profoundly dangerous trend was followed by Jim Jones and David Koresh into deadly endgames for cult members.

The CUT ideology also exhibits a strange nostalgia for the future. The church is building a staging station in Montana, while preparing to expand into a depopulated American landscape scorched pure by the cleansing fire of nuclear fission. The community bomb shelter reveals far more than prudence. CUT's history of accumulating weapons did not arise from a fear of burglars.

What is most deceptive about apocalyptic groups is that individual members can be extremely decent and peaceful people. It is only when their leader descends into psychosis and directs these vulnerable, dependent souls to perform heinous acts that the terrible essence of dystopian cults is disclosed as stacks and circles of human corpses.

The quest for utopia comes with all the admirable and deplorable traits of our kind. Many of our most elegant spiritual and intellectual truths have been born this way. Yet, interspliced like parallel strands of rope, are recurrent, mystifying cases such as the Church Universal and Triumphant. The lasting lesson here is that even our noble wish for geographic salvation is not immune to falls from ethical grace.

I rose from the ground and looked out over the Paradise. School buses passed through CUT's East Gate Work Camp, crossed the iron bridge, and entered a magnificent land. What a lovely place to await a nuclear holocaust.

Suddenly, my CUT pamphlets took on an unexpected meaning. "The Royal Teton Ranch has become a launching pad for thousands of souls to reach the star of their own God presence." Is that part of what they're doing here? Waiting for the payloads?

"Sic transit gloria mundi"—thus passes the glory of the world.

Oh Montana, yours is the one death I cannot bear.

If the nukes were imminent, I wouldn't cower in a sunless bunker. I'd dash over to central Montana's missile silos—to one called "Molten Bones"—build a fire, strip naked, paint myself blue, unsheathe my fishing rod, and wave it at the incoming ICBM's. I'd defend my place with one last, gloriously futile gesture. I'd die a human being in love with the land, as a person unwilling to scurry through the ghastly glowing soot like a singed Paleocene rat in a post-apocalyptic hell. Land or life dammit. Tierra o muerte. No retreat.

CUT sees life after the bombs, and that is dangerous craziness. If the alleged cache of weapons is still there, it has one ultimate use—to defend the CUT faithful, to keep the rest of us irradiated zombies from stealing their jerky and creamed corn. More fearsome is what might happen when the bombs don't come, when a new external threat must be manifested to keep the faithful from straying.

I sat back down on a block of stone. The breeze feathered across my face.

A quarter of a century ago I spent time in a Sikh ashram doing meditation and yoga—the breath of fire. I was in love with a woman who moved there. At first it seemed miraculous. God, love, and health. The hat trick. People who said life was difficult had simply been misinformed.

Then human nature intervened. Yogi Bhajan, the path's head vegetarian holy man, ended up owning stock in McDonald's. One day, he yelled at a woman when her dog barked. It had interrupted him. I watched people in the ashram compete each morning to see who could do a tough yoga posture the longest. The sexism of the life began to chafe. I read that Sikhs from the Punjab assassinated Indira Gandhi.

I left the ashram because I saw this hypocrisy for what it was, and because I knew I deserved better. But not everyone has the strength to leave a religious group when it no longer fits, especially one that is far more controlling than Sikhism.

A few things, the true things, have lasted from those days: a tangible connection to the land, an awareness of my soul, a need for peace and quiet. I understand the search.

Members of the Church Universal and Triumphant have a perfect right to preach and believe anything they choose. I would stand in a picket line to defend their religious freedom. Maybe they'd stand in one to protect my free speech. But religious freedom, like all freedoms, is not boundless. The line gets drawn here: CUT members do not have the right to damage the environment and threaten the peace of the Paradise Valley. The rest is their business.

I looked out over the basin. Cars were passing by down on Highway 89. A steady flow of people passing through.

Utopian communities always lose track of land or life, earth or ethics. CUT has done both in this valley at the northern door of the wild Yellowstone. As Thomas More told us, "utopia" means "nowhere." It now seemed obvious that time and nature will exorcise their presence. Paradise will outlast the church. That is certain.

But what will be their legacy?

In the end, sadly, the final reckoning might be found in the terrible mathematics of the body count.

9

THE ELK'S GOLDEN EYE

AFTER THREE weeks in the Scottish Highlands you get used to climbing mountains in the fog. I rolled out of my B & B next to the Falls of Dochart and drove north to the trailhead at the base of Ben Lawers.

In Scotland a "ben" is a peak. Although Lawers didn't quite reach 4,000 feet, the maps said it had about 3,000 feet of vertical rise. Respectable.

I'd already climbed Ben Nevis, Ben More, Ben MacDui, Cairngorm, and half a dozen other summits. Fog roofed the top of every one. But I was still trying for an open view from the heights before I headed south to "The Big Smoke"—to London.

More than that, I was hoping for my first sight of a red deer. A red deer in this part of the world is an elk to a North American. To Europeans, an elk is what we call a moose. It gets a bit confusing.

By any name, wild creatures seemed to be in short supply.

Over the centuries the Scots have deforested their world and taken a serious toll on wildlife. Vast flocks of sheep (locals called them "woolly buggers") have been turned loose to graze in the altered landscape. Heather rolls across the countryside like lavender surf.

Only a few hundred acres of the original Caledonian forest ecosystem remains. In a weekend you can see every natural Scots pine in the country. This lack of habitat and centuries of overhunting nearly wiped out the Scottish red deer. Elk were reintroduced into the Highlands more than fifty years ago. Some of the animals came from Yellowstone National Park.

Although there were more than 30,000 red deer in the country, in three weeks I hadn't seen even one. But still, I climbed the steep rocky trail up Ben Lawers with my eyes intent on spotting any white rumps that might be moving on the glens and bens of a region called Tayside.

It drizzled off and on but stayed comfortable as I gained elevation. The linear, rippling shape of Loch Tay hemmed things in to the south. Scottish lakes fill narrow glaciated valleys. The valleys are controlled by faults as straight as the crease in a Tory's pants. Loch Shin, Loch Broom, Loch Ericht. Myths of monsters draw millions to Loch Ness.

But after a long stretch away from Montana, I preferred to look for elk.

I made the false summit, descended, and charged up the last pitch to a concrete marker atop Ben Lawers. A group of eight Scottish gentlemen encased in wool hiking clothes were hunkered down in the lee to escape a sudden wet and biting wind.

I ate my pastry and drank my Irn-Bru, an enigmatic and excessively sweet Scottish beverage. Clouds and mist swept in and out on their way toward Norway. I was catching ten-second glimpses of Highland green, pink, and gray. A boulder-strewn valley sank below my boots.

There was no sign of any animals except the hundreds of hearty, loudly bleating sheep dotting the slopes. Each had a blue or red dot spray painted on its wool. You can't brand a sheep.

The men beside me were laughing, taking nips of local whisky, and sharing stories from forty years of hiking on the ben.

"Hello, do you ever see any red deer up here?" I asked cheerfully.

"Aye, from time to time," said a white-bearded man in scratchy brown knickers and tall green socks. His boots were shellacked in oil to keep the water out.

"But mostly you see them on private hunting lands or in fenced pastures," he went on.

"So there are no wild herds around here?" I asked.

"Sorry, laddie—I've heard there are some up by Ben Hope and down at Loch Lomond, but around here they're managed pretty firmly."

"Thanks," I said sadly. "Seems a shame with all these mountains."

"Aye," my bearded friend agreed, raising his flask.

We all watched in silence as the clouds opened to reveal a hundred square miles without a single wild elk.

Cervus elaphus. That's the Latin descriptor for one of the most widespread species within the biological family called "antlered artiodactyls"—deer with racks. The largest is the moose. The smallest, the knee-high musk deer.

Cervus elaphus has a global distribution. These charismatic megafauna are everywhere under many names: Norwegian red deer, Bactrian deer, Barbary deer, Corsican red deer, Swedish red deer, Kashmir deer, Spanish red deer, Tien-Shan red deer, Shou deer, Izubr stag, and the Shingielt. Each is a subspecies of *Cervus elaphus.* This means that if you put them together they can breed and produce fertile offspring. In North America, we think of them all as elk.

Elk wandered across the Bering land bridge from Asia into our part of the world about 120,000 years ago. Early on they were concentrated in Alaska. Climate shifts, vegetation change, and hunting pressure pushed them southward to lower latitudes. Herds became isolated from each other in the vastness of the Americas and gene flow was reduced. This led to morphological, behavioral, and physiological differentiation.

We ended up with six subspecies of *Cervus elaphus*: Eastern elk, Manitoban elk, Merriam elk, Tule elk, Roosevelt elk, and Rocky Mountain elk. All could interbreed, but distance and the strong scents and vague rules of animal culture reduced crossings.

When Europeans landed in the Americas in 1492, there may have been about 10 million elk of various sorts roaming the landscape. By 1910, there were less than 100,000 left. Like the Scots, we developed quite a taste for elk meat. The Indians always had. The Shawnee called the animals "wapiti." The wily wapiti. But tribal hunting did little to reduce elk numbers.

The Elk's Golden Eye

The die-off was our doing.

Eastern elk worked the deciduous forests and oak openings from Ontario south to Louisiana. Intensive settlement and woodland clearing caused their numbers to collapse. In 1851, John James Audubon reported just a few stragglers in the Allegheny Mountains. By the 1870s, the Eastern elk was extinct.

Merriam elk were concentrated in Arizona, New Mexico, and the Sierra Madre of Mexico. Huge bulls bugled from the Mogollon Rim, the Sacramento Mountains, and the wild country of the Gila. Hunters took them all. In 1902, the Merriam elk was extinct.

Tule elk are the smallest of all North American elk. Perhaps a million once roamed the marshes and grasslands of California's San Joaquin Valley. Market hunting to feed miners and railroad crews, competition with livestock, and agricultural land development reduced these immense herds to less than a hundred animals by 1875. A rancher named Henry Miller rounded up the few head that remained and tried to protect them. Wildlife biologist Starker Leopold wrote that by 1910, only about six Tule elk remained. Some say they got down to a single mated pair.

Manitoban elk faced the same human pressures on the Canadian plains. Early in the century just a few hundred remained.

By 1910, the Rockies and the Pacific Northwest were the only places in North America where elk survived in large numbers. Perhaps 10,000 Roosevelt and 70,000 Rocky Mountain elk remained in remote high country strongholds like the Cascades and Yellowstone National Park. Rocky Mountain elk had been wiped out in Utah and Nevada. Fewer than 500 existed in Colorado. Outside of the Yellowstone region, Montana and Wyoming were thin with elk.

In just over 400 years, Europeans had exterminated two of six subspecies, nearly eliminated two others, and killed 99.5 percent of North America's elk. Even the elk of Yellowstone National Park weren't secure.

The park's "Northern Herd" of 30,000 animals wintered in Montana's Paradise and Gallatin valleys. As many as 25,000 from the "Southern Herd" wintered on Jackson Hole ranchlands. The 2.2-million-acre park wasn't nearly big enough to save them.

Poachers were slaying elk by the thousands. This was nothing new. In 1875, three years after Yellowstone was set aside, the Bottler brothers from Emigrant killed 2,000 elk near Mammoth Hot Springs. They kept only the tongues and hides, earning $3 per animal. Poaching became an industry, and elk carcasses littered the ground. Army troops were stationed in the park to protect the herds, but the slaughter continued.

In 1894, Congress passed the Yellowstone Park Protection Act. It included a new set of laws for prosecuting poachers and some progress was made. But in Wyoming, conflicts between wintering elk and cattle ranchers kept heating up.

In 1912, the National Elk Refuge was established in Jackson, Wyoming. Private ranches were bought. At first, this winter range was just 2,800 acres, but eventually it was expanded to 24,000.

The "Southern Herd" at last had some protection. Elk began to be shipped all over the world to repopulate depleted ranges. In the first year, 220 elk were transported to Glacier National Park, South Dakota, and Washington. In 1913, elk were reintroduced to Arizona's Mogollon Rim. The Merriam were gone but the Rocky Mountain subspecies quickly refilled the niche. Elk were sent to Pennsylvania, Utah, Virginia, and Wyoming. In 1914, herds were released in Colorado and Oregon. The next year, elk were again bugling from the heights of New Mexico's Sacramento Mountains. Elk were even sent by steamer to Argentina and Scotland.

We were returning *Cervus elaphus* to reclaim the places where we had foundered. Between 1912 and 1997, some 22,000 elk were shipped from the Greater Yellowstone to the rest of the world. A map of the outflow looks like a starburst.

The Tule elk have also come back. Today, about 1,000 roam California reserves from the Owens Valley to Point Reyes National Seashore. In Canada, 10,000 Manitoban elk graze in Prince Albert National Park and other Canadian preserves. Huge herds of Roosevelt and Rocky Mountain elk share the Cascadian forests. Transplanted wapiti are found in Pennsylvania, Arkansas, New York, Wisconsin, and Florida—nearly every state within their former range.

There are now over 700,000 elk in North America. Extinction is no longer an option. This is best called a success.

Until recently, elk biologist Jack Ward Thomas was the head of the U.S. Forest Service. He coedited the bible known as *The Elk of North America: Ecology and Management*. Few can claim to know as much about the beast. When asked why he was retiring, the burly Thomas gruffly remarked, "Washington, D.C., is awfully poor elk country."

People tend to be enchanted by the animal. The daughter of a friend calls them "the big Bambi." For good reason. Bulls can weigh 900 pounds, with 430 pounds being average for a two-year-old. They're something to see.

Both genders have a reddish-brown summer pelage and a white butt. Males grow a fresh set of antlers each summer. At first the rack is alive, a mass of nerves and blood vessels. In the fall, male hormone levels soar during the breeding season known as "the rut."

During the rut, the necks of bulls literally swell up with lust. They send high-pitched bugling sounds off into the world for potential rivals to consider. Blood flow is pulled back from the antlers to fill more urgent regions of the bull's anatomy. The velvet peels away or is rubbed off on tree trunks and branches. Racks turn to hard bone. They're used to show dominance and as a weapon during jousts with competing males. When it comes to racks, size does matter. Well-endowed, victorious bulls assemble harems of dozens of cow elk. Then come several weeks of rampant and recurrent elk-style unions. When the breeding is done and the genes downloaded, the antlers drop to the ground like spent swords. The calves arrive in late May or early June. They are born as scentless, thirty-five-pound wobbles—all spindly legs and spotted coats.

But such a listing of biological traits is like describing Monet's *Water Lilies* with a chemical assay of the paint. We are devoted to elk for reasons that reside in our souls.

I love elk for their wariness and complete intelligence, for the way they prefer the most beautiful habitats as home. Because, even in Yellowstone Park where you can stand ten feet away, or at the National Elk Refuge where winter feed is alfalfa pellets, they are always unmistakably and courageously wild. I love elk because they don't crowd into clearcuts like deer but walk miles to remain unseen off in the timber. I love them because in seasons when 80 percent of hunters can shoot a deer, only 12 percent of those with elk tags fill them. I love the sudden unexpected sight of them, the primitive adrenaline rush and thumping aorta, the way that no matter how many times you see one you're always eye-hungry for more. I love elk because of a bull a few years ago that managed to walk from the mountains of Colorado all the way to the suburbs of Kansas City without being spotted, dog-bit, or road-killed. He just felt an old migratory pull and acted on it with stamina, savvy, and an overwhelming heart. I love the dendritic beauty of their branching antlers, the curving mass of smooth or rough-dimpled tines, even the eccentric palmated blobs of "non-typical" racks. I love the softness of their double guard hairs. The groans, chirps, snorts, and bugles of an advanced language only the truest hunters can decipher and mimic. I love the taste of their meat even though I could never shoot one. I love that they can learn to survive in country only their distant kin ever saw—because their senses of smell, vision, and intuition dwarf our atrophied will to live outside a world of 2 × 4's, CD/ROMs, and GE refrigerators full of food from habitats we do not know. I love elk because even with all the paintings, sculptures, bronzes, carvings, and taxidermy, their beauty is only seen in the back country where you have to hike, breathe, and sweat to be granted one second of real looking.

Mostly I love elk because, although I could never prove it, they found a way to save themselves.

I first saw an elk in 1973 near Fish Creek, downstream of Missoula. Nothing special, just an average young cow or two working the thawed-out edges of a winter-beaten hay meadow. It was on the Garcia Ranch. Trinidad "Cookie" Garcia lived here in a log house nearly engulfed in lilac bushes and clematis vines. You had to move fast along the bordering road. Cookie was embittered by polio and a solitude too well demanded. He hefted a sizable anger. Word had it he kept a shotgun full of rock salt for lollygaggers.

But I had seen an elk and a shiver told me this was real news.

Enlightenment arrives in little moments like this, when we're otherwise engaged. Elk work their magic on the hoof, out there in the natural world, knowing everything about being what they are, conjuring up noble lives from a swirl of seasons, forage, cover, predators, hunters, sightlines, smells, and urges. I suddenly felt lonely for a grace I could never know. All I could do was lend a hand to conserve those parts of the world they need. There's lots to do. Despite all the reintroductions, the work is hardly over. Managing the herds and securing essential habitat is now the true calling of thousands of conservationists.

In the early 1980s, a group of men were drinking coffee around a kitchen table in the Yaak country of northwestern Montana. Charlie Decker, Bob Munson, a bunch of others—just regular guys who happened to love elk beyond all reason. They had watched elk winter range habitat continue to disappear as subdivisions took their toll. The feds and state Fish and Game people were working hard, but there just wasn't enough money to get the whole job done. So, over coffee, these guys figured that what was needed was a group formulated, consecrated, and dedicated to saving elk. So, in 1984, they thought big and

The Elk's Golden Eye

set up something called the Rocky Mountain Elk Foundation (RMEF).

Things went slowly at first. In 1985, the RMEF held seven fundraising banquets. Rifles, artwork, guided hunts—all manner of elk stuff was auctioned off. About $30,000 was added to the coffers. Two years later, forty-eight banquets netted $575,000. Something was going on here. People from all over the world were coming forward to work for the betterment of elk.

The RMEF's first major project came in 1987. Anheuser-Busch donated $500,000 toward the purchase of 16,440 acres in the Robb Creek drainage of southwestern Montana's Snowcrest Range. An additional 16,000 acres of attached grazing leases brought the total package to more than 32,000 acres. The fledgling group raised the money and bought the land. Several hundred elk could now safely winter on the property.

But the Robb Creek purchase put out a more powerful message. The Elk Foundation wasn't just about elk. In saving big game range, it had also protected the habitat of thirty other mammal species, fifty-seven kinds of birds, and numerous fish, reptiles, amphibians, and bugs. Elk are a "keystone species": if you protect their habitat, everything else in the region comes along for the ride.

I went over to Twin Bridges for the Robb Creek celebration. There was a red-and-white striped tent, barbecue grills thick with burgers, hot dogs, and elk steaks, a live country band, and all the Budweiser beer you could manage. Speeches and the unveiling of a bas-relief of an elk capped off the day.

Of all the sights that day, the one I'll hold on to is Phil Tawney, an attorney for the RMEF, wearing a dog-eared cowboy hat, smiling as big as life, holding a cup of beer. A handmade sign was taped to his chest. It read simply "BUY MORE HABITAT." Phil passed away recently, but not before he saw a world of tangible good come from his work and his life. Conservation legacies are places for walking on. Who knows, maybe we'll find the trail back someday.

After Robb Creek, things just kept accelerating.

In the Bitterroot, the RMEF bought the 3,724-acre Burnt Fork Ranch, one of the prime elk wintering areas in the valley. Then it placed a conservation easement on the property, resold it, and used the money to buy more habitat such as:

• the 2,635-acre Nelson Ranch and the 3,265-acre OTO Ranch in the Paradise country . . .

- 6,182 acres of prime land in the Porcupine Creek drainage of the Upper Gallatin, part of an 83,000-acre complex of transactions in one of Montana's most endangered watersheds . . .
- 11,000 acres in Utah's Book Cliffs, part of a multi-agency plan that saved 370,000 acres of wild land linking the red rock canyons of the Colorado Plateau with the Rocky Mountain ecosystems of the Uinta Basin.

Today, the RMEF has been transformed into an international conservation group which has established the North American Habitat Fund and other programs designed to fulfill the Foundation's main mission—"Conserve Wildlife Habitat." There is no mistaking the job at hand. The Foundation's Seeking Common Ground project stresses cooperation between conservationists and ranchers. Conservation education and classes on safe, ethical hunting are also vital missions.

The Foundation now has a spacious visitor center in Missoula, out on West Broadway next to heavy-equipment dealers and tire stores. This is a group that works for a living. Bob Munson has been President of the RMEF since the beginning. Despite the vital participation of corporate givers and cooperative efforts with public agencies, Bob still describes the Foundation as "a group of little guys with five-dollar bills."

He's right. The Rocky Mountain Elk Foundation has 100,000 individual members sending along what they can afford each year to keep things moving. The idea has exploded since those days around a coffee table up in the Yaak. Some 370 RMEF chapters now exist in forty-three states and Canadian provinces. Over $50 million has been raised and spent on elk in 1,200 projects. The Elk Foundation has now conserved or enhanced wildlife habitat on nearly 2 million acres.

All this because people love to see and, yes, hunt elk. Hunters make up a fair share of RMEF members, but hardly all. I am a "Life Member" because I appreciate the conservation. And I realize that hunters, the best of them at least, care as much as I do about wildlife and the land.

Jim Posewitz wrote of real hunting in his book *Beyond Fair Chase: The Ethics and Tradition of Hunting.* It has sold over 100,000 copies—an astonishing success. "Poz" describes what it means to hunt ethically:

You need to be familiar with the field, the woods, the marsh, the forest or the mountains where you hunt. If you work hard and long at this aspect of hunting,

The Elk's Golden Eye

you can become part of the place you hunt. You will sense when you start to belong to the country. Go afield often enough and it will happen. Little by little you will become less an intruder. More animals will seem to show themselves to you. You are no longer a stranger in their world; you have become part of it. Many people hunt for a lifetime without learning this, and they miss the most rewarding part of being a hunter.

Jim Zumbo, Wayne van Zwoll, and Dwight Schuh are just some of the names of real hunters. They give seminars on doing it right. Thousands pay to hear the message. But there are still far too many road hunters who ride around in pickups drinking, waiting to pick off straying animals. These "happiness is a warm gut pile" types give the pursuit a bad name. So do the poachers—like the moron who got caught killing elk *inside* Yellowstone National Park and making videos of his exploits. Then there are the folks who romanticize the "good old days" before all the limits and regs. Folks who wish they were alive in the days of characters like Sir George Gore. The macho mantra of hunting season also doesn't help. Guys will greet each other with "Got yer elk yet?" This turns hunting into a test of sperm count instead of something with an ancient sacredness to it. The worst hunters are driven to take life, preferably the life of a bull—and the bigger the better—not out of reverence, but out of a nagging weakness inside them that can only be briefly silenced by destroying something powerful.

But people hunt elk for all sorts of reasons: for meat, for trophy racks, for the experience of the wild inside of them, as a test of awareness and competence, as part of their cultural heritage, to cull the herds, and from bloodlust. The rationales are many. Some make sense and are worthy of respect.

But as T. S. Eliot wrote, "The last temptation is the greatest treason: / To do the right thing for the wrong reasons." Only the hunters know their true intent out there in the cold.

The worst of it comes where elk are ranched. There are now over 20,000 captive elk in North America. Write a check, shoot an elk. And make it a big check. On some of these fee operations, you can pay $8,000 for the right to blast a bull elk. Then you can haul the head and antlers back home and lie about what a great tracker you are. On other ranches, velveted bloody racks are sawed off living bulls and ground up for sale as an aphrodisiac to randy Asian buyers.

A few elk ranchers have imported red deer from Europe as breeding

MONTANA GHOST DANCE

stock. Exotic nematode diseases, TB, and other maladies incubate in the crowded herds. Sometimes the animals escape. In a recent study, 14 percent of wild elk in one part of Colorado tested positive for red deer gene pollution.

The work of the Rocky Mountain Elk Foundation and fish and game agencies will never be over. Conserving habitat against the insistent hand of development is a permanent calling.

Yet the elk are back. We could have lost them all. We almost did. But we did not fail.

In that is ample reason for hope.

And the news gets better. Elk are just one form of nature. Other conservation groups are working for the best interests of bighorn sheep, wild turkeys, trumpeter swans, trout, ducks, and other species. When it comes to conserving the earth, it doesn't really matter where you start. Everything curves along the same grand circle. Pick a species that moves your heart, learn what it needs, and work to save that habitat. Any species will do. Walk any arc of the natural wheel and soon you'll encounter everything else—all the different faces of the divine double helix that holds all life together with fur, skin, feather, and scale.

Montana's still got ample room for those sorts of walks. Everyone who hikes this country has a favorite mountain range and drainage. This information must be tended carefully. Solitude is a perishable thing. Names must be changed to protect the innocent.

Once a year I backpack by myself to a certain lake perched in a remote, high basin. One time the hike happened late, at the end of September. I packed my gear, loaded the pickup, and drove toward a distant trailhead. After more than thirty hikes in this backcountry, even the bumpy graveled miles felt like a soft pilgrimage.

The country opened up into a quilt of grasslands, aspen groves, and conifer stands. Sunny side and shady side were playing out in the sure logic of vegetation. I pulled over beside a large clump of aspen for a look. The yellow leaves were trembling, making a sound like polite applause. The understory grasses were still lush even with fall firmly in charge upslope. To the north, the main ridgeline shone like the earth's freshly cut teeth.

Elk sign began wedging into the treads of my hiking boots. Some pellets were still moist and springy when I squeezed them between my thumb and forefinger. They were nearby.

A browse line from foraging elk scarred the aspen trunks to a height

The Elk's Golden Eye

of over eight feet. During winter, elk devour the delicate inner bark for its high content of fat and protein. In time, bite marks oxidize to mottled, black wounds. Same thing happens to human initials scabbing over on the transitory ledger of bark.

I walked to an opening and glassed the foothills for movement. Nobody home. But I just knew they were close, staying as quiet as caves, staring back at me through the dappled branches.

The binoculars were allowed to hang from their strap as I popped an elk-calling diaphragm into my mouth. The thing looked like one of those plastic retainers that orthodontists make snaggle-faced kids wear. Except this just suctioned into the roof of my mouth. Then I raised a two-foot length of grunt tube to my lips and began producing my version of an elk bugle.

It sounded like a clogged drain.

But I kept at it and in a few minutes I heard a bull bugling back. Maybe he was just amused. The call started low and rose in a smooth arpeggio high up into his upper register. I called back and managed to generate a rough approximation of a rival. The bull answered in a magnificent timbre that echoed off the avalanche chutes and out toward Venus. Chills goose-fleshed their way down my neck and arms.

Bugling with elk—a common man's duet with god.

This beat the hell out of the time I bugled off the balcony of a Chicago high-rise hotel. The sound raced over the Miracle Mile, through Grant's Park, and out across Lake Michigan. I knew elk hadn't been heard along that shoreline for 150 years. But the sound of an unanswered call made even the city seem quiet.

Back here in the aspen grove, the bugling continued in earnest. Dominance and breeding rights were being sorted out among several bulls out beyond the trees. It was time for me, the two-legged troublemaker, to back off.

I drove on for a few miles and parked at the trail register. I never sign the silly things. If I break something, so be it. Worse ways to go.

I hefted my pack and crossed the frigid creek on a log bridge. Then up a slight rise to trail signs that laid out the options. I went right, as always, on a five-mile trek up to a small, fishless lake of no particular reputation.

The forests rose and fell with the glacial scours. A few thousand years ago, this basin held a creaking, crevassed river of rock-strewn ice. You could still see the strandlines on the encircling arêtes. Boulder piles marked places where the glacier stopped and melted away its life.

Then the lakes started—tarns—water-filled glacial scoops. A string of round, troutless islands encircled by bedrock. Paternoster lakes. Our father who art in mountains. I watched a moose flee through the shallows, making hollow clumping noises with its amplified hoofs.

Dwarf huckleberry, grouse whortleberry, heather, and sedge. Elk sedge. The subalpine forest was in full form now. Lodgepoles where the burns had been, whitebark pines and subalpine firs where they hadn't. Engelmann spruce filled the frosty pockets. Up higher, a golden verge of larches stood out like neon against the margins of the rock-made world.

Aldo Leopold reminded us that "poets sing and hunters scale the mountains primarily for one and the same reason—the thrill to beauty."

A few miles farther and a fool's hen stood expectantly in the middle of the trail. Like I owed it money. I looked deep into its dark, matt-finished eyes. Zilch. It's amazing the species survives. I eased the bird aside with my boot to keep from hurting the poor thing. Fool's hens—a sure source of backcountry food if the bears get your stash.

Then I climbed the last switchback into the upper cirque. By now I was sweating a bit even in the falling, 50-degree air. The supply of easily gotten deadfall and dry side branches began to thin out. I was getting close to the lake. One last stare up at the summit to regain my wind. Alpenglow was coming on, remaking a high corniced snowfield into a languishing patch of tropical sea. I watched the colors rise as the sun raced toward Baja. In three more months, the fire would winter on the coast of Chile, heating the backs of Atacama lizards and bleaching the bones of ships gone aground and never reclaimed. For months to come, warmth was up to me. I hiked with a purpose for ten minutes, generating enough heat to reach a draw with chilliness.

Then the lake just showed up.

The tenting site meadow, the level-rock kitchen, the fallen-log sofa—they all still existed as flawless as cold beer. I downed my pack and leaned it against one of two deadfallen trees. This was new. Together they formed a perfectly legible sixty-foot "X." Just one year before, I had slept at the crossing point of the oracle sign. Timing tends to matter.

I set my tent up in no time, the same North Face mountain job I've relied on since 1971. When camping, reduce the variables. Then I strode off to gather firewood. Upslope of some Labrador tea I got lucky. It was a huge whitebark pine, dead for a while, covered with

The Elk's Golden Eye

barkless, desiccated branches two inches around. I snapped off what I needed and hauled three armloads of cheer back to my spot. The same modest ring of rocks would do for my fireplace. It seemed unchanged, immortal. I could be twenty or eighty; the circle would be unbroken.

I scrounged some kindling, piled on a few larger sticks, poured on stove fuel, and tossed a lit wooden match onto the mixture. With a welcome WHOOOMP! the fire gained life and soon was crackling and sparking along nicely. Then I stripped off my sweat-soaked T-shirt and armed myself into a long-sleeved thermal shirt and blue pile coat. I scrunched on a green "Anglers Afloat" baseball cap to cover my significant baldness and was soon walking along a small peninsula into the lake.

A single, ice-beaten whitebark pine was drawing out life from a beach of skeletal soils. Upslope of the water, larch trees were in full color. This world has deciduous conifers. Larches are cone-bearing trees that act like maples, turning their needle-leaves to orange and gold when the green mask of chlorophyll weakens and drains away. Carotene pigments finally emerge and glow for a few weeks at the very end of the growing time, after the crowds have gone home for the season. It is this union of beauty and solitude that makes the "larch turn" so essential.

I stared at the perfect colors for a long time. Until the faintest scent of light had gone. Larches sleep as faint gray slivers.

By now my fire needed tending. I walked back over into a shrinking sphere of warmth and piled on more branches, careful not to crowd out the air. A minute later, flames were jumping three feet into the retreating darkness.

I retrieved a green nylon food bag from my pack. Granola bars, M & M's, and oatmeal packets were pushed aside until the main course was pulled from a clear plastic baggie. Dinner would be a steak carved from a cow elk a friend had shot up Wolf Creek. I'd walked that country, seen the same land she'd seen. The steak had thawed perfectly on the hike up. I poked it onto a whittle-sharpened four-foot length of fir. The fire began its work. The meat hung over the fire, sizzling and real. Soon it was done enough. I ate every morsel like a grateful, quiet animal.

After an hour of staring at shimmering coals, I got tired and tucked myself into a soft mummy bag of down. The fire snapped and talked until I fell away into warm dreamless sleep.

Sometime during the night it snowed. Even in my first creaky moments of waking, I just knew. Things were too quiet. I pulled down the front zippers of the tent and found myself at eye level with an eight-inch-deep comforter of heavy, wet snow.

I smiled.

After lacing on boots and yanking on clothing, I rose from the tent and walked uphill to relieve myself a respectful distance from the lake. Subalpine firs were shedding branchloads of whiteness that thumped to the ground. Then a cold silence settled back down. I was the only person on this side of the wilderness, but I wasn't alone.

A huge raven flew by overhead, its wingbeats whock-whocking twice every second. Excessively intelligent creatures, they seem to play at life. Subsistence affluence. This one eyed me for a second but quickly got bored. It disappeared over the brightening divide on some sort of bird business.

I shuffled through the snow back to the campsite. My tracks were likely to be the last human sign this year. A stray goat hunter on horse-back might still make it up this high, but that didn't seem likely. With this snowfall, the cream-coated billies and nannies were probably safe for another year.

My wood supply was pretty soggy so I contented myself with a handful of frozen M & M's. The edges of the lake were icing up. I walked over and tapped a thin plane of glaze with the toe of my boot. The molecules fractured apart, making a high crystal plink. A boulder broke free somewhere up on the headwall. I scanned the slope but saw no movement. The rock thumped and echoed along an unseen path-way toward the birthplace of gravity at the center of the world.

My eyes stayed high and moved along the larches. Their gold was back now, brighter than ever against the salt-colored talus. But the dark bedrock scarps had easily shed this little snowfall.

That's when the shape began to break through.

At first I just let my eyes play with the patterns like a kid with cu-mulus. Golden larch, white snow, gray rock. Shafts and smooshes of color and form.

Snow had edged the lower margin of a slanting outcrop. It was like the side view of something alive. Like a long-muzzled head. A cleft opened northward—a mouth. Above was a dense clump of larches—an eye. The more I looked the more the shape turned true. There was a gracefully curving neck, a hint of ears, maybe even a rack curving up above the fell fields.

It was an elk. An elk with a golden eye. An elk breathing deeply at a

The Elk's Golden Eye

full run, not from danger, but from the absolute animal need to move freely and fast across a perfectly natural world.

I watched the mountainside for an hour.

In a few days, wind would take down the last of the golden needles. In a few weeks, heavy snow would bury the outlines. Soon, the elk would retreat back into the mountain.

But every year since, late in September when the larches are peaking and a dusting of snow falls across the high basins, I know with soft certainty that the elk's golden eye is blinking wide open.

And seeing a world that is still bountiful and good.

10

MEDICINE

I LIVE IN Missoula in a small house surrounded by a stand of large ponderosa pines. Mount Jumbo rises to the south like the reclining body of a grassy elephant. The Salish called it Si Nim Koo ("Big Bump"). On June days you can hike among the waving prairies and watch lazuli buntings color the sky.

On one of those absolute days, I walked up to the saddle of Jumbo. A fuzz of pink bitterroots was rising from a windblown bank. Then I went up an old ranch road through forests and meadows all covered in varying conjugations of green. Soon I reached the summit, flat and horsy, with mule deer hopping off into the fir-scented shade.

I'd seen photos of the mountain taken years back. Fire used to keep it grassy. Trees were seldom. But now the city had spread up to its margin and fire was banished. The forests had grown thick on the old Lake Missoula shorelines, eking out moisture from stray snow pockets and silent seeps.

Some of the pictures showed a huge ponderosa pine that locals called "the Medicine Tree." The Salish and other tribes came up with the idea. Trees whose strong gentility brought the power to heal and see meaning. There are many across Montana: a big one rises next to the East Fork of the Bitterroot. It was said that Chief Charlot went there each year of his life.

But I was looking for a different tree. I'd heard that the Medicine Tree on Jumbo was over 400 years old. It was used by the Salish and, later, by generations of Missoula gamblers trying for an edge at the poker table. This went on until 1949, when two thoughtless young boys from the Rattlesnake Valley cut the pine down. One theory had it that the medicine was finished.

I kept scouting for some sign of a stump. Down a steep fescue slope, across the lupine blues, and into the head of a ravine. Shrubs took over in the moist, shady swale; a thicket of hawthorn, serviceberry, choke-cherry, and wild rose. The seemingly dry mountain had hidden glens like this one, places with three-toed salamanders, western toads, rub-ber boas, and yellow-bellied racers. Deer droppings were everywhere; mule deer and whitetails. In the winter, as many as seventy elk seek refuge on the mountain when high elevation snowpacks pile too deep. You can watch them graze from downtown Missoula.

Mount Jumbo is nearly surrounded by streets, houses, stores, and cement. Yet nature is still hearty and true up here on the open land. The mountain still has bighorn sheep, yellow-bellied marmots, moun-tain lions, bobcats, foxes, and badgers. Black bears are seen within ear-shot of Interstate 90. Over 100 species of birds fly here. Will Kerling has seen them all and written down their languages. There is a rich-ness of butterflies: Milbert's tortoise shells, mourning cloaks, northern blues, yellow swallowtails, orange sulphurs, and painted ladies.

All this right next to 60,000 people.

I hiked down the ravine, glancing at a Xerox copy of an old photo from time to time. I was beginning to wonder if I'd picked the wrong spot. But then, after I pushed aside some branches, a fallen tree ap-peared. The gray bole was nearly submerged in a clump of choke-cherry and penstemons. It was slowly turning to humus. I knelt down and examined the base. There were saw marks. This was it—the medi-cine tree. Almost fifty years dead, a skeleton.

I sat down on the trunk and ran my hands over the body. What are you thinking old one? Does anybody still come here for luck or medicine anymore?

I looked out over the Missoula Valley. You could actually feel the earth's gravity holding you close. The tree was dead, but medicine still coursed through every cell and sand grain on the mountain.

With my feet on the ground, the future looked possible.

To the north was the Rattlesnake National Recreation Area and Wilderness. Bruce Bugbee and many others gave years of their lives to complete a land exchange that created it. The Rattlesnake Greenway, the Mount Sentinel conservation easements, the Kim Williams Trail along the Clark Fork, the Riverfront Park system, the easements on Waterworks Hill and the north benches. Despite all the growth, traffic, and air pollution, Missoulians were saving some key parts of their community. Each project was a ceremony of belonging. And a damn good idea.

Mount Jumbo itself was now secure. Greg Tollefson and The Five Valleys Land Trust had gotten it done. Over 1,700 acres was conserved because people cared. City voters chose to tax themselves to buy parts of it. The Rocky Mountain Elk Foundation, the Forest Service, and the Montana Department of Fish, Wildlife and Parks came through with abundant financial and moral support.

We know how to save our home landscapes. People are doing it. We can keep both the land and our hope alive. Or we can succumb to the old fictions and keep ghost dancing.

Indian people already know there is only one choice. Wovoka— the imagined messiah—has not stirred from his grave beside Pyramid Lake in Nevada. The nations are pragmatically adapting to the changing West while trying to hold on to the best of themselves. Now it's our turn.

I scanned the horizon. I could imagine a quiet day a century ahead, in a time when the wars for the landscape finally abated, when stewardship prevailed over developmental extremism. I prayed this wasn't just my dance.

If this post-boom, stable Montana comes to be, if people choose to create it, a monument will be built. Perhaps in the Big Hole, beside a river once called The Wisdom. This monument will be made of rocks from all over the state: quartzite from the Little Belts, limestone from Mount Helena, argillite from Kalispell, granite from the Beartooth. The plaque will be made of copper. It might read as follows:

MONTANA IS THE HERITAGE OF ALL MONTANANS
SOME ARE LIVING
MANY HAVE PASSED ON
MOST HAVE NOT YET BEEN BORN

I can see this. The image is clear.

The copper has turned greenish with age. A few offerings of ribbons, crosses, and starflowers lie at its base.

A traveler stands, her hat held under one arm. She pauses to read some of the names carved into the rocks. People who spent their lives working to conserve Montana land and life. We would recognize some of them. One entry would be this: "All the Montana landowners who stood by the ground." Room would be left to add the names of those standing vigil, people tending the landscape against harm.

The woman stands quietly. Then a strand of woven sweatgrass is removed from her jacket. She looks first at the names, then the broad sweep of enduring valley. Her small hand lowers the offering into place. She exhales slowly, rises, and wordlessly walks back to her car.

Nearby, kids are playing king of the mountain on a soft cushion of freshly cut hay. A sandhill crane flies toward a nest built in the sheltering bend of a grayling meander.

The woman smiles and drives off past the Big Hole Battlefield into a rising pool of darkness and illumination.